The Diverse Worlds of Unemployed Adults

Consequences for Leisure, Lifestyle, and Well-Being

Mark E. Havitz

Peter A. Morden

Diane M. Samdahl

Wilfrid Laurier University Press

WLU

We acknowledge the financial support of the Government of Canada through the Book Publishing Industry Development Program for our publishing activities. We acknowledge the Government of Ontario through the Ontario Media Development Corporation's Ontario Book Initiative.

Library and Archives Canada Cataloguing in Publication

Havitz, Mark E.
    The diverse worlds of unemployed adults : consequences for leisure, lifestyle, and well-being / Mark E. Havitz, Peter A. Morden, and Diane M. Samdahl.

Includes bibliographical references and index.
ISBN 0-88920-464-0

    1. Unemployed—Ontario—Social conditions. 2. Unemployed—Ontario—Psychology. 3. Leisure—Ontario. 4. Unemployed—Services for—Ontario. I. Morden, Peter A. (Peter Armstrong), 1969– . II. Samdahl, Diane Marie. III. Title.

| HD5708.H38 2004 | 305.9'0694'09713 | C2004-903525-8 |

For Sue, Niki, and Charlie. Thanks for
all of your love and support.— Mark

To Dana Hopson, for creative
problem solving.— Peter

For my father, who worked 47 years
for the same company.— Diane

Table of Contents

List of Appendices, Figures, and Tables... vii

Acknowledgements xi

1 Introduction.. 1
    Content and Format of This Book.. 4

2 Method 7
    Recruitment and Remuneration of Unemployed Participants........... 7
    Questionnaires, Data Collection, and Data Entry 9
    Representativeness of the Sample... 10
    The Participants.. 16

3 Talking about Unemployment
    Participant Classification and Descriptions of Daily Life.................. 21
    Planners... 24
    Vacationers.. 47
    Connectors 58
    Marginalized People 72
    Summary of the Participant Categorization Scheme........................... 95

4 Alternative Perspectives on Unemployment
    Confirmation and Disconfirmation of Daily Life Patterns
    Using Experiential Sampling and Mail-Back Survey Data............... 97
    Television Viewing 98
    Perceptions of Leisure and Non-Leisure... 105
    Satisfaction with Daily Planning... 114
    Highlight of the Day: Content-Analysis of Open-Ended
    ESM Comments... 116
    Respondents' Self-Esteem and Life Satisfaction................................. 133
    Job Importance, Career Socialization, Leisure Boredom,
        Self-Definition through Leisure, and Perceived Freedom
        in Leisure.. 136
    Perceived Constraint on Favourite Leisure and
        Recreation Activities... 139

**5 Integrating the Present Study
with the Literature** 145
Loss of Latent Functions or Categories of Experience......................... 148
Activity During Unemployment.. 158

**6 Perceptions of Unemployment Agencies and
Other Social Services** 161
Interacting with Human Resources Development Canada................. 162
Other Governmental and Community Resources............................... 172

7 Leisure Services Planning and Policy 177
Local Government: Standard Practice.................................... 178
Market Segmentation... 179
The Marketing Mix and Municipal Action.. 180
Participant Categorization: Implications for Local
     Service Providers 188
Provincial or Territorial, and Federal Action 190
Conclusion 193

8 Summary, Conclusion, and Future Directions 197
Concluding Thoughts 200

Appendices 203
References 245
Index 251

List of Appendices, Figures and Tables

Appendices

Appendix A   Phase 1 Initial Interview Guide 203
Appendix B   ESM Questionnaire 207
Appendix C   Phase 1 Follow-up Interview Guide 210
Appendix D   Phase 1 Mail-back Questionnaire 212
Appendix E   Phase 2 Initial and Follow-up Interview Guides 218
Appendix F   Detailed Description of Qualitative Data Analysis 222
Appendix G   Where Were Respondents When Signalled? 237
Appendix H   What Was the Main Thing Respondents Were
             Doing When Signalled? 238
Appendix I   How Task Involved Were Respondents?
             Did Respondents Perceive a Time Limit? 239
Appendix J   Who Were Respondents With? 240
Appendix K   Mood States by Subgroup 241
Appendix L   Price Subsidy Messages 242

Figures

Figure 1   Gender Distribution by Group and Subgroup 18
Figure 2   Age Distribution by Group and Subgroup 18
Figure 3   Education Distribution by Group and Subgroup 19
Figure 4   Ethnicity Distribution by Group and Subgroup 19
Figure 5   Pre-Employment Income by Group and Subgroup 20
Figure 6a   Frequency of Four Common Highlights by Context
            and Subgroup 118
Figure 6b   Frequency of Daily Highlights by Context
            and Subgroup 119

Tables

Table 1   Data Completion Rates for Phase 1 and Phase 2
           of the Study 8
Table 2   Sociodemographic Characteristics of Respondents 11

Table 3   Financial and Job-Related Characteristics
           of Respondents 13

Table 4   Final Group and Subgroup Breakdown 22

Table 5   Respondents' Location When Signalled (by Group) 24

Table 6   The Main Thing Respondents Were Doing When
           Signalled (by Group) 24

Table 7   Task Involvement and Perceived Time Limit (by Group) 25

Table 8   Social Context and Form of Interaction (by Group) 25

Table 9   Mood States (by Group) 26

Table 10   What Were Planners Doing When Signalled? 28

Table 11   Who Were Planners with When Signalled? 30

Table 12   Where Were Planners When Signalled? 36

Table 13   Planners' Perceptions of Time Pressure and Task
           Involvement 37

Table 14   Mood States of Planners 44

Table 15   Who Were Vacationers with When Signalled? 48

Table 16   Where Were Vacationers When Signalled? 50

Table 17   Vacationers' Perceptions of Time Pressure and Task
           Involvement 52

Table 18   Mood States of Vacationers 53

Table 19   What Were Vacationers Doing When Signalled? 58

Table 20   Who Were Connectors with When Signalled? 60

Table 21   What Were Connectors Doing When Signalled? 61

Table 22   Mood States of Connectors 63

Table 23   Where Were Connectors When Signalled? 67

Table 24   Evidence of Daily Social Patterns and Mobility of
           Networkers 69

Table 25   Connectors' Perceptions of Time Pressure and Task
           Involvement 71

Table 26   Who Were Marginalized People with When Signalled? 77

Table 27   What Were Marginalized People Doing When Signalled? 78

Table 28   Mood States of Marginalized People 83

Table 29   Where Were Marginalized People When Signalled? 85

Table 30   Marginalized People's Perceptions of Time Pressure
           and Task Involvement 90

Table 31   Television Viewing Patterns by Group, Subgroup,
           and Individual 99

Table 32   Social Patterns Associated with Television for Nine
           Frequent Viewers 101

Table 33   Percent of Episodes Self-Described as Leisure by
           Group and Subgroup 107

Table 34 Mood States by Subgroup during Self-Described
Leisure and Non-Leisure Contexts 108
Table 35 Mood States of All Respondents by Time of Day, Group,
and Subgroup 110
Table 36 Mood States by Subgroup, Time of Day, and Self-
Description of the Leisure or Non-Leisure
Nature of the Experience at Hand 112
Table 37 Mood States during Nine Common Social Situations 113
Table 38 Responses by Subgroup to the Planning Statement: "I Had
Expected to Be Doing That about This Time Today" 115
Table 39 Expectations Minus Perceptions by Subgroup to the
Planning Statement: "I Had Expected to Be Doing
That about This Time Today" 116
Table 40 Phase 1 Self-Esteem and Life Satisfaction Mean Scores
by Group and Subgroup 134
Table 41 Phase 2 Self-Esteem and Life Satisfaction Mean Scores
by Group and Subgroup 134
Table 42 Phase 2 Self-Esteem Mean Scores by Group and
Employment Status 135
Table 43 Phase 2 Life Satisfaction Mean Scores by Group and
Employment Status 135
Table 44 Scores Reported by Group for Leisure Boredom, Job
Involvement, Career Socialization, Self-Definition and
Perceived Freedom in Leisure, and Family Leisure 138
Table 45 Comparison of the Networker and Rover Subgroups
with Respect to Leisure Boredom, Job Involvement,
Career Socialization, Self-Definition and Perceived
Freedom in Leisure, and Family Leisure 140
Table 46 Phase 1 Perceived Constraints to Favourite Recreation
Activities by Subgroup 141
Table 47 Pre-Negotiation Categorization of Participants by Mark's
Categories and by Peter's Categories 226

Acknowledgements

The initial discussion leading to the development of this study originated some thirteen years ago when Mark and Diane were faculty members in the Department of Leisure Studies and Services at the University of Oregon. Ironically, shortly thereafter we were, along with approximately 100 other untenured colleagues, both pink slipped as part of the University's reaction to a state-imposed twelve percent budget cut. We were fortunate to both secure positions at other universities before our Oregon positions were eliminated. Nevertheless, the very real feeling of being devalued professionally and the sense of loss with respect to our colleagues and academic community were sobering. The downsizing experience gave us renewed resolve and added empathy with respect to studying unemployment and leisure.

We are grateful for the financial support of the Ontario Ministry of Tourism and Recreation, which made this project possible. Also, the gracious support of the staff, especially Barry Daniels, at the Canada Employment Centre was important in the early stages of recruitment and data collection. We would like to acknowledge a number of individuals who have contributed to this research project over the past few years. The principal research assistant for the data collection and data organization phases of the study was Laurie B. Whyte, then a graduate student in the Department of Recreation and Leisure Studies, University of Waterloo.

Data collection, entry, organization, and analysis assistance was provided by numerous students and staff, unless otherwise noted, who were at or are from the University of Waterloo's Department of Recreation and Leisure Studies. This assistance was invaluable in informing the authors as we developed the final product.

Data Collection and Entry

Elaine Brinkert, Denise Cundy, Chris Flood, Johann Friesen, Pam Gahwiler, Kirk Harding, Sue Havitz (UW Department of Systems Design Engineering), Raeann Kelly, Tara Kropf, Lynn Mighton, Elaine Nepsted,

Pauline Raghubir, Laurene Rehman, Michelle Robinson, Christine O'Sullivan, and Wendy Yamamoto.

Data Organization and Analysis

Heather Smith, Sandy DeVisser, Troy Glover, Lowell Williamson (Faculty of Applied Health Sciences), Mary Ingram, Sharon Jacobson, Christine Scolley, and Angela Loucks (the latter three people were with the Department of Recreation and Leisure Studies at the University of Georgia).

Finally, but most importantly, we would like to acknowledge the immense contributions of our study participants. Our participants gave unfailingly of their time, they were open and honest, and many went above and beyond the call of duty to schedule interviews, to complete questionnaires in trying circumstances, and to replace failing batteries in telephone pagers. We believe that their diligence has provided an outstanding data set that will add volumes to the leisure and unemployment literature and which will provide a basis for improving public policy and management strategies. In sum, we hope it will improve lives.

1 *Introduction*

Nature herself, as has been often said, requires that we should
be able, not only to work well, but to use leisure well....

Both are required, but leisure is better than occupation
and is its end; and therefore the question must be asked, what
ought we to do when at leisure? —Aristotle, *Politics*

L eisure is a widely studied phenomenon, critical to the quality of
life for individuals and cultures, and central to the economic
health of communities and nations. Leisure has been examined
from a variety of theoretical perspectives with respect to demographic,
life-stage, lifestyle, and economic circumstances. A substantial body
of literature devoted to work-leisure relationships has developed
(Haworth, 1997; Reid, 1995), wherein issues related to leisure and
unemployment have been raised. That coverage notwithstanding and
in spite of the accumulation of literature specifically focussing on
unemployment, similar in-depth coverage is not available regarding
leisure and unemployment. Exceptions include Glyptis's (1989) book
Leisure and Unemployment and Lobo's (2002) *Leisure, Family and*
Lifestyle: Unemployed Young People. Complicating issues further,
reactions to unemployment at the personal level and the resulting
implications for service delivery are culture- and country-specific;
two of the above texts (Glyptis, 1989; Haworth, 1997) rely primarily
on data and circumstance specific to the United Kingdom, whereas
Lobo's book focusses on Australia. The smaller body of North American research (see Pesavento Raymond & Havitz, 1995, for a summary)
has focussed to some extent on the response, or lack thereof, from
social services (including leisure services) to unemployed constituents
(Havitz & Spigner, 1993; Smit & Reid, 1990) and on recreation participation patterns of people who are unemployed (Pesavento Raymond &
Kelly, 1991; Reid, 1990).

Unemployment is a persistent feature of advanced industrial society, and the Canadian economy is no exception. Matters are complicated, though, by the cyclical nature of unemployment and the difficulty of predicting from one year to the next the scope of the problem.

1

Recently, local unemployment rates have hovered near 6%, and unemployment has not been a prominent political or social issue during the past several years. When our data were collected in 1994, however, a markedly different economic climate prevailed. In the two years preceding the start of this study, unemployment had reached, within Canada and in Ontario in particular, levels not seen since the recession of the early 1980s. Provincial unemployment rates exceeded 10% in 1992 and 1993, and had receded slightly to 9.6% in 1994. The governing New Democratic Party (NDP) endured substantial criticism about its fiscal management, spending priorities, and the economy. Further, the political climate in Ontario at the time—in the run-up to a provincial election—had made unemployment a hot button issue, with the Progressive Conservative (PC) party promising a "common-sense revolution" that would overhaul the distribution of social services, including welfare distributions and unemployment insurance regulation. The preponderance of the rhetoric that emerged during the pre-election dialogue, and that ultimately became the public will with the election of the PC government in 1995, was a harshly negative view of unemployed citizens. Political dialogue focussed largely on the perceived drain they had on the economy and the negative impact upon employed Ontarian taxpayers. For these reasons, among others, we felt it important to undertake an in-depth assessment of a sample of unemployed individuals in Ontario, and to assess their perceptions of the broad social service infrastructure in place to help them cope with their current joblessness.

Over a decade ago, Roberts, Lamb, Dench, and Brodie (1989, p. 229) summarized existing knowledge related to unemployment, well-being, and leisure as follows:

- Unemployment can, and, in present-day industrial societies, often does lead to deterioration in physical and mental health.
- Unemployment tends to reduce the victims' ranges of recreational activities and their levels of leisure spending.
- Leisure activities offer independent physical and psychological benefits.

As a result, if and when leisure activities can be developed or sustained during unemployment, the otherwise detrimental effects of joblessness might be mitigated. Though Roberts et al.'s conclusions are valid based upon the research available at the time, and are largely supported by more current research, it is worth restating that within-population differences make such generalizations suspect at both the community and societal levels.

Despite established conceptual linkages between leisure, unemployment, and health (Brenner, 1984; Spigner & Havitz, 1992), there is little evidence that people who are unemployed are routinely sought, consulted, or served by North American leisure service agencies (Havitz & Spigner, 1993). Further, although some demographic and social commonalities have been identified, it is apparent that people who are unemployed cannot be viewed as a homogenous population from a service delivery perspective. For example, studies of unemployed steelworkers (Pesavento Raymond, 1984) and young inner-city women (Pesavento Raymond & Kelly, 1991) in Chicago revealed striking differences. Although both samples lived in the same broadly defined community, they differed with respect to a variety of demographic, attitudinal, and behavioural characteristics. Likewise, Lobo's (1996, 1999, 2002) recent studies of people experiencing early-career and late-career unemployment revealed distinct between-group differences with respect to leisure and lifestyle.

As noted, in comparison to other topical areas such as at-risk youth or leisure constraints, the literature on leisure and unemployment is not extensive. Nevertheless, several methodological tendencies and shortcomings are apparent. Existing North American literature is largely based on post hoc instrumentation; there are little data focussing on the daily, lived experiences of unemployed adults. In-depth interview techniques have predominated in research related to leisure and unemployment. In general, respondents have been asked questions, based on short- to medium-term recall, related to daily life activity, participation and spending patterns, psychological coping, and social networks. Some studies have also collected time diary or objective inventory-type data with respect to participation patterns and the like. Sample sizes are generally small- to mid-range, and few studies have used standardized indices (for example, those related to self-esteem and life satisfaction). Likewise, few studies to date have used immediate experience measures provided by well-established methods such as Experience Sampling. Finally, few leisure and unemployment studies have combined the various methods listed above in order to improve the reliability and validity of subsequent analyses. Most leisure and unemployment studies have been cross-sectional, and longitudinal data are rare. These limitations have been apparent for a number of years, but little has been done to address the issue. Recently, Creed and Macintyre (2001) noted that "future studies should attempt to include data from multiple sources and be augmented with nonsurvey designs" (p. 330). Although initiated prior to the publication of Creed and Macintyre's observations,

the present research was designed to overcome several of the identified, and still prevalent, shortcomings.

The purposes of this book are three-fold. First, the book describes
the results of a multi-method approach in a study of the effects of
unemployment on leisure, lifestyle, and well-being in an urbanized
Canadian community. Second, using literature collected worldwide,
the book integrates our findings into a comprehensive understanding of the effects of unemployment on these life spheres. Finally, we
propose improvements in public policy and marketing strategies for
unemployed adults and their dependants, and we offer suggestions for
communicating with and understanding the inherent diversity of
these individuals.

Content and Format of This Book

Chapter 1

This introduction articulates the purpose of this study and highlights the need for research relating to unemployment, leisure, lifestyle,
and well-being.

Chapter 2

This chapter describes our sample and details the methods used
to gather three distinct types of data: first, qualitative data were collected through open-ended interviews with 60 participants (Phase 1)
and follow-up interviews with 48 of those participants three to four
months later (Phase 2). The description of the qualitative analysis
includes an articulation of the process undertaken by the two independent analysts that led to the categorization of participants into
relatively homogenous groups.

Second, quantitative data pertaining to social contexts and the *in
situ* psychological states of these individuals were obtained through
Experience Sampling Methodology, hereafter referred to as ESM,
collected in Phases 1 and 2 (4,415 total ESM questionnaires). These
data provide snapshot descriptions of a random selection of events in
these people's lives. Finally, quantitative data were attained through
the administration of standardized psychometric scales during both
Phase 1 (N = 50) and Phase 2 (N = 36). This multi-method approach is,
we believe, one of the major contributions of this project.

Chapters 3 and 4

These chapters provide an overview of response rates achieved for
each of the data collection phases and a sociodemographic "thumb-

nail sketch" of the participants in the study. Following this, a description is provided of the four main groupings of participants, based on the salience of various lifestyle, life-cycle, and psychological characteristics.

The quantitative ESM data provide both confirmation and critique of the lifestyle categorization scheme, and allows further insight into the lived experience of these unemployed adults. The data obtained through ESM afford an examination of factors such as venues of interaction, experience of flow, social interaction, mood states, situational involvement, and perceived obligation/sense of freedom with respect to daily tasks. This analysis was complemented by data pertaining to participants' self-esteem, life satisfaction, leisure boredom, and perceived freedom in leisure; as well, the study examined both unemployed adults' participation in leisure activities and also the constraints they perceived preventing such participation.

Chapter 5

Consistent with standard practice in inductive research using qualitative data, which formed the basis of our analyses, we integrated our findings with the existing body of literature related to unemployment and leisure. Where appropriate, findings from this study that echo previous research are noted, but findings which seem to run against the grain of conventional wisdom or that seem to have not been addressed in previous research are particularly emphasized.

Chapters 6, 7, and 8

In chapter 6 we critique current social service provision standards for people who are unemployed, with specific focus on our respondents' experiences with Human Resources Development Canada (HRDC). In chapter 7, we explore how leisure services might be better integrated into the lives of unemployed adults and their dependents to improve their quality of life and general well-being during their transition into and out of unemployment. Special focus is placed on the role of local agencies, but provincial and federal level support is also critiqued. The final chapter provides an overview of our major findings and offers suggestions for future research.

2 Method

As noted in the introduction, this study is based on three distinct methods of data collection that were repeated three months apart. This chapter describes the recruitment of the participants, the nature of their participation over the course of the study, the data collection methods, and the response rates for each phase of data collection.

Recruitment and Remuneration of Unemployed Participants

Our intention was to study recently unemployed adults who had established job histories. Permission was obtained to recruit participants on-site at the Canada Employment Centre in Kitchener, Ontario. This Centre serves citizens who live in and around the twin cities of Kitchener and Waterloo. In May 1994, in order to discuss the purpose of the study and to answer questions, two group meetings were held with staff members who have direct contact with clients. They were given instructions concerning the desired characteristics of potential participants, advised how best to inform their clients about this study, and asked to inquire whether their clients might be interested in participating. In addition, signs were posted throughout the Centre advertising the opportunity to participate in this study and directing interested people to the Centre's staff. Each staff member was given a sign-up form on which to record the name, signature, and phone number of interested participants. Sign-up forms were collected from the Canada Employment Centre over a six-week period, approximately once every two weeks during May and early June. As a result of this process, the names of 156 volunteers were collected.

Volunteers were then contacted by phone in order to provide more detailed information about the study, answer questions, and obtain their consent to participate in the study. Of the 156 people on the original sign-up sheets, 88 could be reached through the contact information they had provided. The remaining 68 volunteers had moved, had no phone of their own, had disconnected phone service, or were otherwise inaccessible. Each volunteer was called at least five times before his or her name was dropped from the list of potential participants.

Of the 88 contacted volunteers, five decided not to participate. An additional 23 were rejected by us because they did not fit the criteria for the study. The latter category included volunteers who had been unemployed too long, who had recently been full-time students, or who were moving out of the area. This left 60 unemployed volunteers to participate in Phase 1 of the research.

This study was relatively intrusive on people's daily lives and was somewhat time-consuming as well. Therefore, Phase 1 participants were paid for their involvement, receiving $15 upon completion of the initial interview and $25 upon completion of the week-long experience sampling component and follow-up interview. In addition, the names of all participants (regardless of whether or not they completed all data collection components) were placed in a random draw for prizes at the end of Phase 1. Six participants received cash prizes ranging from $50 to $250. A two-page "Midterm Report" was distributed to all participants at this point. The purpose of the newsletter was to thank the participants, summarize some initial results, and maintain their interest for the second stage of the study.

Phase 2 of the study began in September, approximately three months after the completion of Phase 1. At this time the 60 volunteers who had participated in Phase 1 were contacted again. Four participants had moved out of the region, three declined to participate in Phase 2, and five others were not reachable. Six volunteers began Phase 2 but completed only a portion of the data collection; consequently, all six were dropped from Phase 2. In addition, the interview data for two participants in Phase 2 were lost due to malfunctioning tapes, and the ESM data for one participant was lost in an apartment fire. This left 39 volunteers for whom there was complete data from both Phases of the study. Table 1 summarizes the data completion rates for Phase 1 and Phase 2 of this study.

Table 1 Data Completion Rates for Phase 1 and Phase 2 of the Study

Data collection mode	Phase 1	Phase 2
Initial interview	60 (100%)	48 (80%)
ESM	60 (100%)	45 (75%)
Follow-up interview	60 (100%)	44 (73%)
Mail-back questionnaire	50 (83%)	39 (65%)

Although all respondents had been unemployed at the onset of Phase 1, by the time Phase 2 commenced 11 had found full-time work, 17 had found part-time work, and four had returned full-time to school. The remaining seven were still unemployed. Participants were again paid for their involvement in Phase 2, receiving $25 upon completion of the interview and $40 upon completion of the experience sampling study. Another random draw was held and eight respondents received cash prizes ranging from $50 to $250. A two-page "Final Report" was distributed to all participants at the conclusion of Phase 2. This newsletter provided a short summary of findings to date and thanked the participants for their participation in the study.

Questionnaires, Data Collection, and Data Entry

The several forms of data collection, already introduced, are described in greater detail below.

Phase 1

After agreeing to participate, volunteers scheduled a time for an initial interview. The questions used to guide this interview are included in Appendix A. Interviews were tape-recorded and later transcribed verbatim. The average length of these interviews was approximately one hour.

At the end of the interview the Experiential Sampling Method (ESM) was explained and volunteers were asked to begin this on the following day. ESM is a process whereby volunteers describe what they are doing and how they are feeling at randomly selected times throughout the day. Participants were given a booklet of questionnaires (Appendix B) and an electronic pager. They were "beeped" seven times each day for seven days, and were instructed to complete a questionnaire as soon as possible following each beep. Each questionnaire took approximately two minutes to complete. The ESM questionnaires included items relating to the activity, social situation, respondent's mood-state, respondent's perceived role constraints, levels of self-awareness, and situational involvement. Data collection extended for one full week, providing information about the daily routines and experiences of each participant.

Following seven days of ESM, the interviewer returned to collect the booklet and pager, and to conduct a follow-up interview; the interview guide for this interview is included in Appendix C. This interview lasted approximately 15 minutes. Similar to procedures followed for the initial interview, follow-up interviews were transcribed verbatim. Following completion of the interview, the interviewer left a postage-paid mail-back questionnaire. This questionnaire elicited information about favourite leisure activities and perceived constraints, and included standardized scales measuring leisure boredom, work orientation, perceived freedom in leisure, self-esteem, and life satisfaction (Appendix D). It took 10–15 minutes to complete.

Phase 2

The second phase of the study was initiated in September. An attempt was made to contact all Phase 1 participants to determine if they were interested in continuing with Phase 2. As noted above, 39 of the 60 volunteers from Phase 1 were available and completed data collection for Phase 2; four other volunteers participated in Phase 2 but part of their data was lost due to fire or malfunctioning tapes. When possible, the participants in Phase 2 were assigned to the same research assistant who had interviewed them in Phase 1. Data collection procedures for Phase 2 were similar to those described for Phase 1 in that each participant was asked to complete an initial interview, participate in ESM for seven days, have a follow-up interview, and then complete and mail back the questionnaire. The ESM and the mail-back questionnaires were identical to those used in Phase 1, but the interview schedules were modified somewhat according to the current employment status of each participant (see Appendix E).

Representativeness of the Sample

Although initial attempts to recruit volunteers were designed to attract a diverse sample of people who had recently become unemployed, there is no way of knowing how well the actual volunteers for this study represent the sociodemographic diversity of people who use the services of the Canadian Employment Centre in Kitchener. However, the original sample of 60 unemployed volunteers should reflect some of the diversity of experiences shared by unemployed Ontarians.

The loss of participants between Phase 1 and Phase 2 was attributed to several unknown circumstances. It might be safe to assume that the people who no longer had telephones or local addresses had moved away from Kitchener–Waterloo; unemployment may have played a role in their decision to move. These people reflect an important segment of the initial sample that was lost. Approximately one-third of respondents did not complete Phase 2, limiting the sample for whom change over time can be analyzed. Because some respondents did not complete all forms of data collection, the reliability when comparing data from the interviews, ESM, and mail-back questionnaire is, at times, limited. Therefore, the sample sizes used in the analyses reported in subsequent chapters varies from section to section.

While some participants were lost during this study, the remaining participants showed a willingness to be responsibly involved. After Phase 1, several people called in to report that they had moved or changed phone numbers but still wanted to participate in Phase 2. Some participants went out of their way to help the research process by replacing the batteries in the ESM pager, randomly picking times to fill out the ESM booklet on rare occasions when their pagers didn't work, or photocopying the ESM questionnaire when the booklets didn't have enough pages.

Attrition notwithstanding, the sample size remains rather large in comparison to many studies that have attempted to collect this amount of in-depth information from individual respondents. Tables 2 and 3 summarize the demographic, financial, and employment history of all participants. Throughout the book, all reported respondent names and the names of individuals mentioned in quoted material are fictional, having been assigned by the authors.

Table 2 Sociodemographic Characteristics of Respondents

Name	Sex	Age	Education	Ethnicity	Marital status
Aaron	M	20–29	Some HS	Caucasian	Single (GF)
Alison	F	30–39	Coll/Univ grad	Asian	Divorced
Andrea	F	40–49	Some Coll/Univ	Caucasian	Widow
Angie	F	20–29	Some Coll/Univ	Caucasian	Single (BF)
Anita	F	30–39	Coll/Univ grad [professional degree]	Caucasian	Single
Anna	F	40–49	HS grad	Caucasian	Divorced
Barb	F	20–29	HS grad	Other	Married
Bob	M	20–29	Masters	Caucasian	Single
Bruce	M	20–29	Some Coll/Univ	Caucasian	Single
Carolyn	F	20–29	Some Coll/Univ	Caucasian	Common law
Carrie	F	20–29	Some Coll/Univ	Asian	Married
Christina	F	20–29	Coll/Univ grad	Caucasian	Single (at home)
Dale	M	50–59	Vocational	East Indian	Married
Darlene	F	Under 20	Some HS	Caucasian	Separated
David	M	30–39	HS grad	Caucasian	Single
Diane	F	20–29	Some HS	Caucasian	Common law
Dick	M	40–49	Some Coll/Univ	Caucasian	Divorced
Donald	M	20–29	Masters	Caucasian	Single
Donna	F	30–39	Coll/Univ grad	Caucasian	Common law
Frank	M	30–39	Some Coll/Univ	Caucasian	Single
Harry	M	20–29	Coll/Univ grad	Caucasian	Single (at home)
Heather	F	40–49	HS grad	Caucasian	Single

▼

Table 2 (*continued*)

Name	Sex	Age	Education	Ethnicity	Marital status
Jack	M	40–49	Some Coll/Univ	Caucasian	Married
Jackie	F	40–49	Some Coll/Univ	Caucasian	Married
Jacob	M	30–39	Vocational	Caucasian	Married
Janet	F	30–39	Some Coll/Univ	Caucasian	Single
Jeanne	F	40–49	Some Coll/Univ	Caucasian	Married
Jeffrey	M	20–29	Coll/Univ grad	Caucasian	Common law
Jenny	F	40–49	Coll/Univ grad	Other	Divorced
Jim	M	20–29	Some Coll/Univ	Asian	Single (at home)
Joanne	F	20–29	HS grad	Caucasian	Single (at home)
Joe	M	20–29	Coll/Univ grad	Caucasian	Single (at home)
Keith	M	20–29	Some HS	Caucasian	Single
Kelly	F	20–29	Coll/Univ grad	Caucasian	Single (BF)
Kim	F	30–39	Coll/Univ grad	Other	Single
Larry	M	40–49	Some HS	Caucasian	Single
Les	M	20–29	Some Coll/Univ [professional degree]	Asian	Single (at home)
Lynn	F	20–29	Coll/Univ grad	Single	
Marcia	F	20–29	Coll/Univ grad	Caucasian	Engaged
Marianne	F	20–29	Coll/Univ grad	Caucasian	Single
Paul	M	30–39	Masters	Caucasian	Married
Mary	F	20–29	Coll/Univ grad	Caucasian	Engaged
Matt	M	20–29	Some Coll/Univ	Caucasian	Common law (gay)
Melanie	F	50–59	Some HS	Other	Single
Nicole	F	30–39	Some Coll	Caucasian	Separated
Pauline	F	20–29	HS grad	Caucasian	Single
Peggy	F	20–29	Some Coll/Univ	Asian	Single (at home)
Robert	M	30–39	Coll/Univ grad	Caucasian	Common law
Shawn	M	40–49	Some HS	Caucasian	Married
Sheila	F	50–59	Some Coll/Univ	Caucasian	Separated
Shelly	F	40–49	Some Coll/Univ	Other	Married
Stacy	F	40–49	Vocational	Caucasian	Married
Stephanie	F	40–49	Coll/Univ grad	Caucasian	Married
Steven	M	30–39	Some Coll/Univ	Caucasian	Single (GF)
Susan	F	20–29	Some Coll/Univ	Other	Common law
Taryn	F	20–29	Coll/Univ grad	Caucasian	Single (BF)
Todd	M	30–39	Some HS	Caucasian	Single
Tom	M	20–29	Coll/Univ grad	Caucasian	Single
Tracy	F	30–39	HS grad	Caucasian	Single (at home)
Walter	M	20–29	Some Coll/Univ	Caucasian	Single

Note. In Table 2, the Education column, HS = high school; in the Marital status column, Single (GF) means "Single with a girlfriend," while Single (BF) means "Single with a boyfriend." "Single (at home)" means the respondent lived with one or both parents.

Table 3 Financial and Job-Related Characteristics of Respondents

Name	Pre-unemployment income	Dependents	Monetary support	Job loss circumstances	Previous job title	Phase 2 employment status
Aaron	$15,000 or less	No	No	Quit (moved)	Cook/dishwasher	Student
Alison	$15,001 to $25,000	Yes	No	Laid off	Bookkeeper	Full-time
Andrea	$15,001 to $25,000	No	No	Fired	Clerk/secretary	Student
Angie	$25,001 to $35,000	No	No	Laid off	Restaurant manager	Full-time
Anita	$15,001 to $25,000	No	No	Fired	Waitress & retail clerk	
Anna	$25,001 to $35,000	Yes	No	Fired	Sales representative	Part-time
Barb	$55,001 or more	Yes	Yes	Laid off (contract)	Clerk/secretary	Full-time
Bob	$25,001 to $35,000	No	No	Laid off (moved)	Project Coordinator systems design	Full-time
Bruce	$25,001 to $35,000	No	No	Student	Manual labour/ auto line	
Carolyn	$15,000 or less	No	No	Fired	Retail clerk	Unemployed
Carrie	$35,001 to $45,000	No	Yes	Quit (moved)	Retail clerk/supervisor	Part-time
Christina	$15,000 or less	No	Yes	Graduated	Hospitality/front line	
Dale	$35,001 to $45,000	Yes		Laid off	Industrial security	Part-time
Darlene	$15,000 or less		No	Laid off		
David	$15,000 or less	No	No	Laid off (downsized)	Retail shipping/receiving	Full-time
Diane	$15,001 to $25,000	Yes (non-custodial)		Quit	Waitress	Unemployed
Dick	$15,000 or less	Yes (non-custodial)	No	Laid off (downsized)	Warehouse manager	Unemployed

Table 3 (*continued*)

Name	Pre-unemployment income	Dependents	Monetary support	Job loss circumstances	Previous job title	Phase 2 employment status
Donald	$35,001 to $45,000	No	No	Laid off (downsized)	Electrician	Full-time
Donna	$35,001 to $45,000	Yes	Yes	Laid off (contract)	College instructor	Unemployed
Frank	$25,001 to $35,000	No	No	Business failure	Restaurant manager	Part-time
Harry	$25,001 to $35,000	No	Yes	Laid off (contract)	Apprentice electrician	Unemployed
Heather	$15,001 to $25,000	No	No	Laid off (temp)	Secretary	Part-time
Jack	$55,001 or more	Yes	Yes	Fired	Civil engineer/surveyor	Part-time
Jackie	$55,001 or more	Yes	Yes	Laid off (contract)	Human resources	Part-time
Jacob	$55,001 or more	No	Yes	Fired	Mutual fund analyst	Part-time
Janet	$15,001 to $25,000	Yes	No	Quit	Retail clerk	Unemployed
Jeanne	$15,000 or less	No	Yes	Fired	Retail/sales incentives	Full-time
Jeffrey	$15,000 or less	No	No	Quit (moved)	Cab driver	Unemployed
Jenny	$35,001 to $45,000	Yes	No	Laid off (downsized)	NFP fundraiser	Unemployed
Jim		No	Yes	PT summer job	Landscaper	
Joanne	$55,001 or more	No	Yes	Laid off (downsized)	Receptionist	Full-time
Joe	$15,000 or less	No	Yes	Graduated	Librarian	
Keith	$15,000 or less	No	No	Medical leave	Manual labour/construction	Part-time
Kelly	$15,001 to $25,000	No	No	Laid off (contract)	Human resources	
Kim	$15,001 to $25,000	Yes	No	Quit (moved)	Secretary	Part-time

Larry	$15,000 or less	No	No	Fired/quit	Manual labourer	Part-time
Les	$15,001 to $25,000	No	Yes	Laid off	Manual labourer	Part-time
Lynn		No		Laid off (contract)	Computer product tester	Full-time
Marcia	$15,001 to $25,000	No	No	Quit (for school)	Group home counsellor	
Marianne	$15,000 or less	No	No	Laid off (seasonal)		Part-time
Paul	$15,000 or less	Yes	Yes	Moved	Mechanical engineer	Full-time
Mary		P1 no, P2 yes	P1 no, P2 yes	Laid off (contract)	Administrative assistant	
Matt	$25,001 to $35,000	No	Yes	Quit	Night auditor	Part-time
Melanie	$15,000 or less	Yes	Yes	Left job to move	Red Cross homemaker	
Nicole	$25,001 to $35,000	Yes		Quit	Film/video processor	Part-time
Pauline	$15,001 to $25,000	No	No	Laid off (temp)	Secretary/clerk	Part-time
Peggy	$15,001 to $25,000	No	Yes	Laid off (temp)	Mailroom clerk	Part-time
Robert	$25,001 to $35,000	No	No?	Laid off (temp)	Product testing/mechanical	Part-time
Shawn	$25,001 to $35,000	No	Yes	Laid off	Sales estimator, industrial	
Sheila	$35,001 to $45,000	Yes	No	Laid off	Accounting clerk	Unemployed
Shelly	$55,001 or more	Yes	Yes	Laid off (downsized)	Bank manager	Part-time
Stacy	$55,001 or more	Yes	No	Laid off (contract)	Accounting assistant	Full-time
Stephanie	$35,001 to $45,000	Yes	No	Fired	Computer programmer	Unemployed
Steven	$45,001 to $55,000	Yes (non-custodial)	No	Laid off	Trade show display technician	Unemployed
Susan	$15,001 to $25,000	No		Laid off (seasonal)	Telephone operator	Full-time
Taryn	$15,000 or less	No	Yes?	Business failure	Restaurant manager	Part-time
Todd	$25,001 to $35,000	No	No	Laid off		
Tom	$15,001 to $25,000	No	No	Laid off (contract)	Data entry clerk/analyst	
Tracy	Don't know	No	Yes	Laid off	Manual labourer/industrial	
Walter	$15,001 to $25,000	No	No	Quit	Restaurant manager	Full-time

The Participants

As described in the preceding section, a series of interviews was conducted with unemployed individuals accessed through the Canada Employment Centre in Kitchener, Ontario. The purpose of these interviews was to gain insight into the lived experience of people during a period of unemployment, including such elements as their daily routine, leisure behaviour, and interactions with others. As a first step in analysis, the interviews were examined to reveal common threads of subjective experience. Although interview data from Phase 2 are sometimes reported, the vast majority of this analysis was conducted using Phase 1 interview data. When Phase 2 data are used in chapter 3, we are careful to identify such data.

This analysis was undertaken separately by two of the researchers. Analysis began by reading the interview transcripts for each participant several times in an attempt to "get to know" that person. One researcher then used an iterative process of reading and rereading the transcripts until emergent themes were identified that captured salient aspects of each person's experience. These themes were then compared across individuals in an effort to uncover common threads that encompassed the collective experiences of several people in the sample. The other researcher did a more systematic coding of the data using qualitative analysis software but had the same goal of uncovering common themes and experiences among participants. These analyses led each researcher to a classification system in which they grouped participants according to similarities of experience. The researchers then shared their categories with each other and discussed the strengths of each classification system. This discussion led to a melding of categories that best captured the differences and similarities between the participants. A detailed description of this process is reported in Appendix F.

The resulting categorization placed each participant within one of four broad groupings. Those groups were given a "title" indicative of the dominant issues those people faced while unemployed, their dominant perceptions of unemployment, or the overarching motivations that seemed to direct their behaviour. The four groupings that emerged from this analysis are the Planners (n = 18), the Vacationers (n = 11), the Connectors (n = 12), and the Marginalized (n = 18).

Those labels were necessarily broad. Within each group, participants were further classified by various objective and subjective factors that characterized the distinct sets of factors affecting each participant's daily functioning and subjective well-being. The Planners' sub-groups included the Routinizers (n = 7), the Anti-Homebodies (n = 4), and the Efficacy-Seekers (n = 7). The Vacationers' group included subgroups labelled Breaking In (n = 6) and In Control (n = 5). The Connectors' group was subdivided into two groups: the Caregivers (n = 6) and the Networkers (n = 6). Finally, the Marginalized group was similarly composed of three subgroups, including the Rovers (n = 7), the Surplus People (n = 7), and the Lonely People (n = 4). Table 4 lists each participant by group and sub-group.

Figures 1 through 5 on the following pages detail the demographic breakdown of the sample by group and subgroup. Figure 1 displays gender, Figure 2 displays age, Figure 3 displays education, Figure 4 displays ethnicity, and Figure 5 displays pre-unemployment income. Although a cursory glance at the nature of these groups suggests some interesting between-group differences, a more complete discussion of each group is provided in chapters 3 and 4. Each group is described through the common experiences and perceptions those participants shared, with an appeal to the words of the participants to articulate these factors within their life contexts.

Figure 1 Gender Distribution by Group and Subgroup

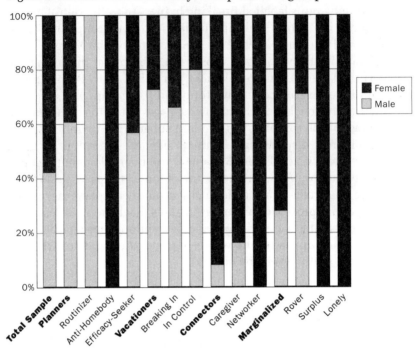

Figure 2 Age Distribution by Group and Subgroup

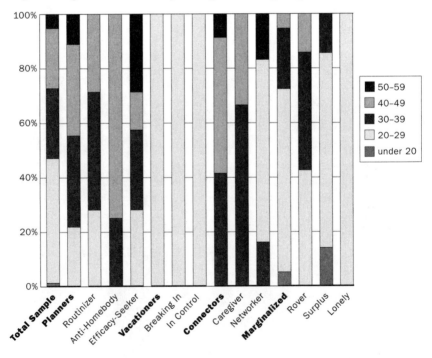

Figure 3 Education Distribution by Group and Subgroup

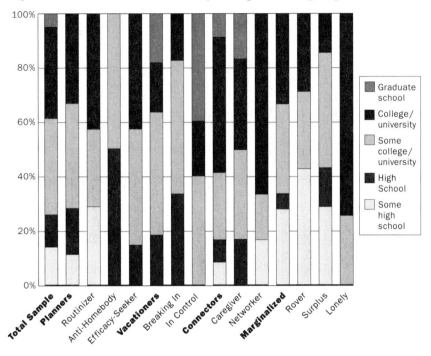

Figure 4 Ethnicity Distribution by Group and Subgroup

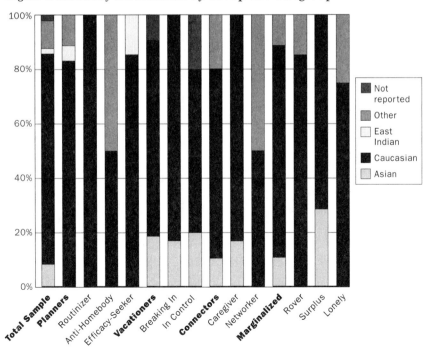

Figure 5 Pre-Unemployment Income by Group and Subgroup

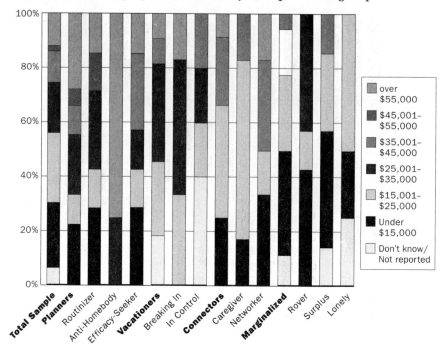

3 *Talking about Unemployment*

Participant Classification and Descriptions of Daily Life

The participants were each placed within one of four broad groups whose "title" indicates the dominant issue they faced while unemployed, their dominant perception of their unemployment, or the overarching motivation that seemed to direct their behaviour. The four groupings that emerged from the analysis of the data are the Planners, the Vacationers, the Connectors, and the Marginalized. Subdividing the usable sample of 59 participants, the Planners and Marginalized each included 18 participants, the Connectors 12, and the Vacationers 11 (Table 4).

Further to this broad categorization, each group was composed of subgroups that included a more homogenous sample of participants. Although representative of the broad group theme, the subgroups were differentiated by various objective and subjective factors that allowed a more meaningful articulation of the distinct sets of factors that came to affect the participants' daily functioning and subjective well-being. The Planners' subgroups included the Routinizers and the Efficacy-Seekers, each of which included seven participants, and the Anti-Homebodies group, which included four participants. The Vacationers included the subgroups Breaking In with six participants and In Control with five. The Connectors' two subgroups, the Caregivers and the Networkers, each included six participants. The Marginalized group was composed of three subgroups labelled the Rovers, the Surplus People, and the Lonely People, which comprised seven, seven, and four participants respectively. A discussion of the objective and subjective features of each of these groups will follow in the proceeding section. Indeed, most of this chapter is devoted to detailed description of the various groups and subgroups. This discussion is supported with numerous quotations from the participants.

This chapter also provides detailed analyses of daily life patterns, using Experience Sampling Method (ESM) data, as reported in Phases 1 and 2 of the data collection process. These are very different

Table 4 Final Group and Subgroup Breakdown

Planners (n=18)

Routinizers (n=7)	**Anti-Homebodies** (n=4)	**Efficacy-Seekers** (n=7)
Dick	Anna	Dale
Jacob	Barb	David
Jeffrey	Jackie	Jack
Shawn	Shelly	Joe
Steven		Kelly
Todd		Nicole
Tom		Sheila

Vacationers (n=11)

Breaking In (n=6)	**In Control** (n=5)
Bruce	Bob
Harry	Donald
Joanne	Jim
Les	Walter
Matt	Lynn
Pauline	

Connectors (n=12)

Caregivers (n=6)	**Networkers** (n=6)
Alison	Anita
Andrea	Jeanne
Donna	Jenny
Heather	Melanie
Janet	Stacy
Paul	Stephanie

Marginalized (n=18)

Rovers (n=7)	**Surplus People** (n=7)	**Lonely People** (n=4)
Aaron	Carrie	Marcia
Angie	Christina	Mary
Kim	Carolyn	Susan
Frank	Darlene	Taryn
Larry	Diane	
Robert	Peggy	
Keith	Tracy	

data from the interview data upon which the groups and subgroups are developed. The ESM data were collected to provide a series of detailed, on-the-spot snapshots of the daily lives of respondents and to provide triangulating evidence supporting or challenging conclusions drawn from the interview data. Respondents carried a telephone pager and a small booklet for a week during Phase 1 and again during Phase 2. A computer was programmed to send telephone signals on a stratified random basis seven times per day. The ESM data were collected as quantitative responses to a short series of questions which respondents answered each time they were signalled. The ESM questionnaire is reproduced in Appendix B.

We expected that interview analyses would be useful in informing the ESM component of the research and, indeed, the four groups and 10 subgroups provided the basis from which this portion of the ESM analysis is drawn. Members of the four groups varied with respect to where they were when signalled, the main thing they were doing, how involved they were with the main task at hand, perceived time pressure, and their levels of interaction with others. The groups also exhibited varying mood states as measured by a composite of four items. Similar differences were also reported at the subgroup level. Tables 5 to 9 provide details regarding these analyses at the group level whereas Appendices G to K provide details at the subgroup level. Collectively, these tables and appendices provided the quantitative basis from which subsequent text-based tables, presented later in this chapter, were developed.

Although percentages and mean scores may not appear to vary between groups when examined descriptively, analyses reported statistically significant differences between groups on every test. The extent to which between-group differences are "real" or of "practical significance" is sometimes clouded by the large number (N = 4,415) of episodes sampled during the study. Nevertheless, we believe that meaningful inferences can be made in the majority of cases, especially by comparing the quantitative data with the qualitative interview data. Written comments drawn from the ESM data are inserted, in tabular form, at appropriate junctures throughout this chapter. In most cases the ESM data provide corroborative evidence for conclusions drawn from the interviews, but in some cases the ESM data appear to contradict earlier findings. Where appropriate, we provide possible reasons for contradictory evidence and offer opinions about which data seem most trustworthy. In this chapter, then, the textual material is drawn from the interviews whereas the tables include data and written summaries of the ESM component.

Table 5 Respondents' Location When Signalled (by Group)

	Total %	Planners N	Planners %	Vacationers N	Vacationers %	Connectors N	Connectors %	Marginalized N	Marginalized %
Home	55	708	60	423	59	496	53	686	54
Work/school	14	113	10	91	13	88	9	141	11
Store/office	5	63	5	42	6	60	6	79	6
Friend's house	5	47	4	34	5	56	6	93	7
Recreation site	5	58	5	35	5	54	6	49	4
Other	16	199	17	88	12	188	20	235	18

Note. $\chi^2 = 47.22$, df = 15, p < .001.
Subgroup data related to this question are presented in Appendix G.
Total ESM (N = 4,415).

Table 6 The Main Thing Respondents Were Doing When Signalled (by Group)

	Total %	Planners N	Planners %	Vacationers N	Vacationers %	Connectors N	Connectors %	Marginalized N	Marginalized %
Family/home related	26	370	32	78	11	266	29	297	24
Employment related	18	185	16	133	19	94	10	191	16
Other tasks	19	239	20	102	14	259	28	207	17
Personal care	15	157	13	195	27	110	12	218	18
Recreation related	22	220	19	206	29	201	22	316	26

Note. $\chi^2 = 258.74$, df = 15, p < .001.
Subgroup data related to this question are presented in Appendix H.
Total ESM (N = 4,415).

Planners

Individuals who are characteristically very strong in their planning orientation and who desire to maintain a high degree of structure in their lives are grouped under the broad category of "Planners." The 18 individuals grouped as Planners vary widely in terms of demographic factors and prior work experience, but all share this strong planning orientation. There are three subgroups within the main Planners group, differentiated by the motivation underlying their disposition to planning and the relative degree of success they achieved in maintaining or producing the sense of structure they desire. The Routinizers sought

Table 7 Task Involvement and Perceived Time Limit (by Group)

	Total %	Planners N	%	Vacationers N	%	Connectors N	%	Marginalized N	%
Task involvement									
Entirely	46	293	40	176	43	295	57	348	47
Mostly	40	323	44	181	44	182	35	262	35
Partially	14	117	16	57	13	37	7	138	18
Time pressure									
No time limit	57	533	45	458	63	626	66	774	61
Some time pressure	32	468	39	226	31	247	26	360	28
Lots of time pressure	11	189	16	40	6	80	8	142	11

Note. Task involvement: $\chi^2 = 61.28$, df = 6, p < .001.
Time pressure: $\chi^2 = 139.69$, df = 6, p < .001.
Subgroup data related to this question are presented in Appendix I.
Total ESM (N = 4,415).

Table 8 Social Context and Form of Interaction (by Group)

	Total %	Planners N	%	Vacationers N	%	Connectors N	%	Marginalized N	%
Presence of others									
Alone	37	394	33	354	49	368	38	434	34
Partner	20	342	29	51	7	136	14	323	25
Friend	23	210	18	190	26	208	22	312	24
Other adults	22	196	16	187	26	210	22	293	23
Children	15	300	25	11	2	225	23	116	9
Pets	13	183	15	28	4	139	14	175	14
Level of interaction									
No	46	566	48	396	55	440	47	552	44
Yes (task related/ formal)	11	129	11	68	10	121	13	137	11
Yes (social/ formal)	11	95	8	44	6	109	12	150	12
Yes (casual/ intimate)	32	397	33	211	29	277	29	423	34

Note. Presence of others: No statistical test was conducted.
Level of interaction: $\chi^2 = 44.94$, df = 9, p < .001.
Subgroup data related to this question are presented in Appendix J.
Total ESM (N = 4,415).

Table 9 Mood States (by Group)

	Planners		Vacationers		Connectors		Marginalized	
	Mean	SD	Mean	SD	Mean	SD	Mean	SD
Mood states[a]								
Bored/ involved	3.77	.92	3.64	.92	4.04	.96	3.66	1.20
Unhappy/ happy	3.54	.87	3.65	.87	3.67	1.23	3.87	1.08
Irritable/ good humour	3.57	.86	3.65	.80	3.87	1.01	3.71	1.12
Anxious/ relaxed	3.41	.97	3.50	1.02	3.54	1.36	3.59	1.21

Note. $F = 6.80$, $df = 3$, $p < .001$.

[a] Mood states were assessed with semantic differential scales using endpoints labelled by these adjective pairs, whereby 1 = the negative end of the scale (bored, unhappy, irritable, anxious) and 5 = the positive end of the scale (involved, happy, good, relaxed).

Subgroup data related to this question are presented in Appendix K.

Total ESM (N = 4,415).

the sense of order and accomplishment that they previously derived from work and were generally successful at maintaining a sense of structure in their daily routines. Anti-Homebodies were motivated in their planning efforts by a strong desire to escape what they perceived to be confining home environments, but the structure they imposed on their lives was neither as far-reaching nor as successful as the Routinizers'. The Efficacy-Seekers missed the routine and structure of work; however, their compensatory planning efforts often fell short of their intentions, and they consequently often felt adrift while unemployed.

Routinizers

The seven Caucasian men in the Routinizer group vary in terms of their age, education, and income levels prior to unemployment. Two were in their 20s, three in their 30s, and two in their 40s. Two had not completed high school, two had some college or university training, and the other three had earned college or university degrees. Pre-unemployment household incomes varied widely. Two Routinizers had family incomes less than $15,000 in the year prior to losing their jobs whereas, at the other extreme, one household had earned more than $55,000. (Demographic and job-related data for each individual in this and other subgroups are provided in Tables 2 and 3.) The common theme among this subgroup was a very strong predilection for planning their daily routines. This planning was primarily motivated by their desire to seek employment, but also manifested in their orientation toward leisure pursuits and indicated their desire to attain the routine and sense of accomplishment that they derived from working. They felt that their age and unemployed status contributed to being stigmatized, and they were concerned and uncertain about what the future holds for them.

The planning orientation of the Routinizers was most strongly evidenced in their job-search activities, which included not only day-to-day activities undertaken in order to immediately find a job but also skills-upgrading activities they undertook in order to be more attractive candidates for employment in the future. Scheduling their activities figured prominently, as Jacob described: "I've been writing out a schedule for each day, what I'm going to look at, what I'm going to do.... Here now I have a routine. I do almost as many hours on my scheduling, job search and doing odd jobs around the house. I do put in a full day's work." This comment was echoed by Dick, who noted, "I try to keep a routine so that I'm always busy and I'm always geared up for what is going to be happening. I don't like just letting things happen as they may." A similar desire to control what happened on a daily basis and to take proactive steps to secure work led Tom to suggest that "you can absorb too much time into hobbies." Tom also mentioned, "I try to structure my daytime activities so at least I figure 'OK, I spent so much time on this I should move on to other things.'"

However, as mentioned, these individuals were not merely concerned with plans that may yield benefits in the present, but also steps that may stand them in good stead on both a professional and a personal level in the future. As Jeffrey explained,

> I'm getting in touch more with myself. It's kind of, you know, I feel that things happen for a reason and maybe are important for a reason and that maybe I should just take this time, to benefit from this time that I have off and maybe I can see this as a time to enrich my skills so that I can be [a] more worthwhile person in the long run, not even as an employee, but important to myself. It's also time to upgrade skills, like I've heard of this place on King and University where if you're unemployed you can go there for free and train yourself on computers.

Others in the group had undertaken the skills development to which Jeffrey alluded. For instance, Tom explained both the content and structure of his training for employment:

> Since I'm in training for blackjack dealership it helps to ... there's a couple of things that you have to know. I mean, just simple things like

shuffling cards, there's a certain way of doing that, so it's just pure repetition, same with cutting chips, you know. I've got the chips and the cards and I go over that, plus I also got a manual about that thick about blackjack dealers so I go over that, making sure everything is just split second decisions and nothing where it's the point, what do I do next? So, in a way, I'm training myself for this job. My actual training is on weekends, it's Saturdays and Sundays, but during weekdays, it's pretty much all for myself.

Todd was also in the process of retraining for his return to the labour force, and during Phase 2 he completed grade 11 and 12 English credits, motivated by his desire to take a journalism course: "It's been twenty years since I've been in school—done anything, even remotely even thought about it, if you had asked me six months ago, '[is] this what I would be doing now,' I would have said, 'no, that's ridiculous. Why would I want to do that?' But, in the overall, what I want to do, then that's what I have to do, so.... And it's full time, eight hours a day."

Table 10 What Were Planners Doing When Signalled?

Consistent with responses to the question regarding where they were when signalled, planners, more often than members of any other group, reported that the main things they were doing related to family/home. Planners reported receiving fewer signals when recreating than any other group and fewer signals when engaged in personal care than did members of most groups.

- Routinizers reported, relative to other Planner subgroups, the highest percentage of signals received when engaged in personal care. It seems likely that some of this may be attributable to fitness-related activity and their propensity to plan, including finding space for "personal time."

- Anti-Homebodies, consistent with their expressed frustrations, attended to a very high number of family-related tasks. This was true not only in comparison to other Planner subgroups, but to the larger sample as well. Anti-Homebodies reported fewer recreational and personal care contexts than did any of the remaining nine subgroups in the study. These data are consistent with their gender, their marital and parental status, and their expressed frustration with being home-bound at times when they would otherwise have been at work.

- Efficacy-Seekers seldom reported family-related contexts even though six of the seven Efficacy-Seekers were involved in relationships or lived with children. Instead, they reported engaging in high percentages of employment-related and "other" tasks. This duality is consistent with Efficacy-Seekers' predilection to planning and with their general level of frustration with remaining focussed and on-task.

In addition to structuring their daily work-search activities, the Routinizers displayed a similar degree of planning related to their leisure. Their leisure was often highly structured, having utilitarian purposes beyond the simple enjoyment that may be derived through participation. As Steven noted in Phase 2, "I try to do a few things of physical activity, you know, play hockey once a week, soccer once a week. I try to keep fit." This preference for planned, physically active leisure was also mentioned by Jacob: "During the winter, myself and a group of friends, we play ball hockey on one day during the week. So we maintain that schedule or we keep that night open during the summer. We usually go over to one person's house, always try and guarantee ourselves one night a week." During the Phase 2 interview, Todd pointed out some of the benefits of such planned recreation, particularly in combination with school, as it helped to maintain work-like structure with regard to his time:

> Well, I still get up, I still work out every morning. We start at ten and go to six so that still gives me time to work out in the morning which is nice, I like working out in the morning. So that's great. And then school, as I said it's from ten to six so that's pretty intense…. But I still pretty much participate in other sports that I want to—I still play hockey, and as I said before, mentioned that I work out. So it's almost like getting a job. It's more involved than what I was doing before, at least I'm doing something now, as opposed to looking around, trying to find something to do. You know.

However, planning for their recreation was not strictly limited to sports or physical activities. Jacob also mentioned that he and his wife "try to do one special event a month. This month it was the Eagles [rock concert]. Next month we're going down to Michigan to catch a NASCAR race." Dick also noted that nonphysical but planned leisure time was central to his routine: "I always, I plan for the evenings. After supper the evenings are for me to do the things that make me feel good and let me relax. Going for walks, getting on my radio, working on my computer, maybe playing some chess on the computer or playing some video games or just doing some log entries. I keep all of my contacts from the radio on disk, so those are the things that I like to do in the evenings, and plan for." In addition to maintaining their fitness and remaining in contact with others while providing structure for their days, as in Dick's case, Routinizers' planned leisure was often a time for learning and self-development, a point made by Todd when he described his voluntary activity refurbishing used bicycles for the underprivileged: "You know, you fix up one bike and whoever wants it comes in and buys it. Primarily underprivileged families, but anybody who needs a bike, or wants a reasonable bike, they sell them for twenty to fifty dollars. They're cheap. But the bikes are all fixed up and repaired—but they want to get them back on the street as opposed to having them sit in garages some place, so that's why—hence, they call them 'Recycle cycle.' So it's good. It's a lot of fun. I learn a lot from being there."

Table 11 Who Were Planners with When Signalled?

Planners spent relatively little time alone (one-third of all signals). All three Planner subgroups spent a fair amount of time with partners. Planners were more likely than members of other groups to be signalled in the presence of life partners. This is not surprising because a high percent of Planners are married. They were less likely than members of all other groups to be signalled in the company of friends and other adults. Planners generally reported, in comparison to other groups, mid-range scores with respect to most types of interaction. They did, however, report the highest levels of casual/intimate interactions when signalled.

- Routinizers were more often signalled when in the presence of partners than were other Planner subgroups. Routinizers exhibited the highest percentage of formal social interactions of the Planner subgroups and reported relatively few casual and intimate interactions.

- Anti-Homebodies were less often signalled when with friends and other adults, and were much more likely to be signalled when with children in comparison to other subgroups in the study. These data are consistent with earlier descriptions developed from interview data. The percent of signals with children present is even double that of people in other groups whose members generally had dependent children (for example, Connectors). The fact that very few signals were received in formal social settings may be a reflection of their relatively diffused social networks and may have contributed to perceptions of isolation.

- Efficacy-Seekers were less often signalled in the presence of partners than were other Planners, but more often than were members of most other subgroups. Both Routinizers and Efficacy-Seekers reported a fairly high number of signals when in the presence of family pets. It is not clear whether the presence of pets is a reflection so much of personal predilections or simply a reflection of life-stage for many respondents. The data suggest that, relative to most subgroups, Efficacy Seekers rarely interacted in formal social situations.

In short, the Routinizers attempted to plan for and control their time use, whether it was for the express purpose of finding work or for somewhat less utilitarian ends. They derived satisfaction from the structure they imposed upon their lives, and also gained a sense of accomplishment and worth from their ability to not let their time slip by or be used in a haphazard fashion. This strong orientation toward routine may be understood in light of the sense of accomplishment they were missing from work as well as their affinity for problem solving. Dick clearly explained what he missed during this period of unemployment:

> It's the personal satisfaction. I've always been a person who's really been keen on achieving…. You go into work some days feeling like garbage, and after you're there for a while, you feel so much better because you're interacting with people, and you're doing your job, and you're seeing that you're accomplishing things, and you take a lot of pride in it, at least I do.
>
> I've loved walking into places and seeing problems, and then dealing with the problems and working with the people to iron out the problems, to create a better environment for people to work in. That's what I miss. If I was working for a company, I'd be able to provide them with all the experience that I have that would benefit their operation and their people that work through the operation. I sit back here sometimes, and I just wonder about that part of my life, when that part is going to get back on track again.
>
> You know you miss that satisfaction of knowing that you really accomplished, ah, something on a day-to-day basis, so I really miss that. I turn it around and I make my little day-to-day accomplishments, ah, stand out to say that I've done something and that you know that I've accomplished something so I feel a sense of worth. But from the job that's what I miss, that day-to-day involvement that, you know, making decisions that you know are the right decisions and dealing with stressful situations and dealing with other people's problems and coming up with the answers and feeling good about what you've done. That's what I miss most.

This missing sense of accomplishment was also noted by Steven during the Phase 2 interview, and he lamented the lack of any concrete results for his efforts while unemployed in contrast with the measurable results at work: "What I missed most about that job was it was, ah, rewarding in the sense that when you started something, I'm speaking more about the actual on-site set-up of the exhibits, it was something like concrete that you could, at the end of, you had to work until it was done, but at the end of it, you stood back and you saw what you had built. You know, like the finished product."

This missing sense of accomplishment was difficult to contend with psychologically, as it engendered feelings of self-doubt and low self-worth. During Phase 2, Todd described his feelings about not working and what was most bothersome: "Um, I think, not having a job, feeling somewhat inadequate, that you should be working, but you weren't ... not able to find employment, rejection. That bothered me.... You would much rather be working. It's always good for your self-esteem just to be able to have a job, to say I have a job."

This sense of rejection and not being a productive member of society was reiterated by Jeffrey:

> Well, I think it's the fact that it's really hard on me as an individual, you know, dealing with well, I'm not productive enough. It's given me a different perspective on what the society is about. It's all fine and dandy to be very productive and it's very good to contribute to society, but to what expense, you know, how much of yourself, how much of your values should you sacrifice. I think also I regret the amount of money I put into finding a job, there's so much money you put in, in time and in effort and emotion, you know, sometimes you take it personal when someone doesn't hire you, that's frustrating.

In addition to the frustrations due to not feeling productive and experiencing rejection at the hands of potential employers, the Routinizers often felt stigmatized and were frustrated by the lack of understanding and the implicit judgements of family and friends. Judgements were seen as stemming from two sources: the first related to taking advantage of the Unemployment Insurance system and the second more generally related to not being a productive citizen. Each of these had adverse effects upon their social relationships. Jeffrey neatly summarized both sources of stigma during the Phase 2 interview by stating, "The longer the time period, the longer I seem to be unproductive to my family [who are] sort of wondering, well you're taking advantage of the system." This sentiment was repeated by Dick who claimed that his friends "can't really accept the fact that I'm living off the government, off the tax-payers when I should be out there working." Tom also noted that unemployment is a subject that he would prefer to avoid due to society's sentiments about working: "I guess [the] social stigma of being unemployed, and you, know collecting unemployment is there. Obviously, you don't want to brag about that, so you still get the feeling that you are what you work so when you're unemployed it's, you can't really brag about it...."

As a result of such perceptions of stigma, participants occasionally limited their social contact, and they also noticed that others have similarly limited their contact with them due to their unemployment. As Dick explained, "It seems to be a stigma—a few of my friends sort of drifted away.... So the whole unemployment process has been a real educational one for me. I never realized that there were so many prejudices out there, because I never dealt with them before."

It should be pointed out that the perception of social stigma related to unemployment may simply have been the participants' interpretation of the attitudes of others rather than an objective reality, as Jacob pointed out: "I think it was just more of me thinking that than other people thinking. Most people seem to be very helpful, a lot of suggestions." However, whether the stigma was indeed grounded in social reality or was simply a matter of individual interpretation of the actions and comments of others, the result is the same: it accentuated the decreased sense of self-worth derived from participants' perception that they were not contributing to society.

The cumulative effect of such self-doubt and perceived stigma gave the Routinizers a very high level of uncertainty about the future. During Phase 2 Steven noted that one of his more significant worries was "just not knowing what I'm going to be doing next," while adding that "uncertainty is not something you want in your life." The uncertainty that they felt was a function of the need to earn a living and, for the older members of the group, their age, as well. Tom pointed out that "there's always that thing in the back of your mind, where's the next job or the next paycheque coming in?" This sense of financial insecurity was also noted by Shawn, who indicated that his age contributed to the negative effect on his mind-set: "You get depressed when you're unemployed. Especially for myself, I find that here I am over forty, and have a set of skills—a set—I don't know how to say it...a set number of skills in a given area, and nonetheless, if I can't come up with or find something that falls within that skill set, I'm unemployed." Dick, also in his forties, expressed largely the same sentiment: "I don't like not having a job (laughter). You know, not only is it a tremendous financial hardship, but psychologically, emotionally, it's tough. There are days you just kind of stare out into space, and you just kind of, like, 'I'm 40 years old and I've got another 20 years, 25 years to put in working.' Some days you just kind of sit back and you shake your head and you go, 'Jesus, what in the hell's going to be happening here?' You know, so it's nerve-wracking sometimes."

The financial insecurity, coupled with their awareness that the job market might not be overly supportive of older workers, occasionally led to a general erosion of confidence in their long-term prospects. As Dick wondered during Phase 2, "What happens if I do find a job, how long is that going to last?" Thus, notwithstanding these individuals' very structured approach to training for or securing employment and the small sense of accomplishment they derived from such action, they did suffer social, emotional, and financial hardships due to their unemployment, and these occasionally led to self-doubt and anxiety.

Anti-Homebodies

The Anti-Homebodies share many affective and behavioural features with the Routinizers. However, this group is made up exclusively of women who, in contrast to the Routinizers, were all partnered and had teenaged children living with them. Three of the four women in this group were between the ages of 40 and 49, and the other Anti-Homebody was between 30 and 39 years old. All had completed high school, and although two of the four had some college or university education, none had earned a degree. The pre-unemployment household income for three of the four participants in this group exceeded $55,000, while the remaining participant earned between $20,000 and $29,999 in the year preceding the study. Two Anti-Homebodies identified themselves as Caucasian whereas two others placed themselves into the "other" category. Significant commonalities among these women included struggling with being at home and consequently taking the "the long view" in their efforts to reintegrate themselves successfully into the employment market. The label Anti-Homebody captures their negative feelings about being at home, particularly when the rest of the family was out; in contrast, time spent with their families during the evening was important to them. Similar to the Routinizers, the Anti-Homebodies suffered from a lost sense of purpose and eroded confidence, and attempted to maintain a daily routine. They typically avoided television during the day, and the potential negativity of their experience of unemployment was mitigated somewhat by the presence of supportive friends and the fact that their reduced family income was seen as more of an annoyance than a threat.

The dominant theme among these four women is that their planning horizon extended far into the future, and their day-to-day activities were not predicated upon the desire to seek employment in the short term. Their ultimate aim was to escape what they perceived as a confining home environment, but they knew what they wanted and were unwilling to settle for any job that might have presented itself. Jackie explained her desires: "I guess right now for the skills that I have it has to be office work. I'm looking into—I would really love to do a library information technician's program at Sheridan [college] in the fall, but I have to speak to unemployment about that to see if they would back me on my unemployment insurance while I did it.... Because I have worked in libraries. That's where I would love to do it." Jackie was still in the planning stages toward upgrading her skills to secure the job she wanted, but Shelly had embarked on training for a new career in real estate, and described the benefits of pursuing this training and striving toward a goal: "But most in my ... the last few weeks, the most of my days have been—I have been devoting it to so many hours each day studying the real estate, and I can honestly say I've faithfully made myself do that. I think it's been good therapy, because in a way I had to go to my little job, you know [laughter], and I think that's why it's probably very important for people who are unemployed and don't know which direction they are going to go into to involve themselves with school courses or something like that...."

Evaluating "what direction they are going" and taking purposive steps to get there were motivated by the women's desire to work beyond the confines of their home. This desire stemmed from their prior positive experiences in the workforce and their wish to re-establish themselves, coupled with the lack of challenges posed by being a stay-at-home mom with older, relatively independent children. Barb clearly articulated this during her Phase 1 interview: "I'm bored. I'm not a homebody. As much as I enjoy it for the kids, like the kids are old enough and I don't feel it that much, going out to work and them, you know, coming home by themselves. I like to be out there." It must be said that the work that they did at home was not without its rewards; however, in the long run these satisfactions were not considered to be wholly adequate, as Shelly noted: "I think I've enjoyed being able to be at home to make dinners—suppers, and uh, oh, keeping up—now, like I say, now I get my housework done [laughter]. Now I'm into making meals and things like that, but, yeah, I'll miss that, but I know I couldn't stay like this, not working and be a full-time homemaker. I just couldn't. I've spent too many years out there in the work force, and I find it hard to—too much break time."

Although they were generally unhappy about being at home, the Anti-Homebodies found it particularly difficult in the mornings once the other members of the household had gone off for the day. They felt that they were "being left behind"; as family members went out to participate in those activities that were their lot, these women strongly felt the lack of any similar destination. Jackie mentioned her strategy for avoiding negative feelings associated with being the last one remaining at home: "I'd say [I get up] between seven, seven-thirty ... I'll get washed and dressed and get him going. And uh ... if I'm taking—if it's my turn—We have a pool, a car pool or a walking pool for the kids, whatever it is, I'll do that. Now, I'm trying to do it every morn-

Table 12 Where Were Planners When Signalled?

In comparison to the other three groups, Planners reported the highest percentage of instances when they were signalled at home. In addition, they were less often signalled at stores, offices, or friends' houses than were members of other groups.

- Routinizers answered a high percentage of signals from home, but they were also the subgroup most likely to be signalled at stores or offices, perhaps indicating that they were often conducting job-search activity when away from home. Recall that the interview data suggested that Routinizers' daily routines were structured, first and foremost, around job-search activities. Routinizers, relative to other subgroups in the full sample, reported receiving a relatively high number of signals while at recreation sites.

- Anti-Homebodies were, in comparison with the larger Planners group, most likely to be at home when signalled. Indeed, theirs was the highest percentage of any of the 10 subgroups and is consistent with their general feelings of isolation and being "left at home" as expressed in their interviews. Also consistent with this general sense of isolation, Anti-Homebodies were least likely of the subgroups to be visiting friends' homes when signalled. Their often-expressed desire to interact more with friends, especially those experiencing similar circumstances, may represent a reaction to isolation. Anti-Homebodies, relative to other subgroups in the full sample, reported receiving a relatively high number of signals while at recreation sites.

- Efficacy-Seekers were the least likely Planner subgroup to be signalled at home and the most likely to receive signals while at work/school settings and at friends' homes. Perhaps these numbers reflect the sense of balance and continuity of routine that Efficacy-Seekers, and indeed, all Planners were striving to achieve. Efficacy-Seekers reported a relatively low percent of signals received at recreation sites; half that reported by both Routinizers and Anti-Homebodies. Data reported later in this book suggest that Efficacy-Seekers were generally not comfortable in leisure contexts.

ing regardless of if the other women want to take him or not, I will walk to the school, 'cause it makes me feel better." Shelly, in contrast, was initially unable to find such means to lessen the impact of not having somewhere to go as did everyone else, and she noted the state in which this would leave her: "Um … and the other thing that I find really hard is not getting up to go to work, because I went through such a stage of feeling sorry for myself, I really don't know how my family coped with it. I was just totally useless. I did nothing … I did nothing. You know? I didn't even do housework. I was too busy moping, you know?" Jackie also stated that, notwithstanding the efforts that she made, being at home alone provided inadequate opportunity for action, and she found it difficult to fill her days with meaningful activity when left to her own devices: "I miss not doing something. I don't mind being at home for a time, but it just begins to get to me after awhile. I don't keep myself busy enough. I know there's things to do, but I seem to do better if I'm with other people around that I…. It seems to give me … but it's…. I find it difficult after, for a long period to be here. I'd rather be out doing something. The wages didn't have to be that great, you know? But, just doing something."

That they were not "out there" and "doing something" made the Anti-Homebodies feel, as Anna noted, that they lost "that sense of purpose really, you know, getting up and having no place really to go in the mornings." The lost sense of purpose was troubling, but as Jackie said, there was the occasional benefit: "Some days I like the fact that I don't—it's nice to know you don't have to rush in the morning like that and rush off somewhere, but it would be nice to have somewhere to go. That you can count on everyday, that you have that place to go to. I wouldn't even necessarily have to work."

Table 13 Planners' Perceptions of Time Pressure and
Task Involvement

Despite being unemployed, Planners were acutely aware of time pressures. Indeed, they were the most likely group to report feeling "a lot" or "some" time pressure. Together these responses accounted for well over half of all reports from the Planners, in contrast to less than 40% among all other groups. There was also evidence that Planners often engaged in, or at least thought about, several things simultaneously as they reported the lowest percentage of instances when they were "totally involved" in what they were doing when signalled.

- Routinizers, like the Anti-Homebodies, were keenly aware of time pressure relative to other subgroups and their level of task involvement was middle to high range in comparison to the broader sample.

- Anti-Homebodies, though reporting higher levels of task engagement than other Planner subgroups, were more likely to report feeling time pressure than were every other subgroup in the study.

- Efficacy-Seekers reported very low percentages of total engagement in the task at hand, by far the lowest of all 10 subgroups. It is possible that their lack of task engagement stemmed from the relatively high percentage of uninteresting tasks in which they were engaged. Relative to other Planner subgroups, however, they felt less time pressure.

Irrespective of the occasional small benefit perceived, these participants' sense of self was not vested in the home but in the workplace, and they missed the external validation that being an employee provided. During the Phase 2 interview, Jackie described her feelings in this regard: "It gives me a sense of what I am or what I can do. I miss that. 'Cause I mean I can clean house and do little things around here all day and there's never anyone saying, 'Hey, you did a good job' [laughs]. 'Thanks a lot,' or something, you know?" The lack of such self-defining activity caused their confidence to wane; this, in Jackie's case, was compounded by negative thoughts related to the circumstances surrounding her dismissal from her previous employment. Jackie explained her reactions to such thoughts: "All of a sudden maybe she [her previous employer] was right. Maybe I was lousy. Maybe I wasn't any good. Maybe I can't do anything. Then I'd drag out my resume. 'Now just a minute. You've done this, this and this. You are capable.' It's hard to convince yourself... You start doubting yourself."

Similar to other Planners, the Anti-Homebodies attempted to achieve a sense of self-efficacy by maintaining a daily routine. This served the dual purpose of allowing them to minimize unwanted breaks in their day and also helped them to achieve the same sense of structure and order that they had had when working. Anna described her planning orientation:

> I've really tried to not let it change too much my day-to-day routine. I get up, get myself showered, dress and ready for the day whether I'm going to sit and look through the paper for jobs or go to the Unemployment or whatever I'm doing but I really.... So I guess I can say that it really hasn't changed that much. I try and do everything I did like before and I have resumes and that sort of thing done up so that if I have a list of places that I'm going to go and take resumes to or...I just try and keep it as much as it was before and fill in the daytime hours with my job search or copying resumes whatever is involved in that sort of thing.
>
> Other than the fact that I'm not actually physically travelling out of town...I had a job to do when I worked for this company and now I have a job to do now, but it's a different kind of job and I'm out trying to, instead of selling them a product I'm out trying to sell myself so there hasn't been that much of a change. I'm just not getting paid as much for it.

Congruent with their desire to maintain a daily routine, the Anti-Homebodies attempted to limit their television exposure, due to the realization that by turning the television on they later had to contend with actually turning it off. As Shelly jokingly said, "I don't turn on the television set and watch TV. I told myself right from the beginning, 'you are not going to do this!' or I knew I would end up probably a soap opera addict [laughter]." In a more serious way, Jackie also commented upon the difficulties inherent in television viewing. For her, such viewing was particularly problematic when she was not in her best spirits: "I'll watch, what is it—maybe a talk-show, one of those Donahue things or something, and I guess a few game shows. If I've done that, I've lost the day. My whole day is like I don't want to do anything. If I get on that routine it lasts—sometimes it's lasted a week, and I have to fight, 'Okay, tomorrow I won't do this. Tomorrow I won't turn the TV on. I'll go to the university and work on a computer or work on my resume … I'll go this place or that place.' It's a struggle."

In addition to planning their daytime activities to resemble a work-like structure and avoiding television when they were able, an important part of the Anti-Homebodies' daily routine was interacting with other family members and friends. Opportunities for such interaction will be missed on their return to work and were experienced as a benefit of being unemployed. As Barb stated, "Being home when my kids come home, that's what I'll miss because I know they like that. Being there for them." She further noted that, due to her unemployment, "I think we're more family oriented. Like we do a lot of things with the family. You know what I mean?" She observed that opportunities for being with her family will be hard to give up. Anna also noted the advantages in this regard, but added a significant qualifier: "There are pros are that I have … that it allows me more time certainly to be here when my children go to school and be here when they come home, that sort of thing. That is a positive thing. I like that and they like it but more than anything it's more of a negative situation for myself personally." In addition to the importance of their families, the women in this group found support and encouragement through interaction with their friends, who often were also unemployed and able to add the insight of experience to their commiseration. The presence of such support was noted as an important component in these women's attempts to cope with their unemployment. As Shelly pointed out in Phase 2, she had been an important source of support, as well: "Actually for the first while I would talk to close friends on the phone but um…. And uh, the irony of that was, she was let go, we both worked for the same company, she was let go three weeks after me. So, um, in some ways we were support for each other you know." Jackie also commented upon the mutual support that was shared with friends: "I thought I always got depressed when

I was at home and she was really bad. We get together and help each other out over the computers and things like that. It's good support. It's a support group. We each know how the other feels."

In addition to having supportive friends who helped mitigate the ill-effects of being unemployed, the women in this group were in a relatively advantaged position financially. That they were financially constrained rather than financially destitute certainly made a difference in terms of how oppressive their unemployment was, a fact that was not lost on Shelly: "Um...each person handles it differently. There's circumstances surrounding the family...I know a man that's got five children and is totally unemployed, and there's no—the wife doesn't work—I mean, I thought I had it bad. At least I had a husband still working. I don't know how—it must be very, very hard." Shelly's comments during Phase 1 also illustrate that the loss of income was experienced more as an annoyance than a threat. She was not alone in this. Describing the kinds of changes that her lifestyle had undergone as a result of her unemployment, Barb noted in Phase 2:

> I think, could be because of financial reasons that umm...I'm probably umm...I probably would have been more...because we always talk about going to play tennis or something like that. I think if the money was there, we probably would've done it right away. That could be one drawback. For now I'm just content to go the Y. Doesn't really bother me, you know what I mean? I think if the resources was there, we probably would have been doing a lot more. Yeah.

That Barb was not able to participate in high-priced recreation was a limitation imposed by her unemployment, but this limitation and its impact were not particularly distressing and, relative to participants in other groups, were of rather less significance. It also indicates the overall experience of unemployment for the Anti-Homebodies: one of limitation but not desperation. Due to their active efforts to secure the kind of work they desired in the long term, the emotional support they received from their family and friends, and the financial privilege that allowed them to minimize the adjustments to their lifestyles, the greatest problem for these women was maintaining their self-confidence and securing a sense of purpose beyond the world of family. Their overall circumstances and proactive behaviour, however, suggest that these were problems that the Anti-Homebodies were well equipped to confront.

Efficacy-Seekers

The seven Efficacy-Seekers varied demographically with respect to gender, age, education, and pre-unemployment income. Four were male, three were female. Two were in their 20s, two in their 30s, one in his or her 40s, and two in their 50s. Six of the seven had some college or university education, including three who had completed degrees, whereas one had no formal education beyond high school. Similar to the Routinizers, pre-unemployment household incomes spanned five categories. At the extremes, two Efficacy-Seekers had pre-unemployment household incomes of less than $15,000 and one had an income exceeding $55,000. Six Efficacy-Seekers were Caucasian and one was East Indian.

Efficacy-Seekers were similar in their planning orientation to the Anti-Homebodies and the Routinizers. However, Efficacy-Seekers' planning efforts often fell short of their intentions, and this was reflected in their rather sporadic approach to securing employment. As with the other Planners, they missed the daily and weekly structure provided by work and, in addition, missed the opportunities for social interaction that their workplace provided. They attempted to use leisure activities to help make up for this lack of structure and social interaction, but these efforts were generally perceived as being a pale substitute, and often they felt a sense of guilt due to their leisure participation. As well, Efficacy-Seekers had a tendency to use television to fill their time, and were relatively less successful than the members of the Anti-Homebodies at avoiding such use. They felt somewhat homebound and were dissatisfied with the isolation that stemmed from having few funds and a lack of readily available social outlets. However, they typically did have some unemployed friends from whom they were able to seek some support. Nevertheless, due to their relatively undisciplined approach to organizing their daily activities, the Efficacy-Seekers tended to be greatly discouraged about their unemployment.

There were many reasons why the Efficacy-Seekers missed having a workplace to go to every day. As Sheila succinctly stated: "I like working, because I like having that structure, and I like having somewhere to go every day. I like feeling productive." The lack of structure and feelings of productivity often took their toll, as explained by Kelly: "Sometimes I get, you know I can spend a couple of days, just feeling guilty or depressed or whatever, whereas before, I think, when I had more structure I don't, I wouldn't slip into those as often, those moods I guess." These feelings typically arose due to the Efficacy-Seekers' inability to find a meaningful daily structure in the absence of work, and the difficulty they experienced undertaking worthwhile tasks in the absence of an extrinsic motivation to do so. Joe commented upon this difficulty, and offered his insights about the necessity of routine:

> Yeah, that, it's much easier for me to force myself to do things that are not necessarily pleasant or fun but are beneficial, like studying or reading or looking for a job when I have a routine. I remember reading a study once where someone had said that people who do part-time work during school sometimes actually keep better marks because they have this you know, six hours, or four hours, or two hours to study and that's it, they make use of it where another person will sit in front of the TV or will, you know, sit around and not do much important.

Given the difficulty that they had structuring many of their daytime activities, it is not surprising that the participants in this group often took things as they came and chose to participate in activities on the spur of the moment and without much planning or forethought. As a group, the Efficacy-Seekers participated in a wide variety of leisure activities, in part due to the spontaneous nature of their participation. As Nicole pointed out,

> I pretty much live day to day. I enjoy every day to the fullest as much as I can, like I go to bed tired and not bored. I do enjoy spending time with the kids, even if it's a movie or something or going out to restaurants for a light meal or whatever, something affordable. Walks with the dog, pretty much live each day as if it … you know, get full meaning out of it…. So it's not always, it's a variety of activities that I like doing, if I … like I don't plan these things, sometimes I do plan them or it's just go with the flow, like I'm not a very organized person that way at all. I don't do things consistently all the time.

In addition to spontaneous leisure participation, however, their varied leisure repertoires often entailed a certain degree of planning and organization, and such recurring activities accrued significant benefits to the participants. Examples of such activities include organized sports. David explained the cathartic benefit he perceived from his participation: "Soccer, that's a lot of fun, I have a lot of outlet there, it's not an organised soccer league, it's just with friends and acquaintances who just like to play soccer and I just have a lot of fun, just sort of blow off some steam. It's not really like to get away from frustration idea, it's just a fun thing to do … like, it's active. Some people like to do other things, but I like to play sports with people who are not too serious. I mean they have skills, I like that, but people who aren't too serious." In addition to allowing the release of stress, voluntary activities were noted as providing a needed focus in their lives. Jack acknowledged benefits that stemmed from his participation in a professional association following the reduction of his working hours:

> I did a lot of travelling last year as president of [a professional] Association...visited every province, so that actually went into part of the full period last year after my own employment started to roll off, so um...there was uh...I think last year I probably spent 60 or 70 days doing association work, and so that...I was on an intermittent basis, so spread out greatly throughout the month, so that provided a bit of focus for last fall. My activity there has started to roll off. I'm still on the governing council, like this weekend I've got a conference...so my wife and I are going, and we'll have four days up there, Thursday, Friday, Saturday, Sunday...so that still does provide some focus.

However, even though psychological benefits were reported from participation in a variety of leisure pursuits, occasional pangs of guilt were felt as the participants perceived that they were not being as productive as they could have been. In the words of Joe, "I do a lot of leisure time activities it seems. I'm wasting my life away!" Wasting time was a recurrent theme with the Efficacy-Seekers, as were the accompanying feelings of guilt. Sheila pointed out: "I'm finding that, um, you sort of waste time when you're not working, at least that's how I feel, like I waste time. 'I should be doing this and this,' and I'd start feeling guilty because I'm not doing this, this, and this, you know. Whereas when I'm working, I don't have that, because I feel that I'm being productive and responsible. I'm doing everything that I should be doing, you know, all the 'shoulds' in your head? [laughter]." Kelly made a similar comment: "Whereas now I find that when the weekend comes...I almost feel guilty, you know, that I haven't maybe put in enough time or enough effort during the week."

Feelings of guilt and nonproductivity led to their occasional overconsumption of television, as David explains: "When I'm depressed I tend not to do anything, just hang around and watch TV, sort of that. I do that for three or four days and I realize that's pretty dumb and I just start living again, going back to routines, going to the gym that sort of thing. Sheila, as well, noted that television may be overly compelling, and spoke of her ambivalence toward the medium: "Downfall is morning TV, because I like the talk shows like Donahue, and um, sometimes I watch um, Maury Povich, and sometimes I watch Jenny Jones, but then I turn the TV off, because I hate football and I never watch acting on TV. But...if I'm feeling lazy or if I don't have anything better to do, I might do that."

Table 14 Mood States of Planners

Planners reported relatively negative mood states in comparison to those reported by other groups. Specifically, Planners reported the lowest scores on the "unhappy–happy" continuum, and their scores on "irritable–good humour" and "anxious–relaxed" were relatively negative as well. By way of contrast, Planners had the second most positive scores among the four groups with respect to the "bored–involved" continuum. Higher scores on this item may reflect higher levels of task involvement, their predilection for planning, their preferences for organized activities, or perhaps their tendency to multi-task.

- Routinizers appeared to be happier than the other two Planner subgroups, but were mid-range in comparison to the full sample. Planners were less anxious than were most other subgroups in the study.

- Anti-Homebodies were more involved and less bored than were Routinizers and Efficacy-Seekers during the duration of the study. However, Anti-Homebodies were the most anxious of the three Planner subgroups. Their scores on this indicator were the lowest of the entire sample.

- Efficacy-Seekers had the lowest score of all ten subgroups on the unhappy-happy item. They were also more irritable and anxious than were most participants.

The Efficacy-Seekers' occasional inability to escape from the glow of the television is congruent with their typical inability to follow through with many of the plans they had laid out for themselves. There was often the desire to pursue a given course of action, but they seemed unable to motivate themselves; as Dale explained, "Yes, it's ah, it's affecting me, I can't do what I like to do. The house needs a lot of work, and ah, I can't seem to get in the mood to do it, and I don't have the funds to put in to it anyhow." Jack also noted the difficulty he has motivating himself, and Joe's earlier comments about the effect that a lack of routine had in this regard:

> Other days ... some days you can just be lazy. Um ... I will say that of course it kind of waxes and wanes a little bit anyway, in my energy level. I find energy levels to be down somewhat over this period. It's harder to get enthusiastic about some things. I find I have to prime the pump more often....
>
> Um ... you're a little less focussed. Um ... with the um, that's a little bit, you know, maybe always been a problem with me in the sense that, the ... having activities forces you to schedule and plan your time. The fewer you have, the more you tend to be sloppy about that process. So, I find myself less focussed than ever before. I find that I accomplish less per unit of time than I normally would expect.

Sheila voiced the common self-recrimination that stemmed from this lack of accomplishment, whether the tasks that they had set for themselves were productive or more leisure oriented:

> It just seems like lately, I don't have the same ... I don't know why! It's me! I must be disorganized ... now that I'm unemployed. I should just say, "Okay, I'm going to sit down and read this book for a couple hours this afternoons but for some reason, my time seems to be scattered. Like, all the time I have an appointment here, and appointment there, I have to do this, have to do that, and I don't know....
>
> I procrastinate all the time, "Oh, I'll do it tomorrow, I'll do it tomorrow." Whereas, you know, there was a time in my life when I was like working full-time, I did volunteer work, I was going to university, I was also taking a course at Conestoga College, and at the house and the kids were smaller and I was able to manage all that and now it's like, you know, everything seems to be like falling apart [laughter].

The generally negative mindset experienced by the Efficacy-Seekers was compounded by their perceived isolation and the lack of social outlets available to them. Joe commented that one of the worst things about being unemployed was "the loneliness, just lack of companionship, ah friends, you know, people to do things with. I have a couple of friends, but they're busy, they're either employed or in school." As pointed out, they did not typically lack friends, but due to others' obligations the opportunities for interaction were limited, particularly during the day when the Efficacy-Seekers struggled to fill their time. The lack of a variety of available friends to spend time with is one side of the issue; the other factor that limited their social interaction was the perceived need to budget their expenditures strictly; at times this led to a reticence to venture out of the house into cash-intensive situations. Dale articulated this point during Phase 2, stating, "Well ah, you don't feel free to go out and ah, spend money for one thing. Ah, you're cutting every corner.... We don't get out as much as before." The perceived lack of opportunity or means to socialize or involve themselves in social situations is all the worse for the Efficacy-Seekers, as they keenly missed the social outlets of their work environments. As Nicole simply stated, "I miss the people that I developed friendships with." However, while the friendships were of importance, work also provided a regular social network in which one received a sense of place, as well as the sense of place within the fabric of society. As Sheila explained,

> I miss the contact with the people and, and knowing, because I worked in the community centre I, I miss knowing day-to-day, keeping up day-to-day with what's hopping and what's going on.

I don't miss the actual work itself, but all that goes with having a job, you know? If I do secretarial administrative kind of work, which is not the most exciting kind of work to do, but it's all the, the sort of social aspect of it and the um the acceptance in society. Like, when you're working you're more accepted, when you, when you're talking to people and they ask you where you work and you say you're unemployed they sort of look at you like you know ... being irresponsible [laughs].

The Efficacy-Seekers missed the social contact at work and lamented the lack of regular opportunities for social interaction when unemployed. Each feeling may be understood as stemming, in part, from the fact that the friendship networks they had developed and the relationships that were of greatest significance were spread over a wide geographical area and were not easily accessed, especially during times of financial constraint. Nicole pointed out, "I have a girlfriend in Barrie and then I have one in Sault Ste. Marie and then I have a couple of girlfriends here in Kitchener and if I really thought I'd probably ... but I don't see them continually so...." Sheila explained that many of the friends that she had made while growing up had moved away, as did she, and that although she did have some good friends in the area, many more were spread throughout Canada:

Yeah, I have uh, I have—well, I don't—they're not all here. I have uh, you know, some real close friends here, but I also have friends all over. All of my friends—I have friends in Brantford, and I have friends in Toronto, and I have a friend in Calgary, and one in Vancouver.... You make friends when you're growing up in Brantford, and then everybody sort of went in different directions, but we've kept ties with a lot of people, so we do have um, two or three people here in Kitchener that I would consider good friends.

Kelly echoed Sheila, and pointed out the importance of her long-time friends relative to the new one she had made in Kitchener–Waterloo: "I've got, you know, say three or four. Most of my friends live in Toronto, just from growing up and stuff. I still keep in contact. And actually the university friends that I made didn't stay in the area. So, they're mostly in Toronto, so I've maintained those friendships probably more. I've made a few friends since I've been here but it's more the older friends, I think, that I keep in touch with."

Thus, although the Efficacy-Seekers did have friends within the area, due to situational factors and the relatively greater affinity they felt toward more long-term friends, they perceived a sense of isolation and loneliness that exacerbated the negativity of joblessness. However, many of the participants in this group did have friends who were similarly unemployed. While such unemployed friends may also have been geographically dispersed, Kelly pointed out that their availability did allow needed social contact, and such friendships were strengthened as a result of the opportunities afforded by unemployment: "I've got quite a few unemployed friends.... In some ways, um, it's brought us closer cause I've a lot more time to see them and to visit with them and stuff because they live in Toronto, most of them. Um, then, you know I can pursue it a little bit more, I can spend more time doing that." Thus, although the participants in this group did have occasional social support, due to their general inability to compensate for the lack of structure previously provided by work the Efficacy-Seekers experienced many difficulties as a result of their joblessness.

As is clear, the Routinizers, Anti-Homebodies, and Efficacy-Seekers each experienced unemployment differently, but had in common the desire to re-establish the sense of control over their lives they felt was lost with their paid employment. The level of success they achieved with regard to this sense of control varied widely among the participants. The degree to which they were able to feel self-determined and purposive in their actions seemed associated with their ability to cope with unemployment and, consequently, was intimately related to their subjective well-being.

Vacationers

Eleven individuals were placed in the broad Vacationers category. All were between the ages of 20 and 29 years and, as may be inferred from the group name, their dominant perception of their unemployment was that it was similar to a vacation. There are two subgroups of Vacationers: those who were "Breaking In" to the world of work and those who felt largely "In Control" of their professional lives.

Breaking In

The six 20-something participants who were breaking in to the world of work were geographically grounded in Southern Ontario, and most of the four males and two females were long-time Kitchener–Waterloo residents. Half of the participants in this subgroup lived with their parents, in part because of their age and the transitional phase in which they found themselves. Their reported household incomes for the year preceding the study varied widely, as did their levels of education. Two reported incomes between $15,000 and $25,000, three between $25,000 and $35,000, and one over $55,000.

Table 15 Who Were Vacationers with When Signalled?

Consistent with expectations, Breaking Ins and In Controls were more likely to report being alone and much less likely to be with partners than were members of any other subgroup. Most were, of course, both single and childless. Given these circumstances, it is not surprising that both Breaking Ins and In Controls were often signalled at times when they were not interacting, either formally or casually, with anyone else.

- Breaking Ins reported high percentages of episodes when they were in the presence of friends and pets. In particular, Breaking Ins were signalled when in the company of friends more often than was any subgroup except Surplus People. Although many Breaking Ins lived at home, the home environment often functioned analogously to a hotel at this stage of their lives. Frequent, intense interaction with parents and/or siblings was rare. Breaking Ins also reported the lowest percentage of signals when they were engaged in formal task-related and formal social situations compared with members of any other subgroup.

- In Controls reported a lower than average number of signals in which they were in the presence of friends. It is useful to remember that In Controls were relatively footloose and their friendship networks geographically diffuse in comparison with Breaking Ins, most of whom grew up in the local area. Relative to the remainder of the overall sample, the percentage of formal task-related and social situations reported by In Controls was mid-range.

Two had ceased formal education after high school, three had some college or university education, and another had completed a university degree. Five were Caucasian and one was of Asian descent. However, significant defining elements for this group are the presence of supportive friends and family, the participants' relatively fluid and unstructured daily routines, and their positive attitudes toward their unemployment and the opportunities available to them in the employment marketplace.

It is noteworthy that the participants in this group had friends who had been or were going through a similar situation; that is, contending with unemployment. For the most part, the presence of these friends allowed the participants the opportunity to share their feelings about the experience, receive emotional support, and occasionally share insights or advice about potential avenues in the search for employment. As Joanne stated, "Yeah, we go out and talk to each other about where we've seen postings where we can like refer each other to apply for jobs that maybe we're not qualified but we know that they are or things like that. So we try and always mention places, or sometimes you'll know someone that works in a company that you could tell them to go and talk to them or something so.... We try to help each other out that way, which is good. You do what you can for your friends too."

Given their groundedness in the community, Breaking Ins typically had no shortage of friends with whom to share their experiences. In addition, the fact that these friends might have experienced a similar loss or lack of employment contributed to the lack of judgement that was reported by participants in other groups. As well as the support and encouragement of friends, local family members were significant providers of such support, and gave the participants a familiar context in which to spend some of their time. With regard to family members providing assistance in the search for a job, Joanne noted,

> I suppose if anything all my family keeps their eyes open so that's different because before you wouldn't really think of it. And I guess my out-of-town family will call up every once and a while to see how it's going and see if I found anything, or say, "Hey I saw this one in the paper and I was thinking, I didn't know if you were qualified but would you like me to send it to you?"... I suppose maybe in that sense we're close but there's a bit more interaction there because they're thinking, "Well she's out of work and let's see what we can think of for her," so I guess in that way it would be different. Immediate family, we've always been really close, so I don't know if there's really anything different.

However, in contrast to Joanne's experience, Harry noted that while he received financial support from his family, the fact that he was still living with his parents occasionally gave rise to a certain amount of stress:

> [I] put a bit more stress on them, because you know I am a bit older now, and I still live at home. Like if you'd told me five years ago that I'd still be living there, like I figured I would have moved out by now. I just wanted to get my license while I was still living at home, my electrician's license. Then I wouldn't need money, I could have afforded to move out. I could have afforded to move out before, but I figured it was easy to live there, it was cheap, so. Now since I've, there's a lot of stress on myself right now, like I talk back to my parents sometimes, you know. I shouldn't, but it happens.

Pauline's experience, perhaps in part because she did not live at home, illustrated somewhat better relations with her family and paralleled some of the sentiments expressed by Joanne. In addition, there was the suggestion that support, advice, and encouragement flowed both ways, as illustrated by her efforts on her brother's behalf:

I'm always at my mom and dad's, but that's only because my boyfriend was away for the past couple of weeks for his job so without him to hang out with, Mom and Dad were like, "Oh, why don't you come on over!" so I'd be there all the time, or I'd be dropping in to say, "I found this out," you know, something for my brother to do with leisure buddy. He's going to be a leisure buddy this summer. So, just trying to keep tabs on what's new in that area and stuff, and it would just happen that I'd be there when my mom gets home from work, and then she just sort of includes me in supper, so then I'd stay even longer and seemed like I was always there.

In sum, support from family and friends contributed significantly to these participants' ability to cope with unemployment, and this support took many forms. While the intrafamilial interactions may not have been universally positive on a moment-to-moment basis, taken as a whole those who were "breaking in" were at an advantage due to the presence and availability of family and friends.

Table 16 Where Were Vacationers When Signalled?

Although Vacationers received a relatively high percentage of their signals at home, they also received more signals at work/school than did members of any other group. This observation is consistent with previously reported information about the school/workplace transition currently being experienced by Vacationers. It should be noted that job-search activities (including interviews) were considered to be "at work" as reported by members of this study. The percentage of signals received by Vacationers while at recreation sites was average relative to those in other groups.

- Breaking Ins were more likely to be signalled at home than were In Controls. The former subgroup was also twice as likely as the latter to be signalled while visiting a friend's house although their percentage for this venue was only marginally higher than that of the overall sample.

- In Controls were three times more likely than Breaking Ins to be signalled while in work or school settings. Though at first glance inconsistent with their designation "Vacationers," it appears that work-related tasks and environments may be more enjoyable for this group than for others. This observation may hold for both subgroups, but seems especially appropriate for In Controls who are highly educated, in the early stages of career development, and generally qualified for challenging and creative jobs.

As a result of the support that they received and their generally unconcerned attitude about unemployment, Vacationers took a fairly unstructured approach to their daily routine and had a laissez-faire attitude toward their job-search. In certain instances, this resulted in television becoming a fairly prominent feature of their lifestyle, although not always without regret. Bruce expressed perhaps the most dramatic illustration of the fluidity and lack of concern that characterized this group's daily functioning in response to a query about his daily routine:

> Well, I have no set schedule for waking up, today I woke up at 12:00 because I have an interview at 1:00 p.m. and I actually have to set my alarm for that I'm embarrassed to say, I was up very late last night. So normally I wake up around 12:00 or 1:00 p.m. and I'd get up if the weather's good, I'll go sun-tanning for a little while and I have a membership at a local golf course, I always go in if the weather is permittable, I always play a few holes. That will take me till 4:00 or 5:00 and then I'd come home and either watch TV or work out and just laze around until supper, have supper, usually on the BBQ because I can't cook, and in the afternoon I just make phone calls. Well either we go to a bar or go out to see a movie, rent a movie, just hang around with friends, it's pretty much what I do.

With regard to the relatively subordinate position that job-search activities assumed, for this group, in the run of a typical day, Matt added,

> A typical day for me is to get up, get up when he gets up, have breakfast, go back to bed, lay in bed, watch some television, do some laundry, you know it's … because, you can only market yourself so much. You go out and you pound the pavement. You hand out all these resumes, and you say, "Hi, my name's Matt, blah, blah, blah…." Like the other day, the only thing I did was drive out to a place on Victoria Street and drop off a resume, because they were accepting applications. That's the only thing I did. For the rest of the day I just uh … cleaned the house … whatever you can find to keep yourself busy.

Notwithstanding the incorporation of television viewing into his daily routine, Matt had some reservations about the activities that were neglected, and he averred that "I think, 'I know I should be doing this. I *should* be doing that.' But I don't want to, I'd rather lay in bed and watch television." A similar sentiment was expressed by Les, who explained that "I shouldn't really say this, but I've been watching too much TV. TV's a big thing now … I'm trying to cut … I'm addicted," indicating the ease with which television might take the place of other activities and the participants' ambivalent feelings about television consumption.

As may be predicted from these participants' relatively fluid routines and level of interpersonal support, they did see some advantages to their unemployment. Perhaps the strongest proponent of not having to work, Bruce summarized the common perception that the

Table 17 Vacationers' Perceptions of Time Pressure and Task Involvement

---

Vacationers were perhaps the least time-pressured of all groups, very rarely reporting "a lot" of time pressure and very commonly reporting that they perceived no time limits regarding their daily activity. Their task involvement scores were generally mid-range in comparison with people in other groups.

- Breaking Ins reported feeling no time limits on over three-quarters of all received signals and a lot of time pressure only 5% of the time. These numbers represented extremes in comparison to all other subgroups.

- In Controls felt more time pressure than Breaking Ins, but less time pressure than the sample as a whole. Relative to the full sample, both Vacationer subgroups reported a tendency toward multi-tasking although it was a bit more pronounced for In Controls than for Breaking Ins.

---

participants' period of unemployment was akin to a vacation by stating, "I love it, I'm having the best summer of my life right now. I'm relaxed, my blood pressure has gone down, I'm eating better and I'm seeing a lot more people, so...." Reasons offered for the participants' overall enjoyment included the freedom to schedule their activities without the time constraints imposed by work and the relative lack of severe financial constraint that allowed them to participate in varied activities, which stood in sharp contrast to participants in other groups.

Pauline voiced her pleasure at the increased freedom that she experienced, and echoed Bruce's implication that the period of not working was perceived as a vacation,

> I like being able to sleep in and do that exercise program. It gives me more energy for the day. And just be busy in the afternoon. Kind of take your time in the morning, relax. It's like a little mini-vacation, you know, go and get some sun or whatever. I could never have enough time to do that before. And actually I get to go and have break with [my former co-workers] in the afternoon sometimes, meet them for lunch or whatever but ... um ... either way. If I could make that kind of money doing this, that would be great!

Table 18 Mood States of Vacationers

Both Breaking Ins and In Controls, consistent with their Vacationer designation, registered above average scores with respect to relaxation. With respect to other mood indicators, however, the two Vacationer subgroups were diverse.

- Breaking Ins generally had more elevated mood states than In Controls. The former subgroup's scores were among the most positive in the entire sample, whereas the latter group's scores were generally mid-range.

- In Controls were more likely to be bored and unhappy than were Breaking Ins, suggesting that lack of challenge and friendship contexts were more likely issues for the former subgroup. In Controls' happiness scores, especially, were among the lowest in the overall sample. Earlier analyses suggest that this observation may be more attributable to their diffuse social and friendship networks than to their employment status.

In addition to financial support provided by parents, unemployment insurance money was identified as providing the necessary financial freedom to do what they wished, as Harry indicated: "When I first lost my job, I had unemployment and stuff, so I didn't have to worry about the money, the financial problem right there. So I could take things a lot, lot easier, you know. Sleep in 'til noon everyday, and stuff. My unemployment cheque was always there, so I didn't have to worry quite as much about things like that." These participants' attitudes toward their unemployment and, by extension, toward finding work, can be understood as the result of their confidence in what the future may hold for them. They generally weren't worried about their potential for becoming employed; as Pauline explained, "There are so many prospects out there right now. Before it was more of a deeper recession, and I didn't have any leads, and I went for months before I had a couple of interviews, and they'd be, 'boom! boom! boom!' and then I got a job so with right now only two weeks, and already four interviews, I figure, 'Well, I'm going to get in soon!' [laughter]" Matt stated that through proactive efforts he may achieve his goals, and the confidence that he expressed about his abilities to do what he felt needed to be done to obtain employment was fairly typical of participants in this group. As he explained,

> Well, I have a three-year goal, and that's—in three years, I want to be at least half way through or almost finished a degree. I want to be in business management, whether that's managing a franchise store of my own, managing a store for somebody, or you know, I want to be in that area. I don't know whether I can work and go to school at the same time, or whether I have to go through summer school, or

however it's gonna work, but um ... in three years, that's where I'm gonna be.

In contrast, Harry did voice some concerns and was not as wholly optimistic as the other participants due to his past experiences as an apprentice electrician: "Back five–six years ago when the boom was on it was really good because there was plenty of work. You could always find work wherever you went, plenty of work, lots of over-time, good money. They always paid you overtime, too. Now you'll be lucky to find the work, if there is any, and usually, like I said, it's only going to last the duration of the job and once the job's done you're gone usually."

Notwithstanding his occasionally wavering confidence about job opportunities, in general Harry was, like the others, not overly wor-ried about his ability to find work in the long term. In sum, due to the support networks available to them, the degree of freedom afforded to them, and the lack of severely constraining financial limitations, these participants were coping with their unemployment well and remained reasonably optimistic about the prospects available to them.

In Control

As with the Breaking In subgroup, the five participants In Control were all in their 20s. Four were male and one was female. Three were Caucasian, one Asian, and one did not report race or ethnicity. Pre-unemployment household income levels varied widely, from one at $15,000 to $25,000 to another at $35,000 to $45,000. Two did not report income levels, however. In contrast to the Breaking Ins, In Con-trols typically had attained a higher level of education. Two of the five had graduate degrees, one had an undergraduate degree, and the remaining two were working toward undergraduate degrees. As a result, and similar to those in the Breaking In group, the participants who were In Control were relatively unconcerned about their bout of unemployment and were confident about their long-term employ-ment prospects. However, in addition to level of education, significant differences between the two groups were evident in the In-Control group's lack of geographical grounding and their consequently dis-persed friendship networks. Furthermore, contract work was com-mon within this group, as was the participants' willingness to relocate in order to find work or assume new employment. As well, their leisure repertoires were fairly diverse and, unlike those in the Break-ing In group, they tended to become involved in volunteer organiza-tions and pursue volunteer work.

The In Controls' sense of geographical dislocation stemmed from a variety of sources, including having moved with their family of origin, having relocated for the purposes of education or work, or some combination of these, occasionally in sequence. The result of such sometimes frequent relocations was that Kitchener–Waterloo in particular did not feel like home. Lynn pointed out, though, that the lack of a sense of home was not limited to her current residence, as she responded to the question, "Is this home for you?": "[Laughs] Oh my goodness, no. I don't think I, no nothing would actually be a home. The area that I've most liked that I've been would be Vancouver. That's the greatest. Gorgeous, gorgeous place." Jim, a Maritime native, commented on the reasons why Kitchener–Waterloo was not "home" for him, and indicated that it was largely due to the difficulties associated with fitting in and the differences he perceived between himself and the majority of people in Southern Ontario: "Uh...we've been here for five years, in this area, and I don't have lots of friends to be honest with you. It's just hard to find friends. We are from East, and eastern people are a lot different than western people, so I kind of don't get along very well...." No matter the source of the sense of dislocation, the members of this group were not committed to remaining in the area for any particular length of time, although it would not have been out of the question if opportunities developed. In addition to their past relocations, feeling that the area was not home to them may account for their present willingness to move for employment purposes. Donald, based on a recent visit, noted that he would happily entertain the notion of moving to Europe: "I got some leads in Germany when I was there on vacation. Word got around that I was there. In particular, I was visiting former East Germany, and since my dad's moving into that area, he's got contacts as well. While I was there, for about a week, I helped set up computers for two different companies. And it went very well. So, I'm thinking I could easily do something like that."

Donald's willingness to move indicates another common factor among these participants: their widely scattered or international work experience and their awareness of the global economy and the opportunities it provides. Bob's comments illustrate this:

> I graduated in 1991 with a [graduate degree and discipline listed], focussing on international development, and my specialty area was housing, housing policy, and since then I've been working on a number of contracts in India, basically out, or primarily out of the University of [name omitted to preserve privacy] and I just recently completed one.... Business is always looking out, and with the contraction of the Canadian economy it's natural and advantageous to work overseas. I would like to get into the business aspect of it.

Bob's experience further reveals how common contract work was among the members of this group, primarily because of their technological training and the nature of employment within this sector:

My last employment was a sixteen-month, actually it was a one-year contract that was, at the end of that one year it was to be extended for four more months and it was through the University of Waterloo that I was, the entire contract was in India at the University of [name omitted to preserve privacy]. I was coordinating a project, an institutional cooperation project funded by CIDA that saw the development of a computer lab and it was my job to organize and conduct a series of workshops and training programs and a student exchange and faculty visits and initiate research programs and dealing with other universities in India and non-government organizations and government departments.

Due to the transitory nature of their places of residence, In Control participants frequently reported that their friendship networks were dispersed and in a state of flux. As Walter noted, "I've uh, never stayed more than four years in any one city at any time. I've lived in London, Guelph, and Kitchener in the last 11 years, I suppose. Probably the only friends I keep up with would be the ones in Toronto." Donald expressed a similar sentiment; when asked where he would consider his network of friends to be, he replied, "St. Catharines, Oshawa, Ottawa, Kitchener–Waterloo, a couple places in Germany, one in England.... They're quite spread out."

Notwithstanding the frequent moves that the In Controls had made, three of the participants, Bob, Lynn, and Donald, had left the Kitchener–Waterloo area for a period of time, only to return after their contract had been completed or their employment terminated. Bob noted that returning to a familiar place was a positive experience, largely due to reconnecting with friends: "Nothing's changed. I came back here and I'm living in this house and so the positive things are that I've been able to pick up on my old network of friends. I haven't seen them for a while and so that's positive." Lynn and Donald, in contrast, had moved in with friends with whom they had gone to school, and the proximity of friends was similarly positively experienced as they adjust to their return to the area. As Donald stated, "It's pretty good because we're keeping each other on our toes. He was unemployed for two and a half years and I sort of helped him through that a bit. She's seen it of course from a different point of view. And putting all of that together, we've got one strange sense of humour in that house."

In short, although the majority of participants in this group were not grounded in the Kitchener–Waterloo community, due to the presence of friends and, in Jim's case, family, for the most part they did not find this troubling. Rather, they construed it as the nature of the current employment environment wherein relocation is expected and not considered noteworthy. In light of this, their lack of concern about their long-term employment prospects is understandable, since in a contract-intensive world of work such layoffs are to be expected and were experienced as a matter of course. Lynn, though, surmised that later in her life she might hold a different view of things: "The worst thing about right now? I can't honestly think of anything. Yeah, um. I suppose I might look back at this negatively if I was in an established job with financial security, and you'd have your future structured, a ten-, twenty- or thirty-year job. None of this bothers me now, but it could be my reaction in the future. The financial insecurity, you know." In addition to foreseeing the possibility of holding different attitudes in the future, the In Controls expressed a certain degree of guilt at not being productive members of society. However, this was typically not cause for serious consternation, but was on the order of passing thoughts related to living up to their own and society's expectations. As Walter noted, "The only time I feel uncomfortable are times when I'm saying to myself, 'I should be working'…. It's not always going to be fun forever, and it's going to come back to you. You have to be productive in some sort of way. I feel that I don't want to be unemployed forever."

In essence, these individuals' reactions to unemployment resulted from their self-directed approach to the careers they had chosen. As such, unemployment was not necessarily viewed as an utter disconnect from the world of work but as a recurrent component of it; indeed, it is a component that held vocationally relevant opportunities. For instance, Donald noted that doing freelance computer work fit in well with his plans for the future: "A friend of mine was asked to do some teaching, Lotus, WordPerfect and that sort of thing. He's got two full-time jobs, so he doesn't have the time, so he told me give her a call and make an appointment. So that's going to happen on Wednesday. At least it will be something, and it sort of fits along with the ideas that in about a year I may be in business for myself."

Walter, in contrast, observed that his period of unemployment was valuable for self-assessment and charting the direction of his working life: "At the moment this unemployment is, for me, a needed break. It's a time in my life when I feel that I'm going to try a new career. It's not something I want to jump into. I'm not going to grab at the first thing that comes up, basically. I want this to last for 10 or 20 years."

As Walter indicated, for the In Control group this transitional period was not characterized by worry or consternation, but was instead construed as a valuable respite. Notwithstanding their lack of geographical groundedness and their dispersed social networks, being laid off between jobs was understood as normal within their conception of a career, and they were relatively untroubled by their unemployment.

Table 19 What Were Vacationers Doing When Signalled?

Vacationers differed markedly from members of other groups with respect to the main things they were doing when signalled. They reported higher percentages of job-search and employment-related tasks, personal care tasks, and recreation-related tasks. These data are not surprising given their collective average age (20-something) and marital status (mostly single and not partnered). They reported, again consistent with their life-stage circumstances, by far the lowest percentage of tasks related to family and home.

- Breaking Ins reported a much lower percentage of employment-related contexts than did In Controls. Breaking Ins reported, in comparison to all other subgroups, the highest percent of signals received in recreation contexts over the course of the study. This finding is entirely consistent with their interview data, which suggested that leisure activity was highly valued both in terms of quantity and quality.

- In Controls reported a much higher percentage of employment-related contexts than did the Breaking Ins, and indeed, higher than that of the total sample. These data are consistent with the relatively strong career orientations of the In Control group and the somewhat laissez-faire attitudes of Breaking In members with respect to career goals.

Both the Breaking In and In Control subgroups seemed unconcerned about their joblessness; for the former this stemmed from their optimism about future employment prospects within the as yet relatively untried employment market, and for the latter it resulted from their understanding of the way the employment marketplace operated. Irrespective of the cause of their outlook, both groups of Vacationers looked favourably upon their unemployment and suffered few of the ill effects noted by other participants in this study.

Connectors

Connectors included two subgroups, comprised of six participants each. The overall theme connecting the two groups was their strong need for affiliation with family and friends. Family members, especially dependants, were central to the lives of Caregivers, whereas friends, including former co-workers and customers, were most often sought by Networkers. As might be expected, given the circumstances which led to their inclusion in this study, maintenance of these connections was more difficult for Networkers than Caregivers.

Caregivers

Six respondents, five of them middle-aged women, were placed into this subgroup. Paul, also middle-aged, was the lone male. The dominant theme among Caregivers was their commitment to dependent people and pets. Five of them had children at home, and three also cared for other people, including infant grandchildren, institutionalized parents, and people with physical disabilities. Paul was married and had young children, but four of the women were single parents; three were divorced or separated, and one was widowed. Among the five women, only one mentioned a live-in partner, her boyfriend, prominently in the context of daily routine or future plans. She was also the only member of this group to report a pre-unemployment income of greater than $25,000. With the exception of one Chinese Canadian, the women were Caucasian. Paul had recently immigrated to Canada from the former Yugoslavia, and cultural transition issues were prominent in his experience. Education levels varied. One Caregiver had a graduate degree, one a had high school diploma, and the other four all had some exposure to higher education, two having earned degrees.

For the Caregivers, despite their relatively low incomes, responsibility to dependants appeared to take precedence over paid employment. This responsibility influenced both their daily routines and their long-term planning. Indeed, Janet left her last job rather than compromise her ability to adequately care for her children: "I made a choice, and I quit the job because he wanted me to work all nights, and I hadn't been doing that, and I didn't think as a single parent I could do that, so …" Donna personified the general mind-set of the Caregivers by noting: "Um, my kids take a lot of my time, and they're really important to me, all three of them…. I sound like a martyr or something here, but that's not what I'm meaning to say. I just put their activities ahead of mine, I guess. And so I never plan on anything for myself."

Caregivers often defined "loss" associated with joblessness primarily in terms of its effect on dependants rather than in terms of their personal needs. For example, they often mentioned missing income primarily because their children, or other dependants, had to make sacrifices. Janet noted straightforwardly that "There's not much money to do things." The following comment by Andrea was typical and

Table 20 Who Were Connectors with When Signalled?

Not surprisingly Connectors were, relative to members of most groups, more often signalled when in the presence of children. Connectors reported the highest number of signals wherein they were interacting with others in formal task-related and formal social contexts. Consistent with their previously reported comments, the ESM data suggest that Connectors structure more of their lives around social contexts than do other study participants.

- Caregivers tended to be signalled more often in the presence of other people than were Networkers; the only exception was that Networkers were more likely than Caregivers to be with a partner. It makes sense that Caregivers were more often with children than were Networkers, but it is puzzling that Caregivers were also more often reached when with friends than were Networkers. Caregivers' percentage of casual/intimate social interaction levels were among the highest of all subgroups.

- Networkers reported more task-related formal activity than did members of any other subgroup. Networkers reported higher percentages of task-related formal and social formal situations than Caregivers whereas Caregivers more often reported casual/intimate interactions, suggesting that Networkers tended to "institutionalize" social interaction (for example, by volunteering and participating in church-related activity).

more detailed: "Yeah, yes to a certain extent because I have an older mom. My mom's in [a retirement] home and I have to sort of help her sometimes, and I don't always have the money to help her. I can't help my daughter. My daughter's a single mom who works part time as a gymnastics coach, and I can't help her with anything." Likewise, Allison described how she cut back on expenses for herself but tried to reduce the impact of unemployment on her son: "But right now, you know, when you have more money, your lifestyle goes up, and when you don't have money, nobody will like to get your lifestyle down. Nobody will like to do, but you have to sometimes. But for me I can, no shopping, no buy clothes, shoes. I can't do that, but I can do that for my son, so I keep everything from myself. When he wants something, as long as I can manage it, it is good for him, I just try." In a similar vein, Paul spoke about the difficulty of not having a car: "At least once every few months [when living in Yugoslavia] we were in the zoo, but here, but that's the problem we don't have a car, otherwise we would go to Toronto, see the zoo or whatever and go back.... Here in this country without a car you cannot live." Donna, by contrast, experienced less financial hardship than did others, and instead put unemployment in perspective with respect to other aspects of her life: "No. Maybe it's too soon. And what's going on in my personal life overshadows everything else. Like to me, unemployment is stressful, but the custody dispute in relationship to it, unemployment is nothing. Like it's just money; you can get money anywhere."

Table 21 What Were Connectors Doing When Signalled?

Connectors reported an above-average percentage of signals when family and home-related tasks were their primary focus. Also consistent with their interview data, Connectors reported relatively low percentages of instances when they were primarily focussed on employment-related tasks and personal care. They reported by far the largest percent of "other tasks" as their main focus indicating, perhaps, a general lack of focus in their daily lives, or simply that their activities were less easily classified by the existing data collection system than were the activities of other groups.

- Caregivers were slightly more likely to be signalled in family contexts than were Networkers. Their family and home-related focus was both expected and higher than that for most other subgroups.

- Networkers reported the lowest number of signals received during employment-related tasks of all subgroups in the sample. They also reported a high percentage of episodes where recreation was their primary focus.

Caregivers also defined "gains" resulting from unemployment in terms of dependants, especially in terms of opportunity to be with children and to experience quality family time. Paul noted, "very often I use the library here, the Kitchener public library ... and the kids have fun. So we do everything for the kids and the family so we don't feel that we are in a crisis." Heather, who did not have children, used her role as a Scout leader as an outlet for this need: "Well, Beavers are so cute and they listen to you [both she and the interviewer laugh]. And the Cubs, they're more challenging. You do badge work and star work and you get to go camping and apple day and that. It's a lot of fun. A lot of work, but a lot of fun." Conversely, Donna expressed considerable anguish over a year-old custody decision, which placed her sons with their father; she was hopeful that an upcoming court date would reverse the decision:

> Um, 'cause over the year that they've been with their dad I've seen so many things that really bother me. Elliott's my son, my youngest son, Elliott, his grades have just gone right down where he was doing

so well, and Herbert has been caught shoplifting and Elliott got caught smoking, and all these things. But I don't hear it from my ex-husband, and I don't communicate, so I never hear it from him. I hear it from either the boys will tell me, or a friend of mine who knows what goes on over there will tell me, "did you know that Herbert got caught for shoplifting?"…And, it was really hard, because my identity for the past 14 years has been mom, and I love that role.

Caregivers were also prone to volunteer. A common choice was coaching youth sports, which allowed them to extend their caregiving and nurturing roles. Heather and her sister took their horses to various events where children were allowed to ride them. In this setting, the horses almost served as an extension of herself. She said,

[I love] seeing the kids smile. You get little ones that are just terrified to get on the horse, and then once they get on the horse, they love it so much they don't want to get off. And just seeing the way that horses interact with the kids, like our horses are really gentle, so they always pet the nose and everything, and last year there was a girl there that had cerebral palsy really bad, and she was in a wheel chair, and he [the horse] seemed to sense that because her hands were like, she got tired of always asking her boyfriend to ask us to bring the horses closer, and the one time she just sort of wiggled her fingers a little bit, and when the horse could sense that she needed extra help, and he went ahead and put his head like right in her lap, and he didn't like fight her or anything. He just let her touch his face and that. Like, he didn't—I didn't even notice it. He was just looking for, to see what he could do to help her or whatever. It was very special.

Although Caregivers were generally successful in perpetuating their desired nurturing roles despite circumstances surrounding unemployment, they often noted a decrease in their self esteem and the challenge of coping with depressed moods. Andrea's comments were illustrative: "It's boring. I find it very boring, very, uh it's not a challenge to me. "What challenge is there in my life? What structure? What am I doing?" I get so frustrated with that…. And I find when you're not working your self-esteem goes down for yourself. Really. It's hard to keep it up when you're not working. 'Cause you start to think well maybe after all there is something wrong with you. But there isn't. But you still feel like that. You think, 'Oh, what's wrong with me, why don't they hire me?'" Paul also noted loss of self esteem: "We usually read newspapers and all the time I'm looking for a job but you cannot find, they all require some experience and many times I call them or send my resume, but you cannot all the time just keep looking for a job because it's very, you're very, big depression because if they say no jobs or we hire somebody else with greater experience, more experience, you just have feelings that you are nobody. So that's also bad."

Table 22 Mood States of Connectors

Connectors reported the most positive mood states of any of the four major groups. Their scores on "bored–involved" and "irritable–good humour" were the highest in the sample. Likewise, they were also among the three groups reporting the most positive mean scores for "anxious–relaxed." Connectors had mid-range scores on the "unhappy–happy" continuum.

- Caregivers in particular, but both subgroups to some extent, were more involved than bored by their overall life experiences during the study.

- Networkers ranked among the most positive subgroups on all mood measures. With the exception of the unhappy–happy measure, on which their scores were average, the same observation applies to Caregivers.

Consistent with their generally social nature, Caregivers seemed to miss interaction with co-workers and customers as much as, or more than, they missed the job itself. In response to questions about what she missed most about work, Donna stated, "The people, a lot. Talking to people. I get really bored fast and I like to keep busy. I don't want my brain turning into marshmallow. I used to say that when my kids were really little, cause I took part-time jobs when the youngest one went into pre-school and I took part-time job. I used to tell people it was because I wanted to talk to somebody with a vocabulary of 25 words or more!" Caregivers stressed the importance of friendship networks. Andrea, for example, noted that "I have a lot of friends. I don't know what I'd do without them." They also agreed that grounding was important and that they felt at home in the Kitchener–Waterloo area. Alison said, "Yeah, I like here. It is hard to find a job, because some people recommend, they say, you know big city, they have more opportunity to find job, but, uh, you know, I like this small city, medium-size city, not far from big city like Toronto, not far from States, you know. It's really quiet, you know. Feel much safer compared with Toronto."

Caregivers did not necessarily schedule job-search activity, so it was often sporadic. Consistent with other aspects of their lives, they tended to job-search later in the day after other high priority duties had been completed. Janet's descriptions of a typical day were illustrative: "I usually do stuff around the house in the morning, and then in the afternoon these days I have been doing some career research, so I do that in the afternoon … just make phone calls, and I did my resume, that kind of stuff … and then about 3:00 or 3:30, I start making dinner. We eat a lot earlier now. So I'll probably make dinner around 3:30 or something, and listen to all the kids' stuff, and uh … then probably just stay home in the evening." Andrea described a similar pattern: "Well, usually I get up and, like I said, I drive my daughter and granddaughter to school, and my daughter to work. So I drive them and I have coffee at Tim Horton's. I might go down to downtown to look at the job board at Jobs Ontario, or at the Unemployment Office, or drive a friend over there. Or go to the park. Some days I go to the park, some days read a book. It's not good, a lot of things I put off."

Although uncomfortable with unemployment and its resulting hardships, especially as interpreted through their various dependants, the Caregivers were reasonably well equipped to handle difficult times. The reciprocal social and emotional support provided by their family and friendship networks was a major contribution to their overall sense of well-being. Nevertheless, their overall self-esteen remained somewhat fragile.

Networkers

Six middle-aged women comprise the Networkers subgroup. Only one member was less than 40 years old. Networkers' educational experiences were diverse, ranging from some high school or vocational training to university. One was single (never married), two were divorced, and the other three were married. Most Networkers had children, but they tended to be older teens or adults no longer at home. Networkers were racially and ethnically diverse. Three were Caucasian and three classified themselves as "other" beyond the four named categories that were offered in the initial interview. Pre-unemployment household income also varied, ranging from two who earned less than $15,000 to one who earned more than $55,000.

Networkers placed an extremely high value on social contact. They strove to maintain social contact in a variety of ways, with mixed success. Those with children still at home were early risers and tended to routinize family activities. They were also quite grounded in the Kitchener–Waterloo community, and most were fairly long-term residents with established friendship networks. Networkers were careful to distinguish between casual acquaintances and true friends. Jeanne's comments were typical:

> They say you have to be a friend to have a friend, and I know there's a lot of people that really care about me out there, but right now we

hang around with some people that, you know, that uh ... we're start-ing to develop a good relationship with, and you have to work on relationships and friendships, and I think that this is something that we're going to be sticking to, because there's a love for these people. I would say there's about five couples that we're friends with.... They go to our church, too.

Stacy also distinguished between friends and acquaintances: "A lot of friends and acquaintances. It's a large network of, uh, it's hard to dis-tinguish from real friends and people that you know from work or school that ... 'cause we socialize with them all a lot. There's always a barbecue going around someplace, or a party at somebody's house or ... you know, and everybody goes."

As Jeanne's statement implied, the social aspects of organized religion were central to the daily and long-term rhythm of her life, and this was universally the case among participants placed in this group. Melanie stated, "I have many friends here ... yeah. quite a few. People from the church ... all my church family is here. It feels like home to me." Anita provided a more detailed account: "Most of my social net-work are friends from church, from different programs, different com-mittees that I'm on, and just they've got some really good social type things that happen through there to help develop connections." And Stephanie, also, described her church as family:

Yes, I'm very involved in my church and so that's sort of my commu-nity which rather than, you know, to say the whole of Kitchener–Waterloo but the church, more of church family which makes it, you know, which is a good network to draw upon and there's always lots of things to do and things to get involved in and that kind of thing.... This week I had a meeting last night and I have a meeting tomorrow night. I'm in the choir so I have choir practise on Thursday night so I do at least choir practise Thursday night every week.... My son was involved in a mid-week program this year, and part of the cri-teria for the mid-week program was that at least one of the parents had to do something towards the mid-week program. They serve a supper as part of the program and so I was on the cleanup teams, so every other week I went to, for cleanup for that. I'm on a couple of committees, the music and worship which looks after stuff, like for the choir and that kind of thing and I'm also an elder and clerk of ses-sion.

Jeanne exhibited a more fundamentalist stance when compared with other group members, mentioning social aspects and gatherings, but emphasizing her personal relationship with God, "First and foremost is my relationship with God, my relationship with my husband, and my children. We go to church on Sunday, and there's a service on

Wednesday night, and uh…like there's intercessory prayer on Tuesday.… That's been a great stability in my life; my faith in God. My belief in Jesus Christ as my Lord and Savior and it certainly has helped through a lot of trauma…."

Volunteerism was also universal among Networkers and, consistent with their dominant theme, they tended to emphasize the social aspects of volunteering. Much of the volunteer activity was church-related. For example, Stacy taught Sunday school, and church was a topic about which Stephanie spoke at length: "Well, the one woman that I'm fairly close to from church, like she really helped me the first couple of weeks, she had lost her job about like a year before that and she…and hers was really traumatic, she really was upset with hers and so I went and talked to her a couple of times, you know, and we commiserated together and that kind of thing. It's left me free to do a little bit more volunteer work and stuff at the church, so I get that in. No it hasn't really changed." Stacy elaborated on other types of voluntary work:

> I'm very involved with my kids. I coach my son's under-nine soccer team, and I'm very actively involved with the Kitchener Minor Soccer. I'm on the board of directors. That again, started out as being too poor to pay my fees for my kids, and they can't turn us down, so I thought, "The least I can do is put some work back into the organization," and I love it anyway. I love coaching the kids. It's a lot of fun, so it's not really too stressful. [Laughter.] My daughter's on a rep [competitive] team, so I do some of the management and administration for her team, plus the programs through the school or the unemployment group.

Networkers had limited financial resources, but they did not perceive financial constraint to be the most problematic aspect of unemployment. In spite of having regular social contact with a variety of people, Networkers consistently mentioned missing co-workers and clients as the most difficult aspect of losing their jobs. Jenny mentioned both groups, noting, "I miss the residents. I really enjoyed working with the seniors. And I miss the residents and I miss some of the staff." Jeanne also spoke about missing co-workers: "Yeah, I go in [to her former workplace] and I say 'Hi.' Like, I really care about Alice and Marg and um…they're uh…Alice's one of my references for jobs. So, I've always been close with Alice, but Alice's been close with everybody. She's just that type of person, you know, she's a good soul." In contrast, Melanie mentioned missing her patients: "I'm in tune with all those ladies I looked after when I lived here. We become family. I visited them in their home. I like visiting old patients. Things

Table 23 Where Were Connectors When Signalled?

Though over half of their signals were received at home, Connectors reported the lowest percentage of signals received in this milieu. They also reported the lowest percentage of signals received in work/school contexts. By contrast, Connectors reported the highest percentage of signals received in "other" contexts. One possible reason for the high percent of other/unspecified contexts may be that Connectors were more often signalled when "in transit" than were members of other groups.

- Caregivers were three times as likely to be signalled at work, school, and recreation sites, than were Networkers. Caregivers were also nearly three times as likely as Networkers to receive signals while at recreation sites. Indeed, their percentage for this venue was the highest of all subgroups in the sample.

- Networkers were twice as likely as Caregivers to receive signals while visiting friends' houses and recorded the second highest percentage of such instances in comparison with all subgroups in the sample. Though seemingly counterintuitive based on the interview data, Networkers were more likely to receive signals while at home than were Caregivers. Networkers reported a low percentage of signals received at recreation sites.

like that. I don't care about my problems. They still recognize me from my past. A 92-year-old woman, she sees me and says, 'Is that you Melanie?' Boy that feels so good. Image that, a lady of that age and she still remembers me!" Melanie went on to say: "I love visiting those folks. Makes me feel good. I get a high, it's just that old person face light up, makes me feel as if I were going to burst up. That gives me a high. I was brought up by grandparents and so I felt comfortable around them, not as comfortable with young people." Like Melanie, Stephanie spoke about the enjoyment she receives from helping an older friend: "I have one older lady, she's about 82 or 83, something like that, that I drive to church on Sunday morning, she lives over near Westmount Place and they closed Mr. Grocer over there now so she doesn't have any place to do her grocery shopping, so I said on Wednesdays I would take her grocery shopping. So that's tomorrow, you know, so there's lots of things."

One interesting feature of the Networkers was their highly mobile daily routine. Perhaps because of their investment in church, volunteering, and other activities, they moved around a lot throughout the day. Four of the six women were regularly signalled for ESM when in transit. Table 24 presents a representative sample of open-ended comments taken from the Networkers' ESM booklets as corroborative evidence for their daily travel patterns and, more importantly, the strong social orientation that drives much of their travel. Please note that Table 24 includes only signals received when travelling to and from various events and destinations, not episodes when respondents were actually at those events or destinations.

Also consistent with other aspects of Networkers' lives, leisure activities were often social in nature. Physical activity and other "utilitarian" forms of leisure were not viewed as being particularly essential. Melanie, for example, stated, "I've never been into sports, except for watching on TV. I have no special interest." Jenny's comments were representative of Networkers' general viewpoint and the diversity of social contact sought:

> I enjoy going to church Sunday mornings because afterwards there's a group of us that sit together and have coffee. And it's a good fellowship time, we're good friends. We don't sit together in church, we all sit in our own spots and afterwards we get together. I enjoy when my son comes home from work because the house does get lonesome being there all day. I do try to get out once a day, so I see something else besides the four walls. I enjoyed the line dancing once a week. And I enjoy dancing so, I have a friend who wants me to go back ballroom dancing. I had taken a year off. And I don't know whether I'll go back to ballroom dancing, but I do enjoy it.

Important as socializing was for this group, a prominent subtheme among Networkers was the need for quiet time. Some, like Stephanie, used reading as a way to withdraw and relax: "I like historical novels, historical biographies kinds of things … and if I'm really down in the dumps I'll read a Harlequin romance novel … Danielle Steele or something. An hour and a half and you're done and you can put the book away, get a little rest. You don't have to think about it, you just read it." Stacy's personal time was regularly scheduled in to her routine: "At eleven o'clock at night, I lock myself in the bathroom, [laughter] and I put on a rip-roaring Beethoven tape, take in a glass of wine, put bubble bath in the tub, and just vegetate for about an hour. I do that about twice a week."

The financial outlook for most Networkers was poor, even in comparison to the broader sample. Three of the women (Melanie, Anita, and Jenny) were not currently partnered, and thus did not have a source of financial support common to many others in the total sample of participants. In addition, two of the three married women had unemployed husbands. In some ways, responses from the Networkers with still-at-home children paralleled those of the Caregivers as their concerns related specifically to the negative impact of unem-

Table 24
Evidence of Daily Social Patterns and Mobility of Networkers

Signal Number	Comment
	Melanie
312	Driving on [highway] 86 near Bridgeport, inconvenient.
315	On my way home.
422	We were leaving for Elmira.
427	Calling in. Chatting with an elderly lady at the MCC Thrift Shop in Elmira. She was 76 years old and still very helpful to her community. My friend and I did a lot together today.
645	I had just drop[ped] [Son's name] to his school.
646	On my way home. I had a very good visit with my friend and her children. I also had a very hectic day.
751	On the road to Grimsby for graduation.
755	We were on Homer Watson Blvd.
527	Collecting our coats [after a church dinner]. It sure was a nice evening. A lovely dinner and gathering. The people was very friendly.
	Stephanie
413	Taking an older lady grocery shopping—did mine as well.
637	Just started home from visiting … sister-in-law.
153	On way to Royal Botanical Gardens for flower show.
155	Coming home from RBG.
376	In car—driving son home from soccer.
413	In car running some errands.
522	[in car] Driving to meet friend for lunch.
631	[car] Driving daughter to school.
743	[in car] Driving son to get bike fixed.
152	[car] Driving to Oshawa for family [Thanksgiving] dinner.
156	[in car] Driving home.
261	[car] Coming home from driving daughter to work.
374	[in car] Coming home from meeting.
	Anita
421	Going to visit friend after an accident.
425	On way to store. Left beeper in car.
531	In car on way to Church to volunteer in office.
534	Driving to a meeting. Very busy. It's amazing how you kept catching me in the car.
642	Yes you caught me in the car again.
644	Ha! You just missed me in my car [parking lot]. I just came to visit where I've been volunteering.
751	Driving to store. [volunteering]
271	Volunteering in Self Help Crafts of the World.
275	Driving.

▼

Table 24 (*continued*)

Signal Number	Comment
	Stacy
311	Hustling children & spouse out to school.
163	Coming home from swimming with kids.
639	[Out running errands] forgot to take beeper.
	Jenny
315	[car] Going to the pick-up area for the boys to catch their bus. Questioning my son about his driving habits while he was driving my car & having unwanted input from his friends in the backseat.
422	Driving car to appointment at Canadian Mental Health Association.
641	[car] Driving to my hair appt. I knew if I was a few minutes late, it would not matter.
742	[car] Driving home from shopping.
264	[car] Driving to Brantford for turkey dinner.
	Jeanne
524	Helping friend move.
633	[car] Driving to beach. This is our special planned day.
635	[in car] On way home from beach. Sleepy as the sun was too much for me. 1st time in sun this year.
152	[in car] On way to Sarnia—family reunion of sorts. A bit nervous, apprehensive as I want to look ok to family, (the old insecurity is sneaking a peak).
153	[in car] Still en route to destination. Feeling good right now relaxed— It's good to be with my son Desmond—It will be good to see family.
159	[in car] On the way home.
266	Walking with hubby. I like walking.... It's relaxing—We communicate about many subjects.
372	[on way to church] Driving in friends car to intercessory prayer. Good fellowship. Positive time in the Lord.
999	[driving to school] On my way to pick up person I give ride to school.
999	Going from 1 classroom to the other. This has been a stressful morning—I have lost my wallet with my Visa card in it.
214	On my way to pick up my car from garage. While driving home from garage my car started smoking so I returned to garage to find that the repair man forgot to put the cap back on the radiator. Life is full of glitzes.
651	On our way to assembly in school auditorium for Remembrance Day ceremony. The assembly was done very well. Respect was given due to those men and women who have given their lives for our freedom. The presentation was thought provoking. There was a play, a song sung regarding the war.

Note. Three-digit numbers denote day of week (Su=1, M=2, Tu=3, W=4, Th=5, F=6, Sa=7), day of study (1 to 7), and page signal number (1=first of the day, 7=last of the day). For example, 311 refers to a Wednesday (3), first day of that respondent's participation (1), first pager signal received that day (1). Nines refer to missing data.

Table 25 Connectors' Perceptions of Time Pressure and
Task Involvement

Connectors felt relatively little time pressure. In fact, two-thirds of their signals were received at times when they felt no time limits with respect to the
activity at hand. They also reported the highest percentage of instances when
they were "entirely" involved with no outside distractions. This may be a
matter of perception as opposed to objective reality. Is seems plausible, based
on interview data, that Connectors would generally view social interactions
as fully involving whereas members of other groups, Planners, for example,
might often see them as intrusions on the task at hand. There were few apparent subgroup differences between Caregivers and Networkers regarding task
focus and time pressure. Therefore, no subgroup breakdowns are provided in
this table.

---

ployment upon their dependants. Stephanie tried to minimize the
impact of unemployment on her children:

> I've tried to keep that pretty much the same, it's hard enough I think
> on the kids knowing that, you know, there's not really any money
> coming in. Well my daughter has a part-time job, she's the only one
> in the family that's working. You know, there's just enough prob-
> lems without kind of.... I've tried to keep the rest of it pretty much
> the same or as much as I could anyway so that ... you know ... I didn't
> want to cause any more problems with ... than they're already hav-
> ing as teenagers, so ...

By contrast, Stacy found it impossible to keep her children from being
affected by the loss of income: "Well the kids really notice it, because
they're always asking, 'Can I have this new pair of runners? Can I go
to the movie? Can I do this? Can I do th—' 'NO!' 'But why? [spoken
in a whiny voice]' We finally just had to literally sit down with them
and go over the budget, and say, 'These are all our expenses, and ...'
'But we don't have any... Mom! Our expenses are more than we—'
'Yes!' [Laughter.]"

In sum, the Networkers struggled with unemployment on both
financial and social levels. Although the former issue was acute
because many Networkers were not partnered and others had out-of-
work partners, the latter issue appeared more profound with respect
to its impact on their overall satisfaction with life. As is evident, Networkers and Caregivers shared a strong social orientation, although the
ways in which this orientation manifested itself in daily life varied.
Insofar as they were able to access sources of social support, the well-
being of Connectors was bolstered. However, given their focus on others, their financial situation was often greatly upsetting, and their

perception that they were not able to provide caused them to devalue themselves and suffer a decreased sense of self-esteem and life satisfaction.

Marginalized People

Three subgroups, Rovers, Lonely People, and Surplus People, comprise the Marginalized group. For the Rovers, social marginalization appeared largely self-imposed and was not necessarily viewed negatively. Indeed, Rovers viewed relief from the workplace rat race as a generally positive side effect of their unemployment. Marginalization was more apparent for the Lonely people and the Surplus people. The latter appeared especially at risk of chronic unemployment based on their lack of education, low self-esteem, and general lack of organizational ability. Lonely people, though more educated and more "employable" than the Surplus people, exhibited rather erratic moods and behaviours. This very expressive group tended to register the lowest "lows" and highest "highs" of the entire sample.

Rovers

Five men and two women, relatively diverse in age, education, and income, comprise the Rovers. Three Rovers were in their 20s, three were in their 30s, and one was in his 40s. Three Rovers had not completed high school, two had some college or university experience, and two others had earned college or university degrees. Relative to most groups, income levels were rather low. Three had pre-unemployment income levels under $15,000, one had earned between $15,000 and $25,000, and three had earned between $25,000 and $35,000. Six Rovers were Caucasian and one self-classified as "other."

Members of this subgroup were among the least grounded in the Kitchener–Waterloo community, rivalled only by the In-Controls from the Vacationers group. This lack of grounding was characterized by Rovers' relatively footloose lifestyles and by their preferences for social distance with respect to family, friends, and acquaintances. Many Rovers commented on their geographic instability and lack of connection to the current community. In response to the question, "Is this home for you?" Larry straightforwardly observed that "My home feels ... my home is in Nova Scotia." Kim made a similar remark, saying, "I'm a single parent. Two girls. I moved here three years ago from Newfoundland ... I still call Newfoundland home, I guess." Likewise, Keith referred to home as the place where he grew up: "Nope. I don't know very many people at all. And when I do know them, I only know two or three at a time ... I've felt comfortable in Waterloo, like the city wise. I mean I miss the ocean [in] New Brunswick. But otherwise, no, it just, I don't know. It's home." Like Keith, Aaron was comfortable in Kitchener–Waterloo but didn't feel very attached to the community:

> I just moved back from Victoria, British Columbia. I'm originally from Brantford, Ontario, where I left around four and a half-five years ago ... I know a few people ... my girlfriend, and a few of the people that she hangs around with, and that's about it. I'm pretty much alone here.... Everybody here's pretty acceptable. It's a bigger town. There's a little bit more opportunity. It's got a nice pace to it, but it's not overly paced like, say Toronto or London. It's not slow paced like, say my hometown, Brantford, is. But it does have a unique culture to it, and a unique flavour because of the universities and because of the art programs that are here in town. Is it starting to become home? Well, eventually. I'm starting to fall into place, so yes and no.

For Rovers, the lack of geographic grounding was compounded by their preferences for social distance. The Rovers were not hermits in the literal sense, but they sought to control social contact, generally going to some length to ensure that it occurred on their terms. Angie's comments were typical: "I moved from Cambridge where I lived for a year when I went to university. Before that I was living with my parents ... in Belgium. I have a few friends. I don't make a whole lot of friends easily ... I have more friends in Toronto than I have here." She noted later, "I went to a dating service, because I didn't know anybody in Kitchener. I was going out with ... they were sending like two guys a week. It was great! Even though most of them annoyed me. Go here, go there ... free! I wasn't payin'! [Laughter.]" Robert spoke of having many friends; most of them were people with whom he shared a past, and many lived outside the Kitchener–Waterloo area: "Yes, it [Kitchener–Waterloo area] does [feel like home]. I would say that the friends I have, I am very close to...but then a lot of my friends are military holdovers, and we've formed very close bonds ... I have a fairly large group of acquaintances ... and uh ... I'd say that I'm socially on par with most people ... about average, I'd have to say. I'd have to say I also have a bit more close friends, but that's just as I said, a holdover from my military days.... They're spread across the world."

Rovers were generally not close, literally or figuratively, to members of their immediate families. They tended to resent the often-unsolicited advice offered regarding jobs and other personal issues.

These attitudes provide a marked contrast to earlier quotations from people in the Routinizer and Breaking In subgroups. Two comments from Keith, the first from Phase 1 and the second from Phase 2, illustrate the point (although Keith's mother may be commenting on his alcoholism as much as on his employment status): "[Do you see your dad very often at all?] No ... I think it's been four years now at least. If not five, four for sure.... [My mom is] in Waterloo ... [I see her] ah, on and off...." Later, during Phase 2, Keith commented,

> Definitely my mother, she's always giving me trouble for not going to work. She wants me married with children right now, actually. She's always saying, "When are you going to have grandchildren, when am I going to be a grandmother?" Well, I'm not bringing a child into the world until I've got my own life straightened out and I'm off the bottle. She doesn't seem to understand that. She doesn't understand that she did it with me until I was 16. So, where's she coming from? My dad did it when I went and worked with him, and so he doesn't expect anything because he understands. He's been there more than my mom. My mom's just dead set, "Get your act together no matter what. You know, you're a piece of shit, do better." Not so angry, but that's basically what she says.

Frank also spoke with annoyance about the questions his family asked of him:

> I think it has [affected relationships] ... I just spent the weekend with them in Georgian Bay, all of them, actually. Some I haven't seen recently, so there are all of those questions of how we are doing and what we are doing. They all know that I was unemployed, but now it's ... "You're still unemployed?" I think they're getting a little nervous, and I think they're beginning to wonder whether I've lost my work ethic or something. They're all very subtle.... When you get suggestions out of the blue as to what you should do; when you're talking about the weather, and somewhere somebody will say, "I understand so and so is looking for people," you know it, uh ... [Laughter.] A couple of them have suggested that perhaps I am being too picky, or that maybe I shouldn't be trying to change the sort of work I'm doing and just take what I can get. That sort of thing. A couple of them have told me how broke they are. I think they're heading off any possibility of my asking for assistance from them, which wouldn't happen anyway. They've never previously given unsolicited evaluations of their financial situations to me.... I was invited to a gallery opening last week, and I didn't go, because I didn't want to be endlessly answering questions with, "I'm currently looking for work." So I don't have very much of a social life right now.

For Angie, the persistent questioning by her parents made her decide to visit them less often: "I might go visit my parents ... I used to go there at least once a month. Not anymore.... Well, there's the cost of gas to get there. It's a three-hour drive both ways.... Before it was a get-away from all the stress and everything.... It's not that I don't want to see them. It's just that I don't want to deal with the questions, either. 'So, how is the job hunt going? Blah, blah, blah, blah....' You know how they care and they want to know, and blah, blah, but it's annoying right now, because it's not going well. When things go better, sure." Aaron put a different twist on this issue, noting that family members avoided him by making offers with the knowledge that his acceptance was not possible:

> So that's what the family and friends ... since they're working, they have a sense of being a little bit better, and you're not equal to them, and so they'll look at that as not being equal, and you do have little hints and all this stuff, you know, like, "We're going on this vacation. Would you like to come?" And you know you can't go, because you don't have the money to do so. Or ... they come in and see your furniture, and it's pretty sparse, and you say, "Well, I can't buy furniture because I don't have the money, because I don't have employment," and then they get to the conversation, "Well, maybe if you do this and this and this...."

Although the majority of participants in the overall sample had left work against their will, all of the Rovers mentioned quitting a job at some point. This phenomenon was consistent with their desire to control various aspects of their lives, including those in the workplace environment. They expressed little to no remorse about those decisions, and diverse attributes including frustration, stress, and burn-out were generally offered as causes. Larry's comments were typical: "Well, the last, my very last job, I worked in a small plastics factory, um. Due to problems in my life and people testing my will, well it broke, so I had to leave." Others offered more elaborate explanations. Frank said, "Well, I got pretty fed up with the restaurant business, I guess. I ran out of hospitality, I think.... Burnt out in the restaurant business, and burnt out in the big city. I just thought I needed a quieter place and a friendlier place." Robert (in his Phase 2 interview) mentioned leaving a job that might have become long term because it just didn't feel right: "I also had another job at a place called [name] which although it could have led to a long-term employment, umm, something about their finances and the type of place they had and that uh, really didn't ... me and them just didn't click well." Aaron left a job on short notice but said his employer was very understanding: "I gave them about a day to two days notice, but they were pretty flexible. They weren't understaffed, and I have a reference from them, and I'll probably have a job if I ever need it … if I ever go back to Victoria, and things are settled down, I probably could possibly have— they're still friends. They understood what was going on, so they made my life very easy, and they gave me a good reference." Keith, in contrast, left after getting into a fight with his boss:

> The boss said I was stealing cheques and all this, so I took a swing at him. It's just the way I am, right. And then he just said, "Cut the shit, no more shit. You're a piece of shit." You know, all the angles. He says, "We know you were trying to get the cheques." Which was totally wrong, like definitely I am not in the fraud. Like, definitely not in that. So, I worked for about another hour and then I just said, "Piss on this." I parked my forklift in the middle of the parking lot and I told the other workers to tell him I quit.

In contrast to statements made by many other respondents, the Rovers did not seem to miss former clients or co-workers. Ironically, although formerly employed in the hospitality industry, Angie spoke at length to both aspects of this issue:

> I was a … technical manager, more interested in making sure the food costs were kept low, the employee labour costs were kept low, the store was kept clean, all the paperwork kept done, up to date, on time, all that stuff, the store was kept in a manageable position, clean, making sure that things were fixed and looking okay, and … the president of the company wanted the managers to be more people oriented, in that he wanted them out in the dining room during the whole meal period…. My staff was not trained properly enough to be able to handle the rush. See with fast food restaurants, you have to have 30-second service. If there's not 30-second service, you'll get in trouble. So it was a toss up between: I stayed back there and make sure we get 30-second service, or I go in the dining room and make sure everybody's happy. Now I figured I was employing "beautiful little teenage girls who had these wonderful little smiles," who'd go out there, and serve coffee, and make them happy. Well, I made sure that the food was done properly, and got out on time, so there was disagreement there. He figured that I should be out there in the dining room, and I figured that I would rather be making sure that everything was kept up to par … there were days I didn't feel like smiling at people. It's just … I didn't feel like it. After, you know, because you had to please your guests, you had to please your employees, you had to please your boss, make sure everybody's happy, and not ever lose your temper, and I'm not a very … well, it's not that I'm not easy going, it's just that I have a temper. The whole day at that caused

Table 26 Who Were Marginalized People with When Signalled?

Similar to Planners, Marginalized People spent relatively little time (one-third of all signals) alone. They were also among the most likely to be signalled while engaged in casual, intimate, and formal social interaction. Subgroup differences were readily apparent and compelling.

- Rovers reported a rather average percentage of signals when they were alone but a fairly high percent when they were not interacting with others. That is, they exhibited a tendency to avoid direct interaction with people with whom they were in close proximity. This gap between presence of others and interaction with others was also pronounced for Routinizers and Efficacy-Seekers in the Planners group. Rovers were less often signalled when with partners or friends than were most subgroups, especially in comparison to other Marginalized subgroups. Although seemingly at odds with the fact that Rovers were most likely to be signalled at a friend's house, it is possible that these interactions represented the total interactions Rovers had with friends, whereas other groups may have interacted with friends in a greater variety of social contexts. As well, Rovers reported the highest level of contact with "other" adults, presumably people that they didn't know or with whom they interacted only on a superficial level. Taken together, these numbers are consistent with Rovers' oft-reported difficulties in sustaining meaningful friendships and relationships and with the relative lack of priority that they place upon friendships. Rovers also reported the highest percentage of signals received when they were with pets, usually cats, but not with other people, a finding consistent with their relatively independent personalities.

- Surplus People reported by far the highest percentage of signals received while engaged in formal social interaction. By contrast, their level of casual/intimate social interaction was the lowest of the Marginalized group and among the lowest in the full sample.

- Lonely People were less likely to be signalled when alone than were members of any other subgroup in the study. They were also, by a substantial margin, the most likely to be signalled in the presence of partners. Lonely People also reported the highest percentage of signals in the entire sample when they were engaged in casual or intimate social contact. These data correspond with the "clingy" tendencies that Lonely People exhibited in the in-depth interview and with the fact that they were more likely than Rovers and Surplus People to be partnered.

---

me stress, so I did not feel like going out there and asking all these little people how they liked their fish. So that was that.

With respect to socializing with co-workers, she added, "I didn't consider that good form. The boss does not go out with the employees. So, no. I still go there. It's ... go there for food ... sort of addicted to the

Table 27 What Were Marginalized People Doing When Signalled?

Marginalized People were, relative to other groups, rather undescriptive with respect to what they were doing when signalled. Their scores were consistently mid-range on all five "main task" indicators.

- Rovers appeared more concerned with personal care than were members of the other two subgroups and Rovers, like other Marginalized subgroups, reported fairly high rates of recreation participation. These numbers are somewhat at odds with their infrequent use of recreation sites, suggesting that members of the Marginalized group often participated in leisure activity not part of the traditional organized leisure delivery system. For example, both Rovers and Surplus People had relatively heavy television viewing habits in comparison to the remainder of the sample.

- Surplus People were, in comparison to other Marginalized subgroups, the least likely to be signalled while engaging in employment and job-search activities and the most likely to be signalled while engaged in undefined "other" activity contexts. This may indicate that they found it difficult to classify certain activities given the available options on the ESM form or, consistent with their interview data, that they found themselves in numerous "wasted" situations. It should also be noted that their scores on this indicator, though high, were not as extreme as those of either of the Connector subgroups or for Efficacy Seekers.

- Lonely People stood out as being less family- and home-oriented than were the other two Marginalized subgroups. Although initially counter-intuitive, this was not entirely surprising as none of the Lonely People lived with dependent children in Phase 1 (some living arrangements had changed by Phase 2), nor were any of them living as dependent "children" with their families of origin. However, this is not to suggest that Lonely People avoided such contexts; in fact, the data suggest that they were keenly interested in developing intimate relationships and families of their own.

---

stuff for awhile…. So, I go back there, and everyone's pleasant and happy, and most of my ex-employees, they miss me, they wish I was back. Of course the boss doesn't think the same, so…I know I was never really friends with them, but uh, we have kept in sort of contact."

Consistent with their lives, Rovers' leisure choices tended to be solitary. This choice was sometimes expressed in positive terms; for example, Frank noted, "I try to make sure that I have at least an hour for myself every day at home. I go in my room, close the door, collect myself…. Catch up with myself, and I try to do that for one hour every day." Others expressed their need for solitude in terms of what they avoided. Angie, speaking to organized leisure activity in general, said, "The sort of gung-ho team atmosphere annoys me. That's all rah, rah, rah … yuck." Rovers were quite expressive in describing their leisure repertoires and their struggles to maintain them. Larry, Kim, and Angie all spoke to this issue, but from divergent perspectives. Larry said,

> I used to play ball, and during the winter I used to be a goalie. So winter's gone and I can't get in between the pipes any more, um. I enjoy riding my bike, well that's how I get around. I never learned how to drive and I probably never will. I really don't like the craziness of the roads these days so my bike riding is my main interest now…. Um, because I live in an area where there's quite a few rivers close at hand, could always go there and do a little fishing. Um, but, being up at 5 o'clock and taking care of oneself, I'm finding it a bigger job that I really thought it was going to be. But, it keeps me busy. My spare time, I love to fish, so when I have any spare time you will find me along a quiet stretch of the river … I will leave Friday night and I will get to, out to the river, and I will spend Friday to Sunday there by myself. Just to get away from the hustle and bustle of everyday living, brings me quite a bit of peace and, um, I enjoy it.

Angie looked forward to going to the health club:

> Mornings I usually just go to the health club and play around there … I lift weights every other day, and, uh, everything else. I don't do aerobics. The rowing machine, the bicycle, the stepper, the pool, the treadmill … I've had a problem with the way that I think my body looks. Right now that is one of my goals since I have the time, to fix it, to see how far I can go with it. I am lifting weights so I can lower my fat level and up my muscle content. So, that is something that is very important to me. It's just something I do everyday. It's something that no one will take me away from. It's something that I want to do.

Frank spoke passionately about his enjoyment of reading: "I read a lot … I like reading biographies. I have very strange taste in reading. I don't read very many popular novels or that sort of thing. Uh … right now I'm reading a book called *The Rediscovery of Linear Perspective in the Renaissance*, which is really very interesting. It's not nearly as awkward as the title sounds. That's the sort of thing I … I read a lot of poetry and a lot of philosophy and a lot of history." Kim, who also enjoyed reading, seemed at a loss to describe many other leisure activities:

> TV… that's about it, because I don't really have any other activities….Yeah. Last week I read a novel, and … one of Danielle Steele's.

I was up 'til five o'clock in the morning, because I didn't want to put the book down. [Laughter.] I haven't started reading a lot of them yet. There's a couple of novels I've started reading, though. When I start reading a book, I can't put it down…. A friend of mine, she just joined a club a couple of months ago. She brought me home a free three weeks' membership. She's trying to get me to go, but … I'm not an exercise person. Went down there and done aerobics one month, and for a week later I had bad pains in my legs.

Robert, describing his bicycling and scuba diving, explicitly described the importance and wonder of solitude:

I enjoy my bicycle … it gets me out and gets me around in a lot faster manner than walking and I can utilize it to, uh, get from point A to point B in a reasonable amount of time and to all extents it's, it's, it's single, it's time I can spend, uh, riding by myself and I might use it for uh just, uh, just personal thinking and that and that's a big thing for me. Especially having a wife. You need some personal time. Not having a job means that you need some personal time…. [In scuba,] you enter a whole new world, alien world and, and look around. It's, I'd have to say it's the closest you can come to flying. And you move in … three dimensions, up, down … is not important anymore, and as you go through the world it's totally alien, it's an adventure, no matter if you're diving in the bottom of a pool, a bottom a lake or the bottom of an ocean. It's an alien adventure. It's good, it's fun.

As might be expected, most Rovers were single by choice. Robert was the only Rover partnered throughout the duration of the study, and his was a common-law relationship rather than a formal marriage. Angie expressed the dominant perspective by noting, "I'd come home and nobody would need me. That's why I have cats and not a dog. Nobody needs me! [Laughter.]" Keith, in language consistent with his aggressive persona, said, "Well, I'd like to have a house, and a car, and a dog, and a wife, and a cat to kick around too, but I mean like I can't have it. No, but that's the way I choose to live, so I have no choice but to accept it."

Substance abuse was a dominant issue for both Larry and Keith. As such, it is rather difficult to sort out the extent to which their fit with this group is innate or simply a manifestation of their addictions. Larry spoke about this:

First of all, I'm an alcoholic. Um, I'd had some personal problems that came back into my life. Some resentments came into it, um, I was having trouble dealing with those and some animosities that I never cleared up. I was butting heads with the foreman a little bit, um. I went back, well I had a big fall. Really fell hard. As a result, I'm now having to go to court and everything. But I went back to AA, got help, trying to help myself, um...the foreman came up to me and started yelling and screaming at me. Um, I couldn't really take it. He pushed all the right buttons; I went into what I would consider a sober blackout. According to the lady beside me, my eyes rolled up into the back of my head, and I turned purple and every vein and muscle in my body popped to a point where I was exploding. When I came to, the fellow was running down for the day foreman who was actually in charge of me. Um, the knife that I was holding in my hand was crushed beyond recognition 'cause it was one of those plastic knives. I calmly went upstairs, got my coat and hat, got on my bike and rode to Health and Safety. And from there I went to an AA meeting. So, a pretty rough ride.

Keith was less vocal about his drinking but he noted its impact on his daily life: "Well, I've moved back to the place where you first met me...and I'm working at my home and when I want to. I have that option, if I don't want to go to work, I don't. Which usually relates to drinking. If I'm drinking I don't go to work and when I'm healthy I go to work." Mental health issues were also apparent, most prominently for Aaron, who stated, "I had a nervous breakdown due to a failed marriage, actually, and in that state of mind, it was really hard to hold a job, and so...plus I had been away from home for the last four and a half years...there was a suicide attempt, unfortunately...." The remaining four members of this group seemed likely to do fine over the long term, as long as they could exert control over their jobs and personal lives, and maintain an acceptable, to them, level of social distance.

Surplus People

Members of this subgroup, though they had established job histories, resembled in many ways individuals prone to chronic unemployment. All seven Surplus People were young women. Six were in their 20s and one was in her 30s. Education levels varied. Two members did not finish high school whereas one had a university degree. Several were still dabbling in school, and several took various courses at some point during the study. Two members were Asian and five were Caucasian. Similar to the other Marginalized subgroups, pre-unemployment household income levels were low. Three earned less than $15,000, two earned $15,000 to $25,000 and one earned $35,000 to $45,000. One did not report pre-unemployment income.

The Surplus People commonly experienced transitional issues related to both job loss and living arrangements. Exacerbating their situations, most lived with their parents during the time of the study, and friction at home was a constant theme. Surplus People tended to describe their home life almost from the perspective of an indentured servant. Gender is likely an issue in this case because Breaking Ins, who were in many respects the male demographic counterpart to Surplus People, rarely expressed such familial expectations or similar frustration. Negative experiences and consequences dominated Surplus People's responses to questions related to the effects of unemployment on familial and friendship relationships. Christina noted: "I can get pretty bitchy, because I'm here all the time. I have nothing to do really. I do a lot of stuff around the house here, but I get tired of doing it all the time. I don't get paid for it. I don't mess up some of the things that they want me to clean up, and things like that." Peggy's comments placed some longitudinal perspective on family-related stress; in Phase 1, she noted, "Yeah, I think it has, but like I do try to keep busy, like you know, exercise, or do some light chores, and try to keep busy, 'cause they're working, and I get bored.... When they do come home, I get kind of grumpy. I feel like since I'm stuck at home, that I'm a slave to everybody, because they think well, I'm not doing anything. They're like, you know, 'Cut the grass' or you know, 'Can you do this or make this or cook this,' and I just kind of get upset with them...." Later, during Phase 2, she added, "Now it's startin' to really [pause] put a toll on it [Short laugh.].... Both my parents and my boyfriend.... With my parents I find that I argue with them more. I'm more withdrawn and I don't like going to family events. With my boyfriend I would find that I do argue with him 'cause he works all day and I don't and then when we do see each other I want to go do something, I want to go some place and he's too tired or can't...." By none of the participants' reckoning did their problems disappear in the absence of other family members. Indeed, those problems appeared to be generally more severe when the respondents were with their families than when they were on their own.

Another consistent theme, already introduced for this group, relates to the general deterioration of their situations, both immediately after their job loss and over time. Boredom, depression, and deteriorating physical health were commonly mentioned and at-risk behaviour was commonly acknowledged. Surplus People generally did not enjoy extra time spent at home as a result of the "forced leisure" associated with unemployment. Tracy, Carrie, and Diane spoke to these issues in Phase 1. Tracy emphasized structural constraints related to money: "Well, I wanted to join a fitness club, and I don't got any money, forget it. It's kind of hard to do anything, to join a club or something, or go join a dance club or something, or take les-

Table 28 Mood States of Marginalized People

Marginalized People had the most positive mean scores of all groups on the "unhappy–happy" continuum and high to mid-range scores on "irritable–good humour" and "anxious–relaxed." Marginalized People reported very high levels of boredom, congruent with their aforementioned disinterest in the tasks at hand when signalled. The three Marginalized subgroups exhibited inconsistent mood scores.

- Rovers generally reported low to mid-range mood scores, but their scores were less extreme than are those of the other two Marginalized subgroups.

- Surplus People recorded the most negative mood scores among all 10 subgroups on two of the four measures, bored and irritable; the latter is especially consistent with their interview data.

- Lonely People had the most positive overall mood states of any subgroup in the study. Their scores were especially high during the Phase 2 data collection. As noted earlier during discussion of the interview data, the Lonely People exhibited wide mood swings, and thus their elevated scores may be a function of the period in which they completed the ESM portion of the study and may not reflect their "objective" quality of life.

---

sons or dancing lessons or something ... the money has to be there before you can do it." Carrie spoke about the difficulties of unstructured time: "It's kind of difficult sometimes because you know, you think about it and you say, before you were willing to do so much and now all of a sudden I don't have a job, I can't do anything, it's just a bunch of spare time with nothing to do. It's not as much ... for me I don't know I think it's not as much getting a job for the money but for getting out and being able to do something else instead of just sitting at home." Diane filled part of her time with non-normative activity: "I don't do too much. Or I'll walk around. This is really crazy, but on garbage nights sometimes I'll go out and see what people have got in their garbage. It's really bad. I used to go around and pluck stuff and fix it up and sell it and at this point I'm kind of desperate so ... I know it's a crazy thing to do but ... that's what I do sometimes...."

However, Diane pulled back in several instances, both recorded in Phase 1, when she felt things were going too far, even if it meant risking relationships and friendships:

> I used to play bingo a lot. It actually got out of hand at one point. I
> got my boyfriend into it. We kind of went crazy about it, you know
> some people got their drugs and alcohol to get addicted, well, we sort
> of got addicted to bingo, which was really bad. Like now we'll go
> maybe 2 or 3 times a month and I look forward to it because, I just

like the excitement and of course we always have the chance of winning.

Um, my girlfriend, she's actually, she's a stripper and she has been for a long time. And uh, she keeps phoning me, she goes, "Oh you should come work with me, you should come work with me. And I'm like, "Oh, I'm sorry nooo [laughs]." You know I'm desperate but, I'm not that desperate [laughing]. Um, yeah, she's really on my case all the time. Other than that like, I don't have too many friends here in Kitchener so it [being unemployed] hasn't made too much difference.

Her pattern had not markedly changed in Phase 2, however. When asked if she regularly planned special events, Diane replied, "Well, there is. Um, it used to be bingo, um, we've sort of climbed the ladder in gambling, um, it's really bad. Actually my boyfriend, really he's, he's the one with the problem, not me [laughs]. You know how everyone points the finger at other people, but no! We play a lot of blackjack now, we follow this casino around. But um, I only take $20 with me and so does he, but he always takes his bank card with him so it gets a little out of hand. But I enjoy doing that, I, I like playing cards."

Surplus people clearly struggled with unemployment and its effect upon their mental health. Peggy's comments illustrate the cumulative effect of unemployment over time. In Phase 1, she commented, "I try not to think about it because sometimes it can be depressing, but I try to keep as busy as possible ... kind of fill up the little slow gaps ... I hate sleeping, and I can't, you know. I just want to keep busy, so I just...." Later, during Phase 2, she added, "I think before I was more tryin' to keep busy, now it's just, I'm kinda just moped I think.... Just become more depressing at home. I don't really like them very much, um, it's very stressful. Health-wise I feel I'm becoming more sick, more weak. I don't feel like eating or doing anything so. Yeah. I do find it's kinda puttin' a toll on me." With a few exceptions, Surplus People also had difficulty establishing meaningful daily routines. Although they generally did not enjoy time at home, they spent a lot of time there. They planned few organized activities and rarely participated in physical activity. Surplus People often lamented their overall lack of contribution. For example, Carolyn stated, "I just ... I don't know ... I just feel useless sometimes." Peggy added more detail regarding her daily routine: "Um, tryin' to figure out what I'm gonna do during the days.... Um, well I use to enjoy like walking, like swimming, um ... I used to be in like a dance group, um, just things like

Table 29 Where Were Marginalized People When Signalled?

Relative to other groups, Marginalized People reported fewer instances when they were at home and the lowest number of times when they were signalled at recreation sites. The latter number is consistent with their oft-reported frustration related to lack of financial resources with which to participate in their preferred leisure activities.

- Rovers, relative to the other Marginalized subgroups, tended to report similar patterns with respect to location when signalled. Oddly, Rovers were the most likely of all subgroups in the study to report receiving signals at friends' homes, data that ran counter to other indicators that have suggested that the Rovers were, by choice, a relatively solitary lot.

- Surplus people, by contrast, reported one of the highest rates for staying at home. This observation may be attributable to their general tendency to sleep in and watch a lot of television, and to their relative social isolation. It also may explain in part why conflicts with family members were common among this subgroup. Surplus People reported one of the lowest rates at work/school settings. Surplus People were twice as likely to report receiving signals at recreation sites than were members of the other two Marginalized subgroups.

- Lonely People were least likely of the three Marginalized People subgroups to receive signals at home. Indeed, Lonely People were less likely to receive signals at home than were members of the other nine subgroups. Lonely People reported the highest percentage of signals received at work/school settings, a number consistent with their employment status, especially in Phase 2 (wherein all were re-employed full-time) and the highest percentage of signals received at recreation sites.

---

that.... [But now] Um ... nothin' really ... just work on my night courses kinda just studying but nothing as in any physical activity or anything like that." Diane framed this as having too much free time: "I think, right now I have more free time than ever before and ... I don't know if I'm just getting better at things so I'm doing them faster, I, I don't know what it is. I seem to have too much free time on my hands right now. I find myself walking back and forth, just walking around this apartment you know, with no clue what I'm doing. I'm just sort of walking around, and it's pretty pathetic actually." Christina noted that she fills some of this extra time by sleeping later: "Oh, yeah. I used to go out a lot more and do a lot more social things, I guess. I still slept in, but now I find I'm sleeping in a little later. I used to get up at like eight or nine. Now I have no problem sleeping 'til like noon, so yeah, it's changed."

Surplus People were not, as a rule, well connected to the broader community. As noted earlier, though many lived at home, friction was common between them and family members. In addition, friendship networks were often limited and/or strained. Darlene straightforwardly noted that "Friends don't want much to do with me," whereas Tracy stated that "I still live with my folks.... Not too many [friends] right now." However, she also acknowledged some ties to the community: "I don't think I would ever move. I like it here. It's nice." Consistent with Tracy's comments, several others expressed hope that their social networks, though limited, were improving. Diane said,

> Well, I've been out of work for about a month now and I'm going crazy sitting in an apartment. It's hard to find work. I have three children, they don't live with me though.... They're eight, six and five ... I don't have too many friends in Kitchener but I like it, like I have enough.... When I first moved here, I was like kind of lost but it's such a different ... from Toronto to Kitchener, the community is completely different ... but now yes, I consider it home. [Even though family are] all out [in] Toronto, Whitby.

Several participants mentioned missing the social aspects of work and lamented their current lack of connection with former co-workers. Tracy spoke fondly of "the people that I worked with. They're very nice. I got along with them...." Carolyn added, "I still see them though, like if I go in there; if I see them on the street, but it's still not the same."

Members of this subgroup were, at the conclusion of the data collection, still struggling on a variety of levels related to self-esteem, life satisfaction, personal and family relationships, and financial solvency. It was clearly an at-risk group with respect to long-term job prospects as well as long-term physical and mental well being.

Lonely People

Four young women, all in their 20s, were placed into this category. Three were Caucasian, and one classified herself as "other" with respect to race and ethnicity. Lonely People had relatively high levels of education. All had some college or university experience, and three had earned degrees. Pre-unemployment household income levels were low, and none reported incomes above $25,000. Lonely People were very verbal, effectively articulating their ideas during the interviews which ran half-again to twice as long as those of most other study participants. Lonely People generally exhibited manic-depressive tendencies as they were often very down, especially during Phase 1, or very up, especially during Phase 2. Three were engaged to be married during the course of the study, and the fourth was involved in a serious relationship.

Lonely People, like those in other Marginalized subgroups, found themselves especially constrained by lack of income. Mary's retrospective observations recorded during Phase 2 were typical:

When I was unemployed, I didn't know what to do with myself. I was just at a, at an end. I could stay in the bed, I, I just had a, a really bad attitude. And um, I didn't care. I didn't care how I talked, I didn't care how I dressed. I didn't care if I slept till 11 o'clock. Who cares? Um, I didn't have any money, I was depressed. I couldn't do anything. Um, I was very bitchy and hard to get along with. And um, I don't miss any of that. I don't miss the aggravation and ... I don't miss the embarrassment of having to go to the degrading experience. Going to a food bank, and, and, and going to welfare, and um, fighting with all these people and um, going to job interviews and screwin' them up, and um, going to the unemployment office, and, everything I did, every time I got in the car, I'd worry about worry, worry, worry. Um, fret about, you know, my friend ... if I want to go to Cambridge and do something. I'd fret do I, I don't have the gas, I can't go to Cambridge. Everything I did, everything I touched, everything I bought, you know, I had shopping experiences where I'd pick, every item I picked up I put back, I put back away by the end of the trip 'til there was next to nothing.

Income constraints were manifested in a variety of ways. Mary spoke about negative impacts on social activities:

Yep. Definitely, because you don't have the money to go to the, they say, "Hey, let's go to Toronto, let's go to *Phantom of the Opera*." I've been dying to see that. That's $100 a ticket. Can't do it. So it takes my social life away. It's a reality check in what I do. Can't go to the movies every week like I used to do, every Tuesday night, cheap Tuesday, $4.25. You know, can't do that any more, can't afford it. And it's like pride, like my friends have been taking me out for the last, I don't know, since November, they've just taken me out. And they don't make it seem like it's charity, but they know that I can't afford to do it, and that I want to do these things. My friends have gathered around me and helped bring me up, and said ok, like you know, they know things are bad, they invite me for dinner a lot. And its changed our relationship in that it's made it unfair, unlevel with my friends. It's not, friendship is not always level, but it's give and take. And it's like they're giving a lot more and I'm taking a lot more. It's like there's not as much give and take. For a long period of time, it would be very unhealthy. If you were doing something, just mooching off of them, you know.

Their favourite leisure activities, especially movies and shopping, were also constrained. Susan described an active leisure lifestyle prior to becoming unemployed: "[When working] Weekends we went out a lot, we went browsing, shopping, fix up the apartment, we did a lot of stuff on weekends. Thursdays, Fridays, and pretty much all day Saturdays we were out [to] the stores. Some days I worked so we didn't go anywhere and we rented a lot of movies. Now we don't rent movies." Marcia was also quite active in her leisure prior to unemployment. Many of her activities entailed spending money:

> Well at work, my free time I basically just went to the mall or I had a membership at the Y there, too, so I went to aerobics a lot. Like I'd basically go to aerobics or go to a movie. There was one house parent who was really nice. She'd always want us to go out for movies and stuff like that. So I'd go with her and things like that. And we'd go shopping to the States and stuff.... On Saturdays I love like going to, we go to garage sales and stuff like that ... shopping ... well lately the last few Saturdays, yeah I've gone. I didn't go last Saturday. I went to the market instead. But usually I do something, either go to garage sales or the market on Saturday. And umm ... well I just go out. It's nice to go out and drive around, and it's kind of fun, you can find good deals and stuff. Well there's this one other girl, I went with her, one other friend of mine. Well she is a friend of mine but I met her through Andy's friend basically. She's really into it so we were having a pretty good time going out, spending all our money, buying all this junk. So you know it's kind of fun. I don't know it's just gives you some...I like to get out.

Mary had become employed by Phase 2 and she spoke about returning to leisure activities that she had given up while unemployed:

> Um, I find I'm always busy doing something, and then, um, I, I read the Bible for about a half an hour before I go to bed. Then I say my prayers, and I go to bed, 11, sometimes 12 ...I don't watch TV any more. I do a lot of reading. Um, spend a lot of my time with friends. People. Shopping, um, caring for myself. Taking better care of myself. I started sewing. And I've started cross-stitch, and um, picking up things that I used to do from the past, and, and learning new things.... Like I'm going to take um, I want to get, I want to start skiing again. Like I want to get into outdoor things again and I'm, I've got a pair of skates; I'm going to start going skating again ...I go to the park ... about four times a week ... it's still my favourite.

Two of the Lonely People admitted to watching too much television, an admission that seemed to bother Marcia: "I don't like to be in the house. Like if I can get out and doing something and then come back. You're here all day, you know. I don't like being here all day cause then I end up watching TV all day. And I don't want to do that so, it's like, "Ohhh don't turn it on!" I don't want Andy to think all I do is lay around and sleep and watch TV all day, so I have to do other things." Susan wasn't bothered by her television viewing, perhaps because she was primarily interested in one show: "If I can't watch it, I tape it and that's like my soap. I never miss my soap. Even when I was working I used to tape it and watch it at night. Other than that not really. I don't plan anything because everything's sort of like, well on sort of how you feel, like what do you feel like doing? I don't know...."

All of the Lonely People made repeated references to being very "up" and very "down" at various points in the study. Susan introduced herself in the initial interview by noting that even changes of season affect her moods: "I'm engaged to be married ... I've two cats that are my babies. I hate winter. I love summer, so in the winter time I'm like this incredibly blah person. I don't go anywhere, I vegetate, I watch TV, don't do much, and in the summertime I like outdoor activities and stuff and like camping, hiking, walking, whatever except watching TV." Mary spoke to this issue repeatedly. Her Phase 2 interview comments were typical:

> I'm in full-time counselling. I go one day ... one day a week ... three weeks, three weeks, three weeks out of the month ... either two or three times a month and it's going really well. I'm dealing with my past and ... and dealing on how parts, things about me that I don't like.... My defensiveness sometimes. My ... um, just my mood swings and if I'm really working on things that aren't so good about myself and I'm facing things about my past that aren't so good and ... um I'm doing it professionally so it's sacrifices but ... um, I feel real good about myself. I have a really high self esteem which when you first met me I didn't have.

Consistent with their up-and-down nature, the Lonely People tended to sleep in when unemployed and their days were relatively unstructured. For example, Susan noted,

> ... well I guess they're all about the same. OK, get up around 9:00 or 10:00, you know, depending on the day of the week. We'll get a paper because, you know, not every day of the week, the paper is like worth it. Get a paper, call messages, and if there's no applications to go out, I don't know, wait till 2:00, watch my soap opera and well, do housecleaning, do laundry, whatever's needed to be done, whatever can be done. Sometimes we just go cycling or make long distance phone calls. I don't know, we watch a lot, way too much TV, you know, and at night go for a walk if it's nice, go for a cycle. If we have gas money, go visit the neighbours as I call them even though they're not neighbours. That's about it. We go to bed late. instead of going to

Table 30 Marginalized People's Perceptions of Time Pressure
and Task Involvement

In comparison with members of other groups, Marginalized People reported the highest percentage of signals where they were only partially involved in the task at hand. This collective response may relate to the high percentages, relative to other groups, of casual and intimate interactions and formal social interactions when signalled. It may also reflect their general lack of interest in the tasks at hand. With the exception of Planners, Marginalized People also reported a higher percentage than other groups of situations where they felt considerable time pressure.

- Rovers exhibited the most interesting pattern with respect to task involvement. Whereas most respondents in the sample reported equally high levels of "entirely" focussed and "mostly" focussed task attention, Rovers' responses were bi-polar, showing a high percentage of entirely focussed and partially focussed responses, and a much lower percentage of the middle-range response common to the other nine subgroups.

- Surplus People's reports on time pressure and task involvement were often mid-range relative to other subgroups and hence not particularly compelling.

- Lonely People reported a higher level of time pressure than did the other two subgroups whereas their task involvement scores were relatively low.

---

bed around 10:00 or 11:00, we go to bed around 11:00, 12:00 or 1:00, and so that means that we get up later, stuff like that.... When I was working I was getting up at 7:00 in the morning, going to work for 9:00 or 8:30 depending on which shift it was....

Lonely People were a relatively ungrounded group. None were originally from the Kitchener–Waterloo area and their family networks were dispersed. Family friction was often evident, though not universally reported. Marcia described the geographic dispersion in her family: "Well, I grew up in St. Thomas, which is near London. And then I went away to Bible college in Saskatchewan. And then halfway through that my parents went to BC. Then when I would go home for summer holidays, I would go to BC. So it was kind of weird, but I love it out there. So now my mom and dad live in British Columbia, I have two brothers that live in British Columbia, a sister that lives out there. And then I have a brother and sister in St. Thomas. So I have quite a big family." Mary described her family as dysfunctional and was intentionally avoiding interaction with her parents:

I lived in Exeter for about a year. Before that I was in the hospital for about six months; I was suffering from depression. I had a baby, and

I was suffering from depression and I also, my husband also left me during that time too, and has my child, so, our child rather, so I was going through a lot of stuff. My parents weren't helping me. Basically, they blamed me for all the problems, and I was having enough stress in my life without them. And I just, basically, they are very dysfunctional people, my family, my parents. Not the rest of them, but my parents. And I just decided to say good bye, not in those words, not near that polite. And I haven't had anything to do with them since November, mid-November of last year. And my life just radically changed. 'Cause I wasn't getting dumped on, "You can't do this, you're stupid, blah, blah, blah, blah." All that negativity stuff, dumping on me all the time.

Taryn also felt tension with her mother: "Um, especially with my mother. My parents are living in Newfoundland, my mother and my stepfather right now. And, uh, for a long time she couldn't understand why I was unemployed, to the point where she felt I wasn't looking hard enough."

Despite the family friction, and even though all had experienced recent moves, they tended to agree that the Kitchener–Waterloo area was beginning to feel like home. Having some relatives and friends in the community helped Susan feel settled: "Well, it's becoming home, I'm originally from Montreal, Quebec, so all my friends and family basically are back there, so I write a lot of letters and make a lot of long-distance phone calls. I have a brother and a sister-in-law here and a new-born niece so she keeps us occupied, and I've got a girlfriend and her husband and her daughter as well. So it's an adult or family kind of circle and that's about it and we go out to their place mainly. We don't do much else and I'm happy to be here. I'm just happy to be away from Quebec." Marcia had also begun to feel at home in this community:

Well, I never really thought of Kitchener as my home, but now I kind of do. Well, Andy and I are going to get married in September. We're going to live here for a little while, but we plan to move up to British Columbia. Up to Vancouver area, maybe in one or two years. I actually haven't had really a home that I felt that I was at home at for awhile. Because when I was at university I was living with a bunch of people. And I was living with another roommate, she just got married last weekend. And when I was working at my other job, I lived at three different group homes. Like each week I went to a different one. I just lived out of a suitcase basically. And so, I think I probably feel most at home here, in this apartment, even more than my own.

As previously noted, the Lonely People actively sought out social contact. This need was manifested in their friendships, through the central role that Christianity played in their lives (with the exception of Taryn), and in their intimate relationships. For example, Taryn mentioned that all of her roommates were part of the same social group, especially valued given her ongoing perception of social separation:

> ... when I was growing up in Nova Scotia I was one of those kids that was never picked, never fit into a clique in high school. I tended to be quite sociable but I wasn't into the in crowd, so I met up with a bunch of friends and we kind of stuck together. We're all kind of, the type of people that didn't fit anywhere else when we were together, and that's what I found when I came here. I met everybody through this science fiction fantasy club at Laurier [University].... We all seem to be people that don't fit in anywhere else. We've got along great together so....

Similar to formalized friendship links articulated by Taryn, organized religion was an avenue through which other Lonely People sought to forge social ties and a context in which they developed friendships. Mary noted in Phase 1 that, "I'm newly a Christian ... I didn't grow up as a Christian. Um, so I'm doing Bible study with a lady that I got contact through the Carpenter Shop. And I do that once a week. I've been doing that for four weeks now, and I'm going to do that as long as a can, as long as I want to." She later added in Phase 2, "I don't shout anymore and I just ... I just have my act together, Amen. Been a Christian almost a year now that ... that's very important to me...." Marcia's academic interests and career aspirations were also related to her spiritual side: "I went to another college in Saskatchewan for four years, so I have two BA's now.... It was a Christian college, so it was a bachelor of arts in Christian ministry.... And every Sunday we always go to church in Ingersoll. During Phase 2, Mary spoke at length about her closest friend:

> And the next day she picked me up for church. And from then on I've been going to church every day. And I became a Christian. I was baptized, um, as a believer, um, May 2nd this year. But I've been going to church steadily from December 21st. From the time she met, I met, we met. She is now in Ottawa. I haven't seen her for, oh, I haven't seen her for, three weeks now? She started a job in Ottawa with the, um, blood, Red Cross blood donor clinic. It's really good pay job so, um, I'm going to be seeing her on the 10th of December. 'Cause she's coming back for the weekend or whatever. But um, anyway, yeah! That's how it all started with one person that gave a shit!

Just as they quickly developed devotion to religious belief and activity, Lonely People quickly and wholly immersed themselves into intimate relationships. Mary, for example, was involved in a serious relationship that ended during Phase 1, and yet over the span of three months had become engaged to someone else. During Phase 2, Mary explained the circumstances when she met her new partner:

> ... I met him at a dance, a singles' dance. Parents Without Partners.... He was dressed as a cow! [laugh] He was a cow and was really cool, he had udders and everything, it was, it was real cool. It's a really neat outfit [laughing]. He had this really [pause] he's got this really handsome face, boyishly handsome face and he had this little cap on with these little ears and the horns and these udders, it was just ... it was just great. It really was [pause], moooove over. It was great, it really was. Moooove over, it was great, I'm going to milk it for all it's worth ... there's definitely a good thing. No, we love each other, we fell for each other right from the very beginning, oh yeah [pause] but um, he's right for me....

Reflecting of their somewhat dependent nature, the Lonely People exhibited some caregiving tendencies. This trait was not universal, perhaps because few of them had dependants. Notwithstanding the absence of dependants, though, Taryn's comments during Phase 2 regarding her baking illustrated this caregiving tendency:

> Um, I guess it's because well, I guess it kind of applies to, to the guys in the house when we go.... It's something we do not just because we enjoy baking but because we enjoy creating something that everyone in the house or our friends can enjoy. Like we don't just bake, like there are occasions where we bake for the sake of baking, like we'll bake the loaf of bread rather than go buy it kinda deal, but um, it's more done for treats like, um, I love making desserts. That's what I tend to make if I make anything, and I'll do it purely for everyone else. Like right now I'm on a cholesterol-restricted diet so I can't eat any of the stuff that I'm baking but it doesn't stop me from doing it anyhow just because you know, I know people enjoy it, enjoy what I make and so I enjoy doing it for them.

Nevertheless, it seems plausible that these women will adopt caregiver roles in later life. Mary, the only woman in this group with children currently in her life, foreshadowed this potential:

> Um, Jason and I have the same values. Um, we're not into watching the kids watch TV. And the kids don't watch TV. And we're not into, um, going to the, um entertaining them, like his, his ex-wife does. They, they, every weekend they take the kids to Canada's Wonderland or African Lion Safari or the zoo. They let other people entertain the

kids. We, we sit down with them, we, no matter what, we, if the dishes get done after they go to bed they do.... They know to help because if they want our time for a whole hour, the, we, we, we'll say to them depending on what time it is, you know, we guarantee them a half an hour of what they want to do. And if it starts at 8 o'clock and it ends at 8:30, it means they gotta get their pyjamas on, and be absolutely ready for bed so that when 8:30 hits, they're into bed and that's it, no more complaints. It's like that's it. But they're very happy 'cause, um, and Jason's never spent as much time with the kids as he has now. Quality time. And you learn a lot over a board game about their lifestyles and about us and about how you problem solve and how ya, it, it works out really well, and um, I've started doing cross stitch over there, and um, we, we go to the parks together as a family, the only thing that's changed is instead of me doing all these activities that I like to do on my own, I have family that does it with me.

The Lonely People commonly saw organized recreation services as coping mechanisms. Marcia's and Mary's comments were illustrative. Marcia, for example, emphasized the social aspects of participation, congruent with the overall disposition of this group to seek formalized opportunities for personal interaction:

Well, I would have been on a ball team, but they ended up not having it. Like at our church, we usually have a baseball team every summer, well, like a softball or something. And I really like playing, but I missed the first practice because I went to BC for three weeks. My parents live up that way, so I went to visit them. And then they said they didn't have enough people come out and stuff. So they weren't going to do it. So I was really disappointed because I really like doing that. But, umm ... it's nice to get out and be with different people. I like playing baseball so that's fun. It gives you a chance to go out and do, enjoy the weather and be doing something with some other people basically. And it's fun, so that's what I like.

Mary, by contrast, emphasized the range of benefits that she derived within organized recreation contexts:

Okay, when you're unemployed. Okay, ah, I can say from my experience personally, when I was unemployed, I couldn't for, do squat. And you know what, that's when I really needed a membership at the Y to work off that stress. To swim it off, to, to run it off, to sweat it off. To keep in shape! I also needed, in combination with that, the proper food, because you work out and you don't have the food. Like it was the combination, I needed, ah, you know, I needed a little bit, I needed good food, and to work out, and a, a tutor. That's the trinity. Those three things to pull it together.

Finally, and not surprisingly given the above discussion, Lonely People commonly mentioned missing former co-workers. Taryn said, "Um, the girls that we worked with were waitresses and our waiter was wonderful. They were, like I helped him [her boss] hire some but he made the final decision, but I got to meet them all and between the two of us we discussed who we wanted to hire, so we got people that were bright, good personalities, we all clicked really well...."

Lonely People were, as a group, very upbeat during the second phase of data collection. Their personal lives appeared to be largely in order and their employment situations had improved. We remain cautious, however, in predicting long-term prosperity or relational stability for members of this group. As their social and economic marginality was especially pronounced early in this study and dependency especially pronounced later in the study, long-term satisfaction in either of these dimensions seems to not be assured.

Based upon this discussion of the Marginalized People, it appears that the diversity of experiences and orientations toward unemployment were perhaps broader in this group than any of the other groups. However, the combination of forces that affected the way Marginalized people approached their daily lives supports integrating these subgroups under one heading as the sum effect was one of mild to profound marginalization from the rest of society. It must be noted that such marginalization was neither permanent nor beyond the effective control of the participants, as has been clearly demonstrated by the participants themselves. However, it must also be acknowledged that such marginalization created many hardships for the members of the Marginalized groups, such that their psychological well-being during their period of unemployment was frequently minimal.

Summary of the Participant Categorization Scheme

We believe that the four-group, ten-subgroup categorization scheme described to this point, while not perfect, serves a valuable purpose in systematically reducing the large amount of interview data. Clearly, some individuals epitomize the groups and subgroups to which they were assigned whereas others are on the fringe, perhaps defying placement into any particular group or perhaps sharing characteristics important to more than one group. The scheme should, therefore, be viewed as a heuristic device rather than as a definitive statement about the lives of the individuals or collective involved.

Multiple forms of data were collected subsequent to the initial semi-structured interviews upon which most of the preceding discussion was based. The over 4,400 quantitative ESM data episodes related to daily lived experience have been only partially examined thus far. In the next chapter, we more fully explore the quantitative ESM data and introduce three additional data forms: a mail-back questionnaire about leisure participation, leisure constraints, and standardized questions related to self-esteem and life satisfaction; qualitative ESM data (written commentary accompanying the ESM data sheets); and semi-structured interviews related to respondents' experiences with various social service agencies during their time of unemployment. Analyses of these data will add depth to the above descriptions of study participants and will either support or call into question decisions made about the group and subgroup placements of those participants in the categorization scheme.

4 Alternative Perspectives on Unemployment

Confirmation and Disconfirmation of Daily Life Patterns Using Experiential Sampling and Mail-Back Survey Data

uilding on data introduced in chapter 3, the next component of the ESM analysis includes an exploration of the role of television, perceptions of planning, and the presence of leisure and non-leisure episodes in the daily lives of respondents. We also explore the relationships between these contexts and respondents' mood states. This section involves additional analyses at the subgroup level exploring issues specific to each subgroup. For example, the interview data suggested that members of the Anti-Homebody subgroup had particular difficulties remaining at home in the mornings after other family members had left for work or school. The ESM data allowed us to explore the morning moods of that subgroup in comparison to their mood states at other times during the day. Surplus People, by contrast, often spoke of being especially stressed when interacting with other family members in the home environment. Once again, the ESM data allowed an exploration of subgroup moods in situations where other family members were present versus when they were not present.

The final component of ESM analysis involved comparisons of open-ended comments from the ESM questionnaire and points made during the in-depth interviews. Respondents had several opportunities to comment in situ when filling out ESM questionnaires. The first opportunity occurred at the start of each page when they were given space to "describe the situation in a few words" and the second occurred at the end of the page when they were asked "What else would you like to mention about this situation?" At the end of each day the ESM booklet also included a page where respondents were asked to comment on "the *one* situation that was the best part of the day for you" and "Is there anything else you want to mention about today?"

This chapter concludes with descriptive analyses of responses to standardized batteries of questions related to respondents' perceived levels of self-esteem, life satisfaction, job importance, career socialization, leisure boredom, self-definition through leisure, perceived freedom in leisure, and recreation-activity constraints. These data were collected through mail-back questionnaires given to study participants at the conclusion of Phase 1 and Phase 2. Similar to the quantitative and qualitative ESM data, these standardized batteries were used to triangulate with the interview data that provided the basis for initial analysis of the study participants and their placement into groups and subgroups.

Television Viewing

The ESM data provided an interesting, if incomplete, picture of respondents' television viewing patterns. The data are conservative in the sense that television viewing was recorded only if respondents chose to specifically note that activity on an open-ended section of the ESM questionnaire (see Appendix B, item 2 and items 10–13). There was no closed-end response available for television, so it is possible that television viewing was recorded only if it was the respondent's primary activity when signalled. The data do include, however, instances wherein respondents were watching taped material, including rented movies, on their televisions.

Global observation of the full sample initially suggested that, with some exceptions, respondents did not watch a lot of television while they were unemployed (Table 31). On average, respondents reported watching television during receipt of just over 12% of all signals. Although this number appears small in an objective sense, it is nearly double the 6.6% reported by Kubey and Csikszentmihalyi in their widely cited 1990 book *Television and the Quality of Life*.[1] In addition, and consistent with Kubey and Cskikzentmihalyi, most of the reported television viewing in the present study occurred during evening and weekend hours. Only 2% of all signals were received when respondents were watching weekday, daytime television.

Some diversity was evident among various groups and subgroups. With respect to overall television-viewing patterns, and consistent with expectations, Vacationers and Marginalized People watched more television than did Planners and Connectors. With respect to subgroups, Breaking Ins, Rovers, Routinizers, Surplus People, and Anti-

Table 31 Percent of Situations Watching Television (Total and Prior to Dinner) by Group, Subgroup, and Individual

Group

Planners	11	2
Routinizers	**15**	**2**
Dick	17	2
Jacob	13	0
Jeffrey	0	0
Shawn	12	2
Steven	8	2
Todd	37	8
Tom	17	6
Anti-Home	**11**	**1**
Anna	6	2
Barb	18	3
Jackie	16	3
Shelly	3	1
Effic-Seeker	**10**	**1**
Dale	20	0
David	10	0
Jack	8	0
Joe	2	0
Kelly	7	0
Nicole	—	—
Sheila	11	2

Vacationers	15	3
Breaking In	**19**	**4**
Bruce	20	4
Harry	32	7
Joanne	7	1
Les	12	2
Matt	27	6
Pauline	18	4
In Control	**10**	**1**
Bob	2	0
Donald	7	1
Jim	22	1
Walter	11	0

Connectors	10	1
Caregivers	**9**	**1**
Alison	8	1
Andrea	7	1
Donna	12	2
Heather	13	1
Janet	6	1
Paul	8	1
Networkers	**10**	**1**
Anita	12	0
Jeanne	0	0
Jenny	17	3
Melanie	10	0
Stacy	13	0
Stephanie	10	0

Marginalized	12	4
Rovers	**16**	**5**
Aaron	3	0
Angie	31	10
Frank	5	7
Keith	21	7
Kim	28	17
Larry	0	0
Robert	28	3
Surplus people	**11**	**4**
Carrie	18	2
Carolyn	10	2
Christina	15	4
Darlene	7	7
Diane	2	1
Peggy	27	15
Taryn	2	0
Tracy	5	0
Lonely	**10**	**2**
Marcia	12	3
Mary	1	0
Susan	18	3

Notes. The first column depicts television viewing (including taped and rental movies viewed using a VCR) as a percent of total ESM signals received. The second column depicts television viewing (including taped and rental movies viewed using a VCR) as a percent of ESM signals received prior to supper time on weekdays.

Homebodies were the most frequent television viewers. Routinizers and Anti-Homebodies represent subgroups for which these data were surprising because we expected that their planning orientations would steer them away from unstructured activities of this type. It was most surprising among Routinizers because they did not say much about television in their interviews, whereas Anti-Homebodies acknowledged struggling to avoid daytime television. True to expectations, however, Surplus People, Rovers, and Breaking Ins watched the most weekday, daytime television. Peggy, Kim, Angie, Todd, Harry, Robert, Keith, Matt, and Pauline stood out from the remainder of respondents as prolific television viewers. These nine respondents reported that they were watching television during at least 25% of signals received. Four of these people were classified as Rovers, three as Breaking Ins, one among the Surplus People, and one as a Routinizer. At the other extreme were Networkers, Caregivers, In-Controls, Lonely People, and Efficacy-Seekers. Indeed, five of the six Networkers and five of the six Efficacy-Seekers did not report watching any weekday, daytime television over the course of the study. Networkers clearly preferred face-to-face dialogue as opposed to the passive and entirely receptive communication of television. The Efficacy-Seekers' ESM data seem inconsistent with the interview data, where they expressed concern about watching too much television. It is possible, though, that this discrepancy is a result of altered television viewing habits subsequent to the initial interviews or that the Efficacy-Seekers' heightened awareness of the "television trap" led them to overstate their concerns.

The ESM data suggested that social patterns of television viewing varied from individual to individual (Table 32) but there was some intragroup consistency. Two Breaking Ins, Matt and Pauline, were more likely to watch television with their partners, whereas three Marginalized People, Kim, Keith, and Peggy, most often watched with friends and family members. However, the patterns of the most frequent viewers showed little pattern: Angie only watched television solo or in the presence of pets; Todd, Robert, and Harry also watched television on their own well over half the time. Although two of them are Rovers, no definitive pattern is evident here, as these four individuals are drawn from three different groups. In nearly all cases, however, weekday, daytime viewing was disproportionately done alone.

Table 32 Social Patterns Associated with Television for
Nine Frequent Viewers

	Day Signalled	Time Signalled	Social Context
Peggy			
P1	**Wednesday**	**early afternoon**	**with friends and/or relatives**
	Saturday	late morning	alone
	Saturday	early afternoon	alone
	Saturday	late afternoon	alone
	Monday	**early afternoon**	**with friends and/or relatives**
	Monday	late evening	with partner
	Tuesday	mid-evening	with friends and/or relatives
P2	**Tuesday**	**late morning**	**with friends and/or relatives**
	Tuesday	**early afternoon**	**alone**
	Wednesday	**late morning**	**with friends and/or relatives**
	Wednesday	early evening	with partner
	Wednesday	late evening	with partner, friends and/or relatives
	Thursday	**late afternoon**	**with friends and/or relatives**
	Friday	**early morning**	**with friends and/or relatives**
	Friday	**early afternoon**	**with friends and/or relatives**
	Friday	mid-evening	with friends and/or relatives
	Friday	late evening	with partner
	Sunday	mid-evening	with partner, friends and/or relatives
	Sunday	late evening	with partner, friends and/or relatives
	Monday	**early afternoon**	**with friends and/or relatives**
	Monday	mid-evening	with partner
	Monday	late evening	with partner
Angie			
P1	**Tuesday**	**late afternoon**	**alone**
	Wednesday	**early afternoon**	**alone with pets**
	Thursday	**late afternoon**	**alone with pets**
	Friday	**late morning**	**alone with pets**
	Friday	**late afternoon**	**alone with pets**
	Friday	early evening	alone with pets
	Saturday	early evening	alone with pets
	Saturday	late evening	alone with pets
	Monday	early evening	alone
P2	Thursday	mid-evening	alone with pets
	Friday	**early afternoon**	**alone with pets**
	Friday	**late afternoon**	**alone with pets**
	Saturday	mid-evening	alone with pets
	Saturday	late evening	alone with pets

▼

Note. Bold face indicates weekday, daytime television viewing.

Table 32 (*continued*)

	Day Signalled	Time Signalled	Social Context
Angie, *continued*			
	Sunday	mid-evening	alone with pets
	Sunday	late evening	alone with pets
	Monday	**late afternoon**	**alone with pets**
	Wednesday	**early afternoon**	**alone with pets**
	Wednesday	mid-evening	alone with pets
	Wednesday	late evening	alone with pets
Kim			
P1	**Wednesday**	**early morning**	**with children**
	Wednesday	**late morning**	**with children**
	Wednesday	**early afternoon**	**alone**
	Wednesday	**late afternoon**	**alone**
	Wednesday	late evening	alone
	Thursday	**early morning**	**with children**
	Thursday	**late afternoon**	**alone**
	Thursday	mid-evening	with other adults
	Friday	**early morning**	**alone**
	Friday	**late morning**	**with children**
	Saturday	late afternoon	with children
	Sunday	late evening	with children and other adults
	Monday	**late morning**	**with other adults**
	Monday	**early afternoon**	**with other adults**
	Monday	**late afternoon**	**with children**
	Monday	early evening	with children
	Monday	late evening	with other adults
	Tuesday	**early morning**	**with children**
	Tuesday	**late afternoon**	**with children**
	Tuesday	early evening	with children
Robert			
P1	Wednesday	early evening	alone
	Wednesday	mid-evening	alone
	Thursday	**late morning**	**alone**
	Thursday	**late afternoon**	**alone**
	Thursday	early evening	with partner
	Thursday	mid-evening	with partner
	Thursday	late evening	with partner
	Friday	**late afternoon**	**alone**
	Friday	early evening	alone
	Friday	mid-evening	alone
	Friday	late evening	with partner
	Saturday	early morning	alone
	Saturday	early evening	alone
	Saturday	mid-evening	alone

▼

Table 32 (*continued*)

	Day Signalled	Time Signalled	Social Context
Robert, *continued*			
	Sunday	late morning	alone
	Sunday	early afternoon	alone
	Sunday	mid-evening	alone
	Sunday	late evening	alone
P2	Saturday	early afternoon	alone
	Saturday	mid-evening	with partner
	Sunday	late morning	alone
	Tuesday	early evening	with friends and/or relatives
	Thursday	**late afternoon**	**with other adults**
	Monday	mid-evening	alone
	Tuesday	**late afternoon**	**alone**
	Tuesday	early evening	alone
	Wednesday	mid-evening	alone
	Wednesday	late evening	alone
	Thursday	**late morning**	**with friends and/or relatives**
	Thursday	**early afternoon**	**with friends and/or relatives**
	Thursday	mid-evening	alone
	Friday	early evening	with friends and/or relatives
Harry			
P1	Thursday	mid-evening	with friends and/or relatives
	Friday	**early afternoon**	**alone**
	Friday	**late afternoon**	**alone**
	Saturday	late morning	alone
	Saturday	late afternoon	alone
	Saturday	early evening	alone
	Sunday	late morning	alone
	Sunday	early evening	alone
	Monday	**late afternoon**	**alone**
	Monday	late evening	alone
	Wednesday	early evening	with friends and/or relatives
P2	Monday	early evening	alone
	Friday	mid-evening	with friends and/or relatives
	Saturday	early afternoon	alone
	Sunday	early afternoon	with friends and/or relatives
	Sunday	late afternoon	with friends and/or relatives
	Sunday	late evening	alone
Keith			
P1	**Wednesday**	**late morning**	**with children and pets**
	Wednesday	**late afternoon**	**alone**
	Thursday	**late morning**	**with friends and/or relatives and pets**

▼

Table 32 (*continued*)

	Day Signalled	Time Signalled	Social Context
Keith, *continued*			
	Thursday	mid-evening	with friends and/or relatives and children
	Friday	**late morning**	**with friends and/or relatives**
	Friday	**late afternoon**	**with friends, relatives and other adults**
	Friday	early evening	with friends and/or relatives
	Saturday	late afternoon	with friends and/or relatives and other adults
	Saturday	early evening	with friends and/or relatives and other adults
	Saturday	late evening	with friends and/or relatives and other adults
	Sunday	late afternoon	with friends and/or relatives
	Sunday	mid-evening	with friends and/or relatives
	Sunday	late evening	with friends and/or relatives
	Monday	late evening	with friends and/or relatives
	Tuesday	late evening	with friends and/or relatives
Todd			
P1	**Wednesday**	**early morning**	**alone**
	Wednesday	**early afternoon**	**alone**
	Wednesday	**late afternoon**	**alone**
	Wednesday	late evening	alone
	Thursday	**late morning**	**alone**
	Friday	mid-evening	alone
	Friday	late evening	alone
	Saturday	late afternoon	alone
	Saturday	early evening	alone
	Sunday	early afternoon	alone
	Sunday	late afternoon	with friends and/or relatives
	Sunday	late evening	alone
	Monday	mid-evening	alone
	Monday	late evening	alone
	Tuesday	late evening	alone
Matt			
P1	Saturday	late morning	with partner
	Tuesday	**late morning**	**alone**
	Tuesday	**early afternoon**	**alone**
	Tuesday	mid-evening	with partner
	Tuesday	late evening	with partner
	Wednesday	**late morning**	**alone**
	Wednesday	late evening	with partner

▼

Table 32 (*continued*)

	Day Signalled	Time Signalled	Social Context
Matt, *continued*			
	Thursday	**late morning**	**alone**
	Friday	mid-evening	with partner
	Friday	late evening	with partner
Pauline			
P1	Saturday	early evening	with partner
	Sunday	late evening	with partner
	Tuesday	late evening	with partner
	Wednesday	mid-evening	alone
	Wednesday	late evening	with partner
	Thursday	mid-evening	alone
	Friday	**late afternoon**	**alone**
	Friday	early evening	with partner and pets
	Friday	late evening	with partner, friends and other adults
P2	Friday	late evening	with partner
	Sunday	mid-evening	alone
	Tuesday	**late afternoon**	**alone**
	Tuesday	early evening	alone
	Tuesday	late evening	with partner
	Thursday	**late afternoon**	**alone**

Perceptions of Leisure and Non-Leisure

Consistent with participants' interview data, the ESM data suggest that unemployment was not, on a day-to-day basis, considered a leisurely experience by most members of our sample (Table 33). Leisure was measured on a 7-point scale response to the statement "I would call that leisure" wherein negative numbers (–3, –2, and –1) were classified as non-leisure and positive numbers (+1, +2, and +3) were classified as leisure. Scores of +3 were considered to be unequivocal leisure. Episodes with neutral ratings (0) on this question were not included in these analyses. Fewer than 21% of episodes (872 of 4,213 reported in the ESM data) were self-described as "leisure" by respondents. This percentage is considerably smaller than statistics reported elsewhere in the leisure literature. For example, taking out "neutral responses," two previous studies that used the identical "I would call that leisure" statement (Samdahl, 1992; Samdahl & Jekubovich, 1993) reported that respondents considered their experiences to be leisure in approximately 45% of reported episodes.[2] It is ironic, but revealing, that a sample of unemployed adults would report substantially fewer leisure episodes than have other samples comprised primarily of employed adults.

Members of the present sample, though all were unemployed at the outset of the study, tended to compartmentalize leisure into traditional time periods. Indeed, fewer than 20% of episodes recorded before 5:00 p.m. were described as leisure, in contrast with about 30% of episodes reported after 5:00 p.m. There was, however, considerable within-sample variation when examined at the group and subgroup levels (Table 33). At the group level, Planners reported the lowest percentage of leisure episodes, and they also reported the smallest percentage of unequivocally leisure episodes in comparison to members of the other three groups. Planners reported unequivocal leisure in fewer than 6% of all signals. Connectors and Marginalized People reported higher percentages of leisure episodes in their daily repertoires. They also reported the largest percentages, both over 11% of all signals, as unequivocal leisure episodes. Although data for the Planners, Connectors, and Marginalized People are intuitively understandable, the low overall percentage of leisure episodes among Vacationers is both noteworthy and counter to expectations.

At the subgroup level it was not surprising that, given their efforts to maintain regular work-like routines, Routinizers and Efficacy-Seekers reported the lowest percentages of leisure episodes (Table 33). Both Efficacy-Seekers and Routinizers placed only about 10% of daytime episodes into the leisure category. Efficacy-Seekers, in particular, reported an especially low number of unequivocal leisure episodes, just over 2% of all signals received. This also applies to In Controls who, given their strong career orientations, account in large measure for the low leisure orientation among the Vacationer group. At the other extreme, Caregivers and Lonely People reported, by far, the highest percentage of leisure episodes in their daily lives. Indeed, Surplus People were the only subgroup within the larger Connector and Marginalized categories who reported fewer than 20% of all episodes as leisure. Surplus People, however, stood out in the sense that over 75% of their self-described leisure episodes fell into the "unequivocal" category suggesting that their leisure experiences, though infrequent, were unmistakable.

The relationship between perceptions of leisure, non-leisure, and moods is also intriguing. In this analysis, mood was measured using four semantic differential scales (see Appendix B, question 8). The semantic differential anchors included unhappy–happy, bored–involved, anxious–relaxed, and irritable–good humoured. Each scale had

Table 33 Percent of Episodes Self-Described as Leisure by Group and Subgroup

Group/Subgroup	Percent of leisure episodes			
	Somewhat agree "this is leisure"	Agree "this is leisure"	Strongly agree "this is leisure"	Cumulative percent of leisure episodes
Planners	7.8	3.2	5.8	16.8
Routinizers (n = 431)	4.9	2.1	4.2	11.2
Anti-Homebodies (n = 282)	11.7	3.9	13.8	29.4
Efficacy-Seekers (n = 421)	8.3	3.8	2.1	14.2
Vacationers	6.0	4.8	6.7	17.5
Breaking In (n = 416)	6.0	5.3	7.7	19.0
In Control (n = 298)	6.0	4.0	5.4	15.4
Connectors	9.1	6.9	11.2	27.2
Caregivers (n = 460)	10.0	7.0	16.3	33.3
Networkers (n = 459)	8.3	6.8	6.1	21.2
Marginalized People	4.9	5.9	11.7	22.5
Rovers (n = 563)	5.7	8.2	8.2	22.1
Surplus People (n = 379)	1.1	2.1	12.7	15.9
Lonely People (n = 322)	8.1	6.2	16.8	31.1

Note. Total N = 4,011 (leisure N = 847, neither leisure nor non-leisure N = 535, Non-leisure N = 2,629. Item non-response and sub-group non-placement totalled N = 353.

a 5-point response where 1 = extremely negative mood states and 5 = extremely positive mood states. The reported mood measure reflects the aggregate mean scores for these four items. As expected, there was a positive relationship between self-described leisure experiences and respondents' mood states (Table 34); participants felt better when in leisure contexts. However, closer examination of the data reveals important within-sample differences. Leisure activity seemed to have very positive effects on the moods of about half the respondents and little to no effect on the moods of the remainder. Five of the 10 subgroups reported significantly elevated mood states in leisure contexts as compared with non-leisure contexts. Not coincidentally, these five subgroups were drawn entirely from two groups: Marginalized People and Vacationers. Perhaps members of these groups experienced more "success" in leisure contexts than in non-leisure contexts. That is, relative to non-leisure contexts, in leisure they perceived greater levels of self-determination, autonomy, feedback, and so forth, and these variables are typically associated with greater pos-

Table 34 Mood States by Subgroup during Self-Described Leisure and Non-Leisure Contexts

Subgroup	Non-leisure activities (n = 2,629)	Leisure activities (n = 847)	t	p =
Planners				
Routinizers (343, 48)	3.60	3.76	1.34	0.18
Anti-Homebodies (177, 73)	3.58	3.60	0.29	0.77
Efficacy-Seekers (280, 60)	3.49	3.31	1.39	0.17
Vacationers				
Breaking Ins (262, 79)	3.63	3.92	3.4	0.001
In Controls (218, 46)	3.44	3.77	4.18	0.001
Connectors				
Caregivers (268, 153)	3.53	3.55	0.18	0.86
Networkers (280, 97)	3.59	3.77	1.34	0.18
Marginalized People				
Rovers (326, 124)	3.53	3.94	4.63	0.001
Lonely People (204, 100)	4.16	4.41	2.97	0.003
Surplus People (286, 60)	3.35	3.83	3.72	0.001
Overall	3.60	3.86		

Notes. 535 episodes were scored neutrally on the "I would call that leisure" item (recorded as 0 on the −3 to +3 scale). Those episodes are not included in this table, nor are episodes (n = 172) wherein item non-response and subgroup placement (n = 181) was an issue. Numbers in parentheses after subgroup names are, respectively, the number of non-leisure and leisure episodes reported. Mood states were measured on a 5-point scale where 1 = negative affect and 5 = positive affect. Scores reported here represent means for four items (see Appendix B, item 8). Negative t-values indicate that the non-leisure mood mean was descriptively higher than the leisure mood mean.

itive affect. Note that the data reported in Table 34 relate to perceived quality of experience in non-leisure and leisure, compared to Table 33 that reported the frequency of occurrence of non-leisure and leisure. In that regard, members of some subgroups, such as Lonely People, had more success generating frequent leisure episodes than did others, for example, Surplus People. Likewise, for groups reporting comparable frequency of leisure episodes, some groups, such as In Controls, had more success generating positive mood states in those leisure episodes than did other groups, such as Efficacy-Seekers.

The relationship between leisure and positive mood did not hold for all subgroups. Four groups did not have a significant difference in mood states between non-leisure and leisure. These included the Networkers, Routinizers, Caregivers, and Anti-Homebodies. This lack of relationship may be at least partially attributable to the childcare responsibilities dominant in group members' lives. For example, 46% of the self-described leisure of Anti-Homebodies occurred in the presence of children, suggesting that Anti-Homebodies may have experienced lower levels of perceived freedom in leisure contexts than did other members of the study. That is, they were more likely doing fun things for their children rather than for themselves. The Efficacy-Seekers were the only people for whom mood states were perhaps depressed in leisure as opposed to non-leisure contexts. Although a pattern is apparent, this is a descriptive observation as the statistical test was not significant. Nevertheless, the divergence of the Efficacy-Seekers from the general pattern is worthy of note, although the root cause(s) of such a pattern are not readily apparent. One may speculate, though, that Efficacy-Seekers' general inability to fill their time effectively with what they considered meaningful activity caused them to be more discouraged about their leisure, in comparison with participants who may have achieved greater success on this front.

Respondents reported relatively low mood states early in the day (Table 35). Moods improved, as a rule, as the day progressed, and the statistical test for the full sample was significant. This general pattern was shared by four subgroups, Breaking Ins, Routinizers, Efficacy-Seekers, and Caregivers, although only for Breaking Ins were differences statistically significant throughout the course of the day. Three other subgroups, Rovers, Lonely People, and Surplus People, also exhibited a gradual improvement in moods over the course of the day. However, rather than finishing on a positive note, their moods suddenly declined in late evening. Differences were apparent, but not statistically significant at the conventional 0.05 level in all three cases; however, the divergence from the pattern seems worthy of note, particularly as it involved all three Marginalized subgroups. Finally, mood states for three subgroups, Anti-Homebodies, Networkers, and In Controls, remained relatively constant throughout the course of the day. In all three cases there was a noticeable, but not statistically significant, high point which occurred sometime in the evening.

Table 35 Mood States of All Respondents by Time of Day, Group, and Subgroup

Time of day	Overall sample	Planners			Vacationers		Connectors		Marginalized People		
		Rout-inizer (58–65)	Anti-Home Bodies (35–44)	Efficacy-Seekers (65–70)	Breaking In (46–68)	In Control (39–45)	Care-Givers (66–72)	Net-Workers (64–71)	Rovers (69–82)	Surplus People (49–65)	Lonely People (46–49)
Early morning	3.54	3.47	3.51	3.30	3.52	3.52	3.43	3.53	3.37	3.57	4.13
Late morning	3.57	3.56	3.56	3.48	3.58	3.67	3.42	3.59	3.52	3.53	4.22
Early afternoon	3.60	3.50	3.63	3.40	3.54	3.46	3.43	3.72	3.51	3.42	4.28
Late afternoon	3.55	3.66	3.54	3.31	3.65	3.48	3.36	3.50	3.50	3.20	4.09
Early evening	3.62	3.66	3.69	3.41	3.67	3.52	3.50	3.60	3.55	3.33	4.15
Mid-evening	3.78	3.67	3.59	3.49	3.88	3.66	3.58	3.69	3.83	3.55	4.51
Late evening	3.78	3.73	3.64	3.61	3.92	3.58	3.78	3.59	3.65	3.34	4.37
F	9.97	1.04	0.58	1.3	3.55	1.12	0.88	0.29	2.04	1.44	1.9
p =	0.001	0.40	0.75	0.26	0.002	0.35	0.51	0.94	0.06	0.20	0.08

Note. Total N = 4,183 (item nonresponse = 51 for time of day, 181 for subgroup). Numbers in parentheses represent the range of signals received by subgroup and time period. In general, there was little subgroup variation in number of signals received by time of day. Exceptions include Breaking Ins (who were least likely to respond early in the morning), Surplus People (who were least likely to respond late in the evening), and Rovers (who were least likely to respond in early evening). Mood states were measured on a 5-point scale where 1 = negative affect and 5 = positive affect. Scores reported here represent means for four items (see Appendix B, item 8).

The relationship between time of day, perceptions of leisure or non-leisure, and moods is also interesting (Table 36). Planners and Connectors often reported lower mood states during self-described leisure activity than during non-leisure activity. Table 36 shows 70 comparisons of mood states for leisure and non-leisure throughout the day. For Planners and Connectors, over half of the comparisons (21 of 35 comparisons) for these two groups, self-described leisure moods were equal to or lower than self-described non-leisure moods. This was especially true early in the day. Indeed, all five Planner and Connector subgroups reported lower leisure moods than non-leisure moods during the early morning time period.

Table 36 also includes a total of 35 mood measures for the Marginalized and Vacationer groups. In contrast to the findings for Planners and Connectors, only one Marginalized subgroup (Rovers) and no Vacationer subgroups reported lower morning leisure moods than morning non-leisure moods. Members of the Marginalized People and Vacationer groups usually reported better moods during leisure than during non-leisure experiences. Vacationers and Marginalized People were much less likely to report better moods during non-leisure time. In fact, this phenomenon occurred in only four of 35 possible instances. This positive gap provides corroborative evidence of the frustration experienced by members of some subgroups (for example, Surplus People, Lonely People, In Controls, and Breaking Ins) over the lack of resources for recreation and leisure pursuits, whereas such frustrations were less often expressed by people in the Planner and Connector groups. The data may simply be a manifestation of the fact that members of the Planner and Connector groups enjoyed their leisure less than did Marginalized People and Vacationers. Consistent with their low mood states during almost any kind of leisure experience, Efficacy-Seekers were the only subgroup to report lower leisure than non-leisure moods during mid- and late-evening hours.

A final look at respondent moods was conducted in the context of nine common social situations (Table 37). The social situations included here represent the most frequently reported situations from among some three dozen possible combinations. Together, these nine contexts accounted for over 85% of the 4,415 episodes reported in the ESM data. Several conclusions can be drawn from these descriptive data. First, the Vacationer group (this was true of both subgroups, In Control and Breaking In) reported experiencing a narrower range of social contexts than did members of other groups and subgroups. This finding makes sense given the relatively early life stages of these respondents.

Table 36 Mood States by Subgroup, Time of Day, and Self-Description of the Leisure or Non-Leisure Nature of the Experience at Hand

	Time of day[a]	Non-leisure moods	Leisure moods[b]		Time of day[a]	Non-leisure moods	Leisure moods[b]
Planners				**Vacationers**			
Routinizers	1	3.49	3.38	Breaking In	1	3.57	3.75
	2	3.53	3.72		2	3.56	3.63
	3	3.44	3.66		3	3.48	3.59
	4	3.73	3.55		4	3.50	4.00
	5	3.67	3.86		5	3.56	4.06
	6	3.60	4.07		6	3.88	3.82
	7	3.75	3.86		7	3.87	4.05
Anti-homebodies	1	3.54	3.47	In Control	1	3.40	4.05
	2	3.62	3.33		2	3.37	3.39
	3	3.62	3.61		3	3.34	3.72
	4	3.51	3.56		4	3.38	3.86
	5	4.00	3.66		5	3.52	3.60
	6	3.52	3.70		6	3.68	3.83
	7	3.63	3.65		7	3.48	3.93
Efficacy-Seekers	1	3.39	3.33	**Marginalized People**			
	2	3.47	2.00	Rovers	1	3.43	3.31
	3	3.52	2.95		2	3.51	3.86
	4	3.43	3.25		3	3.51	3.48
	5	3.45	3.57		4	3.54	3.98
	6	3.60	3.61		5	3.51	4.10
	7	3.63	3.50		6	3.89	4.09
Connectors					7	3.46	4.22
Caregivers	1	3.63	3.44	Surplus People	1	3.55	3.85
	2	3.62	3.24		2	3.52	3.75
	3	3.61	3.23		3	3.27	4.11
	4	3.34	3.32		4	3.19	3.00
	5	3.52	3.39		5	3.34	3.56
	6	3.29	3.94		6	3.49	4.00
	7	3.75	4.09		7	2.93	3.93
Networkers	1	3.53	3.53	Lonely People	1	3.96	4.10
	2	3.45	4.27		2	4.13	4.31
	3	3.80	3.78		3	4.18	4.48
	4	3.67	4.05		4	4.10	4.20
	5	3.64	3.36		5	4.13	4.26
	6	3.79	3.81		6	4.41	4.63
	7	3.54	3.59		7	4.29	4.63

Note. Mood states were measured on a 5-point scale where 1 = negative affect and 5 = positive affect. Scores reported here represent means for four items (see Appendix B, item 8).

[a] Where: 1 = early morning; 2 = late morning; 3 = early afternoon; 4 = late afternoon; 5 = early evening; 6 = mid-evening; 7 = late evening.

[b] Leisure mean scores, especially for morning time slots, should be interpreted with caution because some are based on a small (n < 10) number of episodes. Total N = 4,011 (item nonresponse = 51 for time of day, 181 for subgroup, and 172 for leisure/non-leisure). For total number of episodes received by subgroup, see Table 36.

Table 37 Mood States during Nine Common Social Situations

	Overall sample	Planners			Vacationers		Connectors		Marginalized People		
		Rout-imizer	Anti-Home Bodies	Efficacy-Seekers	Breaking In	In Control	Care-Givers	Net-Workers	Rovers	Surplus People	Lonely People
Alone (n = 1,809)	3.45 (0.85)	3.33 (0.69)	3.55 (0.51)	3.32 (0.82)	3.48 (0.60)	3.44 (0.53)	3.88 (1.00)	3.39 (1.22)	3.18 (0.99)	3.23 (0.85)	3.78 (0.72)
Others (n = 700)	3.61 (0.80)	3.57 (0.53)	3.78 (0.42)	3.36 (0.61)	3.80 (0.55)	3.48 (0.51)	3.48 (1.33)	3.63 (1.16)	3.57 (0.83)	3.52 (0.68)	4.16 (0.88)
Friends (n = 572)	3.76 (0.96)	3.23 (0.83)	3.93 (0.45)	3.70 (0.99)	3.73 (0.67)	3.53 (0.65)	4.52 (0.78)	3.49 (1.70)	3.85 (1.06)	3.30 (0.85)	4.29 (0.66)
Partner (n = 484)	3.82 (0.98)	3.85 (0.77)	3.52 (0.49)	3.13 (0.88)	4.06 (0.77)	4.32 (0.55)	2.39 (1.30)	3.62 (0.66)	3.60 (1.25)	3.91 (0.92)	4.40 (0.73)
Children (n = 281)	3.50 (0.95)	3.76 (0.62)	3.50 (0.53)	3.55 (1.01)	3.75 —	— —	3.01 (1.29)	3.18 (1.34)	3.68 (0.33)	— —	4.06 (0.389)
Friends & others (n = 206)	3.63 (1.16)	4.67 (0.29)	— —	3.46 (0.85)	4.12 (0.47)	3.61 (0.75)	2.68 (1.50)	3.85 (1.39)	4.22 (0.84)	3.09 (0.52)	4.50 (0.68)
Pets (n = 164)	3.74 (0.66)	3.52 (0.70)	3.33 (0.58)	3.44 (0.42)	3.88 (0.57)	— —	3.44 (0.51)	3.73 (0.72)	3.81 (0.60)	3.96 (1.07)	3.33 (0.32)
Children & partner (n = 141)	3.55 (0.92)	3.78 (0.72)	3.39 (0.54)	3.58 (0.52)	— —	— —	2.44 (1.36)	4.19 (0.66)	3.00 —	3.25 —	4.68 (0.43)
Partner & pets (n = 137)	3.77 (0.86)	3.78 (0.88)	3.75 —	3.24 (0.66)	2.25 —	— —	2.89 (0.19)	3.83 (0.61)	4.09 (0.69)	3.63 (1.25)	4.11 (0.48)

Notes. 1 = negative mood state, 5 = positive mood state. Standard deviations in parentheses. This table accounts for 85.5% (3,774 of 4,415) of social situations reported by participants during the ESM portions of Phase 1 and Phase 2.

As reported previously, the most common social context in which respondents found themselves was "alone." This context occurred in just over a third of the reported social situations. Not surprisingly, mood states were lowest overall in this context in comparison to the other eight social contexts. However, two subgroups, Anti-Homebodies and Caregivers, reported better moods in solitary contexts than they did in many social contexts involving other people. These data make sense because both subgroups have substantial caregiving and family-based responsibilities and solitary time may be especially welcomed. However, the data are less consistent with the Anti-Homebodies' oft-expressed frustrations at being the last ones out of the house in the morning. Nor are they consistent with the nurturing roles so often described by the Caregivers. Indeed, mood states of Anti-Homebodies and Caregivers appeared to diverge from those of the broader sample in many of the contexts examined. Rovers' low mood scores when they were alone also seem incongruous, given their oft-stated attempts at to maintain social distance from others. Those low scores may be partially attributable to the fact that most of the Rovers were single and childless for most of the study. Perhaps they were experiencing "too much of a good thing."

Interactions with friends were almost universal in generating positive mood states, the one exception being Routinizers. This subgroup appears particularly sensitive to the social stigma of their employment status. Public social settings involving interactions with both friends and other adults were also generally positive for most members of the study. Surplus People and Caregivers, however, experienced relatively negative moods in these contexts. Partners, pets, and combinations of partners and pets elicited positive moods from most respondents. A notable exception was the Efficacy-Seekers subgroup, for whom moods were often low in these contexts. Interactions with children often generated relatively poor moods, a generalization that also holds for many subgroups when partners were added to a social mix that included children. Caregivers, especially, reported very low scores here, perhaps due to respondents' frustrations at having to sacrifice both perceived frills and perceived necessities in deference to their employment status. Networkers' low mood states in the presence of children may be attributable to the same phenomena.

Satisfaction with Daily Planning

Respondents were generally dissatisfied with their ability to plan and pace their daily routines (Table 38). Only three of the 10 subgroups

Table 38 Responses by Subgroup to the Planning Statement: "I Had Expected to Be Doing That about This Time Today."

Subgroup	N	Mean	Standard deviation
Planners			
Routinizers	390	−1.11	1.7
Anti-Homebodies	260	0.12	2.15
Efficacy-Seekers	332	−0.82	1.7
Vacationers			
Breaking In	340	−0.41	1.9
In Control	262	−0.58	1.92
Connectors			
Caregivers	406	0.01	1.94
Networkers	373	−0.4	1.98
Marginalized People			
Rovers	447	−0.46	1.96
Surplus People	334	−0.54	2.11
Lonely People	304	0.01	2.19

Note. A +3 response indicated total agreement and a −3 response indicated total disagreement. Total N = 3,448 (item nonresponse = 967).

reported neutral to positive scores on this aspect of their lives: Lonely People, Caregivers, and Anti-Homebodies. It is worth noting that there is only one male among the 13 total members of these subgroups, suggesting that women may have felt less frustration than did men in this regard. The remaining seven subgroups reported negative scores on this item, though we should also note that the standard deviations were somewhat large, indicating some moderate variability among individual responses.

Perhaps the most interesting aspects of these data are the dichotomous positions of the three Planner subgroups. Anti-Homebodies were most likely to agree with the statement "I had expected to be doing that about this time today," whereas Routinizers and Efficacy-Seekers were most likely, by a fair margin, to disagree. Initially, we expected that all Planners would score high on this item, in keeping with their basic predispositions. The Anti-Homebodies' daily routines may indeed be the most predictable based on their relatively heavy family obligations. We suspect that the contrary positions of the other two groups, however, represent a large measure of frustration with any deviations in their normally planned routines. For example,

Routinizers were particularly vocal in expressing frustration with red tape when dealing with various employment-related social service agencies. The interview data suggested that Routinizers were, perhaps, less tolerant of institutional delays and unplanned interruptions to their routines than were other respondents.

Table 39 suggests that this perceived incongruence between expectations and reality persisted throughout the day for members of all four groups. We subtracted perception mean scores from expectation mean scores, so any deviation from zero value indicates some level of incongruity with respect to daily planning ideals. These incongruities remained acute for Planners late in the day whereas other groups were more prone to midday disruptions. This may reflect the Planners' propensity to fill their time with scheduled tasks; they might therefore have been more immersed in activities at midday than members of other groups, whose daily planning was somewhat less regimented and who therefore were more often at "loose ends" during the day.

Table 39 Expectation Means Minus Perception Means by Subgroup to the Planning Statement: "I Had Expected to Be Doing That about This Time Today"

Group	Time of day	Mean	Group	Time of day	Mean
Planners	1	−0.49	**Vacationers**	1	−0.42
	2	−0.42		2	−0.62
	3	−0.82		3	−0.68
	4	−0.69		4	−0.38
	5	−0.70		5	−0.60
	6	−0.64		6	−0.45
	7	−0.66		7	−0.23
Connectors	1	0.00	**Marginalized People**	1	−0.31
	2	−0.27		2	−0.34
	3	−0.45		3	−0.57
	4	−0.43		4	−0.49
	5	−0.16		5	−0.46
	6	−0.18		6	−0.55
	7	−0.23		7	−0.39

Note. Where: 1 = early morning; 2 = late morning; 3 = early afternoon; 4 = late afternoon; 5 = early evening; 6 = mid-evening; 7 = late evening.

Highlight of the Day: Content-Analysis of Open-Ended ESM Comments

Some 70 pages of single-spaced, 10-point transcripts were created by entering open-ended commentary provided by respondents on their ESM questionnaires. Two headings were included on each ESM sheet:

at the beginning, "Briefly, describe that situation in a few words," and at the end, "What else would you like to mention about this situation?" As often as not, respondents did not add written comments to supplement the quantitative data that they provided. When they did, the majority of written comments were rather vague descriptions of situations such as "in the car" and "watching TV." At the end of each day, respondents were given space to respond to three additional open-ended questions (see Appendix B):

1. Of everything that happened today, what was the *one* situation that was the best part of the day for you?
2. What was so special about that situation?
3. Is there anything else you want to mention about today?

Responses to these questions, though again provided only sporadically, accounted for over half of the 70 pages in this transcript. These end-of-the-day retrospective comments tended to be richer and more descriptive than those provided on the spot, and they were useful in providing another means of triangulating conclusions based on previously discussed data. Where reported here, direct quotations from respondents are transcribed verbatim without editorial comment related to spelling or grammar.

Figure 6 provides a graphic summary of the social contexts surrounding the self-described "one best situation," hereafter referred to as "highlight of the day." Based on participants' answers to this question, 12 categories describing the context of their interaction were developed. Three categories involved the presence of others (family, friends, and pets). For purposes of this analysis, acquaintances identified as boyfriends or girlfriends were described as family, not as friends, reflecting the participants' tendency to think in these terms. Explicitly mentioned leisure contexts (workouts, watching television, walking, reunions, etc.) were combined into a recreation heading. Six other contexts included school/work (including job-search activity, course work, part-time jobs and the like), shopping, household (painting, doing dishes, fixing a car), personal (getting a perm, taking a bath), volunteerism, and church-related and/or spiritual gatherings. Food (an exceptional meal, a dinner out) also constituted a category in and of itself. If respondents specifically stated that they were alone, this was considered a separate context as well. Most comments mentioned just one of the 12 just-described categories, but multiple contexts were noted when appropriate. For example, "coaching my daughter's soccer team" was coded three ways as family/recreation/volunteerism, whereas "spending time with my good friend Carol" was coded under the friends category. Finally, respondents occasionally

Figure 6a Frequency of Four Common Daily Highlights by Context and Subgroup

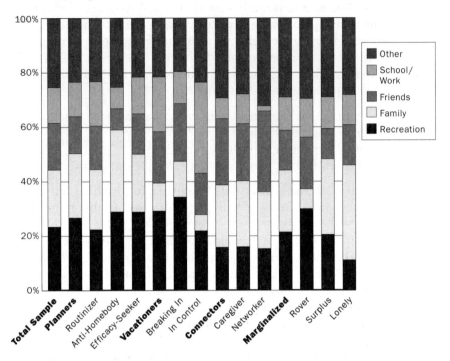

made an explicit point of noting that there was "no highlight of the day." These instances were coded under a thirteenth category, titled "No Highlight."

The first four categories (family, friends, recreation and school/work) accounted for between 65% and 80% of all highlighted social contexts for all subgroups. There was considerable group-by-group diversity, however. As evident in Figure 6a, family interactions provided the plurality of daily highlights for members of four subgroups (Lonely People, Surplus People, Caregivers, and Anti-Homebodies), although contexts involving friends were a close second for the Caregivers, and contexts involving recreation were a close second for the Anti-Homebodies. Similar to the Anti-Homebodies, Routinizers reported an equal number of daily highlights related to family and recreation. Recreation was the context most likely to produce daily highlights for three subgroups (Breaking In, Rovers, and Efficacy-Seekers). Networkers stood alone as the group most likely to derive daily highlights from interactions with friends, whereas In Controls were the only group to report a plurality of daily highlights related to

Figure 6b Frequency of Nine Less Common Daily Highlights by Context and Sub-Group

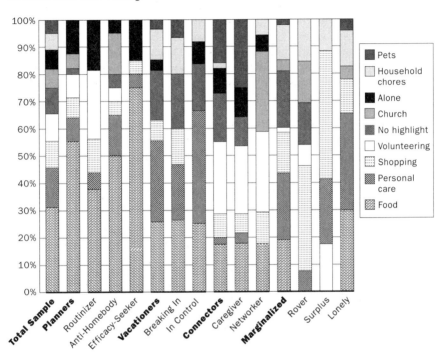

Note. The nine categories of daily highlights in this figure represent an expanded version of the "Other" category in Figure 6a.

school/work. Less common daily highlight contexts are documented in Figure 6b and discussed, where appropriate, in subsequent pages.

Planners

Not surprisingly, people in the Planners group often reported daily highlights associated with getting things done and maintaining control over their schedules:

> *Highlight of the day:* I went to lunch with my son, my husband and a colleague of his.
> *What was so special?* It was a nice change—a break from the routine of the day.
> *Anything else you'd like to mention?* I spent the morning in my husbands office cleaning up some of my paper work and working on my older boys resume on the computer. I like that. I felt as if I had accomplished something! (Jackie—Phase 1)

Highlight of the day: Watching the kids at Fred's party have so much fun in the Haunted House we made for them.
What was so special? We worked really hard to create an atmosphere that was spooky but not too scary. It worked, the kids loved it. The neighbours 2 older boys dressed as Dracula and came over to help set it up and play with the kids. They were really tremendous. *Anything else you'd like to mention?* I was very irritated for a while because my plans didn't go quite the way I wanted. But in the end, it all turned out okay! (Jackie—Phase 2)

In contrast to other groups such as the Connectors, Planners were, as a group, less likely to report daily highlights related to interactions with friends. That is not to say that friendship networks were unimportant, but that Planners' predominant daily highlights clearly related to interaction with family and recreation. As Anna's comments illustrate, family and recreation were sometimes intertwined:

Highlight of the day: Family barbecue at children's school.
What was so special? This is an annual event which we look forward to each year. It's always nice to get together with the parents, children, and teachers in a relaxed atmosphere. (Anna—Phase 1)

Highlight of the day: Going out with my son to the driving range.
What was so special? Spending time together—no one else. We both enjoy hitting golf balls. It is a good chance to communicate. (Anna—Phase 1)

Routinizers, though occasionally mentioning guilt during otherwise peak daily experiences, were more likely than the other two Planner subgroups to express feelings of confidence and mastery in recreation contexts as well as in both training and work contexts:

Highlight of the day: Waking up in the morning HA HA. But really being with my girl friend spending time together relaxing and carrying on with a normal life.
What was so special? Not working makes me feel that my life is not complete. Being with my girlfriend makes me feel that I still have a purpose. (Dick—Phase 1)

Highlight of the day: When I was eating the meal that I had prepared, and it was very good, I enjoyed the fact that my girlfriend thought it was excellent too.
What was so special? I got a certain feeling of satisfaction upon the meal turning out to be a success. The work I had put in to it had paid off. (Steven—Phase 1)

Highlight of the day: When I was playing soccer. It was very enjoyable as well as being an excellent form of exercise.
What was so special? I have only recently taken up soccer as a sport,

and today I noticed a marked improvement in my play. (Steven—Phase 1)

Highlight of the day: Training to become Black Jack dealer.
What was so special? Enjoyed the work it was a combination of work/pleasure. (Tom—Phase 1)

In the case of the Anti-Homebodies, family and recreation contexts more often served to counterbalance each other. Though family was important in their daily routines, Anti-Homebodies often described daily highlights that centered around private or personal time:

Highlight of the day: Exercise.
What was so special? My time. (Barb—Phase 1)

Highlight of the day: The best part of the day was finally being able to sit down at night, relax with no children around and watch one of my favourite TV shows.
What was so special? It was the only time I felt really relaxed. There were no demands being made on me or my time. (Jackie—Phase 2)

Similar to the Anti-Homebodies, the Routinizers and Efficacy-Seekers described daily highlights involving family and recreation that served to counterbalance educational and job-related efforts that took first and top priority in their daily routines.

All of the Planner subgroups displayed recurring themes related to planning, productivity, purpose, and accomplishment. However, the Efficacy-Seekers tended to experience less success in these efforts than did members of other Planner subgroups, as shown in these comments:

Highlight of the day: Sitting in backyard after it cooled off, reading book on creative process and choosing my direction.
What was so special? I feel like I am getting closer to making a commitment to the direction I want to take.
Anything else you'd like to mention? I felt a major lack of energy due to heat. Also felt very conscious of how much time I spend alone. (Kelly—Phase 1)

Highlight of the day: Moving skids.
What was so special? It was the only time during the day in which I felt that my work had any real fulfillment. The rest of the time work was boring.
Anything else you'd like to mention? I felt that my free time was spent in a rather boring fashion. I wanted to go to the gym but I felt too depressed to "treat myself." Instead I ended up over-eating to comfort myself. (David—Phase 2)

Highlight of the day: Taking my son's new car out for a drive.

> *What was so special?* He was happy & excited.
> *Anything else you'd like to mention?* Stressful & boring day. (Sheila—
> Phase 2)

This is not to suggest, however, that Efficacy-Seekers did not report positive moments. Similar to other Planners, they felt positive when they achieved a sense of accomplishment:

> *Highlight of the day:* I had made some contact with job strategy with an organization to help me with a career change and employment.
> *What was so special?* This organization will help me know what it is that I do want to do for a living.
> *Anything else you'd like to mention?* It was a good day! (Nicole—
> Phase 1)

> *Highlight of the day:* The last part of the day, relax and watch TV with family.
> *What was so special?* My efforts are concentrated on the well being of home and family.
> *Anything else you'd like to mention?* Did get a few things done and/or settled plus a future possibility or two. (Dale—Phase 2)

Efficacy-Seekers commonly reported guilt related to most aspects of their current situations, a trait common to the larger Planners group. However, the Efficacy-Seekers expressed greater doubts about their prospects than did members of the other two Planner subgroups:

> *Highlight of the day:* Walk in evening with my wife.
> *What was so special?* a) Pleasant, undemanding conversation; b) friendship & intimacy; c) enough exercise to relieve my "guilt" feelings of working at electronics hobby (sedentary) later. (Jack—
> Phase 1)

> *Highlight of the day:* Doing calculations on computer.
> *What was so special?* It was about the only really productive time.
> *Anything else you'd like to mention?* Fragmented & unplanned. Not productive. (Jack—Phase 2)

> *Highlight of the day:* Applying to four places.
> *What was so special?* Well, though I have an ice cubes chance in hell of getting the jobs, made me feel like I was doing something.
> *Anything else you'd like to mention?* Wore a suit for most of it. (Joe—
> Phase 1)

Planners' need to be productive also manifested in the extremes that they often went to in order to maintain control. Kelly's comments, for instance, demonstrate the satisfaction control could give. However, her conclusion is very typical of the Efficacy-Seeker subgroup of which she is a part:

Highlight of the day: When I was in library reading I was hungry (skipped lunch) but I didn't leave (let it control me).
What was so special? I got *really* into what I was reading—a rush of energy.
Anything else you'd like to mention? This feels like the hardest time of my life right now. (Kelly—Phase 1)

Vacationers

Members of this group were unique in that many of their daily highlights were relatively task-oriented rather than people-oriented. This observation may be attributable to life stage as well as personal orientation. Members of the Breaking In subgroup most often cited recreation contexts as the highlight of their day:

Highlight of the day: Sitting in the sun, reading a magazine by myself, in the afternoon. (Oh, the dog was outside too).
What was so special? I felt relaxed, there was nothing else to do, I enjoyed reading the magazine. (Pauline—Phase 1)

Highlight of the day: Reading a book for a few hours this afternoon.
What was so special? Time to myself.
Anything else you'd like to mention? Good day, very relaxing. (Joanne—Phase 2)

Highlight of the day: Buying scalped ticket for Edgefest [an annual multi-band outdoor rock concert near Toronto] at cost.
What was so special? I had expected to either pay through the nose or not get a ticket. (Bruce—Phase 1)

Nearly all of Les's highlights related to recreation, especially workouts. The subtle changes in word choice from his Phase 1 to Phase 2 are intriguing:

Highlight of the day: The best part of the day was working out.
What was so special? The special thing about working out for me is keeping fit. To me that is important. (Les—Phase 1)

Highlight of the day: The best part of the day was working out at the gym.
What was so special? I feel really good after. It acts as a release. (Les—Phase 2)

The from "keeping fit … is important" to "acts as a release" suggests an increased awareness of the value of leisure.

For Vacationers, interactions with friends and (when they occurred) with family often took place, not surprisingly, in the context of leisure and team sports. Nightlife was also a common theme.

The following comments were made by people in the Breaking In subgroup:

> *Highlight of the day:* Playing tennis w/ roommate.
> *What was so special?* I've been meaning to get back into the game (I also won). (Bruce—Phase 1)

> *Highlight of the day:* Going out to the club with my boyfriend Greg.
> *What was so special?* We hadn't gone in a while because of our recent move from London to Kitchener. I like being out with him.
> *Anything else you'd like to mention?* This activity is what we normally do on the weekend if we haven't decided to go out of town. (Matt—Phase 1)

Vacationers' Phase 2 comments were consistently upbeat and unqualified, even if the respondent was still unemployed or underemployed:

> *Highlight of the day:* Going out with my friends.
> *What was so special?* We have a lot of fun together.
> *Anything else you'd like to mention?* I could not hear the beeper when it went off at night—the music was too loud! (Joanne—Phase 2)

Members of the In Control subgroup were, by a fairly large margin, the only subgroup to identify school/work contexts as daily highlights:

> *Highlight of the day:* Afternoon meeting was productive.
> *What was so special?* My opinions were appreciated. (Bob—Phase 1)

> *Highlight of the day:* Friend needing help in German.
> *What was so special?* It reminded me that I do have something special and that there are people who can make use of my skills. (Donald—Phase 1)

> *Highlight of the day:* Being at the Toastmasters meeting seeing Carol complete her last speech to meet the requirements for her ATM award and congratulating her.
> *What was so special?* I look up to her, and I enjoyed seeing her do so well as she moves higher and higher.
> *Anything else you'd like to mention?* By Carol achieving ATM status in Toastmasters, that makes our group more recognized and more successful. I felt proud to be part of the group. (Pauline—Phase 1)

Evidence of the global nature of both In Controls' professional networks and their world views was also forthcoming in many daily highlights:

> *Highlight of the day:* Meeting with representative from Stuttgart University.

What was so special? Interesting discussion. (Bob—Phase 2)

Highlight of the day: Receiving a phone call from Germany—work may begin on Monday. [This] a.m—Cambridge. [This] p.m.—Ann Arbor, Michigan.
What was so special? I may be employed in next week. (Donald—Phase 2)

For members of the In Control subgroup, recreation settings were the second most common venue for daily highlights. That Donald allowed himself not one, but two, organized recreation experiences in a single day without any evidence of remorse or guilt provides additional evidence that Vacationers had different views than members of many other subgroups:

Highlight of the day: The personal relaxation time I spent on myself. First, the fitness club—I did quite well for me; second—I was really early for soccer, which allowed me to sit and enjoy the earlier game! (Donald—Phase 1)

Highlight of the day: This was giving out goodies to all the kids. [On Halloween night]
What was so special? Memories of myself—the kids were great. (Walter—Phase 2)

Vacationers, largely as a function of their life stage, also reported a fairly high number of daily highlights related to personal care compared to members of most other groups and subgroups:

Highlight of the day: Cold bath. [Temperatures hovered near 40°C during the first week of the study.] (Bob—Phase 1)

Highlight of the day: Had my haircut today & people commented positively about it.
What was so special? It's nice to hear people say good things to me.
Anything else you'd like to mention? It was a good day since I managed to get everything done that needed to be done. (Walter—Phase 2)

Connectors

For the most part, these data supported earlier conclusions about Connectors. The Caregivers often recorded daily highlights that reaffirmed traits that prior analyses had revealed. Not surprisingly, their comments revealed that Caregivers were first and foremost just that— caregivers. They consistently identified daily highlights stemming from opportunities to serve other people, primarily family members. These contexts seem important in mitigating other frustrations related to unemployment and underemployment:

Highlight of the day: When I took my mom out today. That was very special.
What was so special? She seemed so pleased that I took her out. (Andrea—Phase 1)

Highlight of the day: Playing with kids in the park.
What was so special? Both I and kids are happy when we are in the nature. We need it. Only then do I really forget all my troubles.
Anything else you'd like to mention? In sense of my career, another lost day. Filling this book gives me impression that I am doing something, that I am somehow employed. (Paul—Phase 1)

Highlight of the day: Playing chess with my son at home this evening.
What was so special? I've not spent a lot of time with him for a while. I really enjoyed to be with him.
Anything else you'd like to mention? Today, my life is more colourful than yesterday. I like chatting with friends, sitting in the library, reading the paper. (Alison—Phase 1)

In addition to the large number of highlights provided by familial and friendship contexts, Caregivers, like the Networkers, reported a lot of satisfaction from volunteer work and were the only group to prominently mention interactions with pets as daily highlights (this is attributed to Heather's interests):

Highlight of the day: Just watching the [horses] interact with the kids.
What was so special? One boy asked if he could own Mocca my black and white horse. I said he could own them for as long as the ride and he was having so much fun that his father bought two more tickets so his ownership lasted a little longer. (Heather—Phase 1)

Highlight of the day: Interacting with my Beavers.
What was so special? They are just such sweeties and we had a good meeting. (Heather—Phase 2)

Nevertheless, several daily highlights among the Caregiver subgroup were described as special because they allowed the individual to be removed from friends and family. This suggests that personal space and opportunities for personal growth were also cherished among the Caregivers:

Highlight of the day: Watching the movie this morning by myself, before anyone was awake.
What was so special? It gave me the opportunity to watch a movie that I like without anyone disturbing me & it didn't eat up my day because it started at 8:45 am.

Anything else you'd like to mention? Difficult & tense day because I saw how ill my father in law actually is. Didn't know how to react. (Donna—Phase 1)

Highlight of the day: The unexpected opportunity to visit a close friend without children.
What was so special? The opportunity does not often arise that I can go out without my youngest child.
Anything else you'd like to mention? I was pleased with my math test I wrote in the morning. (Janet—Phase 2)

As expected the Networkers subgroup often described daily highlights that revealed the importance of social contact and friendships:

Highlight of the day: My visit with my good friend Carol.
What was so special? She is such a kind hearted soul, may God always bless and keep her always!
Anything else you'd like to mention? The first part of the day weren't very productive. (Melanie—Phase 1)

Highlight of the day: Garage sale was a success.
What was so special? Social time with neighbours & made a little money—got rid of some junk. (Stephanie—Phase 1)

Highlight of the day: Line dancing.
What was so special? Interacting with people & exercise and dancing.
Anything else you'd like to mention? Visiting my [ex-boyfriend] reassured me I made the right decision 8 yrs ago. A good friend he is and/but gambler he will always be. (Jenny—Phase 2)

Consistent with their desire for social contact, people in the Networker subgroup found many daily highlights in organized religion and, relative to participants from other groups, in volunteering. The following comments were characteristic:

Highlight of the day: I helped my friend.
What was so special? She asked Jesus into her heart as her Lord and Saviour. (Jeanne—Phase 2)

Highlight of the day: Volunteering at the school with preparation for school play of the grade 2 class.
What was so special? Able to use my skills even though I don't get $—pay for it. I get *love*. (Stacy—Phase 2)

In summary, data collected regarding the highlight of the day were very consistent with the Connectors' interview data.

Marginalized People

As with other groups, data on daily highlights also confirmed patterns in the lives of Marginalized People. Rovers consistently reported experiencing "no" daily highlights. Indeed, their "no highlight" total was only one short of the combined total of the other nine subgroups. "No highlights" are counted as such only if a respondent explicitly wrote something to that effect on the questionnaire. Two of the Rovers, Frank and Aaron, left the daily highlights question blank during the entire ESM portion of the study (21 days total as Frank completed only Phase 1). They were the only respondents in the study to do so. With the exception of the first quotation from Susan, all of the following are from Rovers:

> *Highlight of the day:* There was no situation that was special. It was a dull, boring depressing day. Even watching the movie was boring because I've already seen it 4 times. (Susan—Phase 1)

> *Highlight of the day:* No comment.
> *What was so special?* No comment.
> *Anything else you'd like to mention?* No comment. (Larry—Phase 1)

> *Highlight of the day:* There was no "Best" part of the day today. (Angie—Phase 1)

> *Highlight of the day:* No. (Robert—Phase 1)

Rovers generally found more daily highlights in recreation activities than in any other context. Angie, for example, mentioned swimming, workouts at the gym (several times), and walking among her highlight repertoire. The Rovers often found pleasure in physical activity, in contrast to the other two Marginalized subgroups whose highlighted recreational contexts were often passive, especially television and movie viewing. Lonely People and Surplus People were also more likely than other respondents to mention specific television programs and times, an indication that their viewing habits were consistent rather than sporadic:

> *Highlight of the day:* Best part of day was sitting watching the comedies in the evening.
> *What was so special?* I just love comedy shows and watch them every Thursday. (Carrie—Phase 1)

> *Highlight of the day:* Watching *Son-in-law* and playing with the dogs.
> *What was so special?* It made me forget about my operation tomorrow. I'm a little apprehensive about it. I have never had stitches & tomorrow I am not looking forward to it. (Christina—Phase 1)

Highlight of the day: I watched *Eastenders*.
What was so special? It is a great show, I look forward to it every Friday. (Carrie—Phase 2)

Gambling was popular among the Rover and Surplus People subgroups. Kim, for example, reported on five different occasions that the highlight of her day was playing Bingo:

Highlight of the day: Playing Bingo.
What was so special? Gave me a chance to get out of the house. (Kim—Phase 1)

Highlight of the day: I finally won at Bingo. [$150]
What was so special? Well, I really needed the money, plus I needed a break from all the stress of moving. (Diane—Phase 1)

Family contexts provided the majority of daily highlights for members of two of the three marginalized subgroups, Surplus People and Lonely People. Many highlights were qualified, however:

Highlight of the day: Dinner with boyfriend.
What was so special? We were alone and I felt happy.
Anything else you'd like to mention? Very boring day. Felt like I was worthless, useless. (Peggy—Phase 2)

Highlight of the day: Family dinner, everyone was home and my boyfriend was there. Everyone was in a good mood. Great conversation over dinner. Felt very happy and relaxed.
What was so special? We were all together and very cheerful.
Anything else you'd like to mention? Found some job listings and I applied for. Felt very good about myself. (Peggy—Phase 2)

Highlight of the day: When I was at home watching TV with my boyfriend, relaxing.
What was so special? It was just sort of a lazy day because of the weather and we were nice and cozy on the couch.
Anything else you'd like to mention? I was annoyed that I wasted my free passes on a movie that was kind of boring. (Diane—Phase 2)

Although Surplus People mentioned partners in relation to daily highlights, they often mentioned other family members as well. By contrast, Lonely People most often spoke specifically of interactions with their partners, and wedding themes were common. The comments below are from Lonely People:

Highlight of the day: Sitting on the balcony, chatting about different things: money, the wedding, the weekend.
What was so special? It's one of the ways we spend together without distractions from television, phone calls, things like that have to be done, like grocery shop, job hunt, etc. (Susan—Phase 1)

Highlight of the day: Just spending some time with Gary when he got home from work. At first we had a bit of an argument but after we made up we spent some time working on the wedding invitations and it was nice.
What was so special? It was nice to spend some private time with Gary.
Anything else you'd like to mention? It was a usual day—running around doing errands & spending a lot of time alone. (Marcia—Phase 1)

Highlight of the day: Working with Fred painting the living room.
What was so special? Team work; quality time together. Making our future come true.
Anything else you'd like to mention? Purchased wedding bands today. We are getting engaged on Christmas Day. (Mary—Phase 2)

In contrast to other Marginalized subgroups, Rovers, rarely mentioned family members in daily highlight contexts, so Robert's rather tender sentiments represent an exception for that subgroup:

Highlight of the day: Spending day with girlfriend.
What was so special? Caring for someone. (Robert—Phase 1)

Second to interaction with family, friends were often mentioned in daily highlights reported by people in the Marginalized group. Surplus People and Lonely People had seemingly drifted away from many friends and tended to emphasize the past in their interactions with friends:

Highlight of the day: Going to my friend's place & spending some time with.
What was so special? Talking about the good ole times. (Tracy—Phase 1)

Highlight of the day: When my girlfriend called me.
What was so special? Well, I was thinking 'bout calling her all week, but since she's an acquaintance from my former employment, I figured that it wasn't mutual, but it was.
Anything else you'd like to mention? Saturday night is a typical movie-nite at the neighbours. Wedding dress shopping was a first. Aside from the lousy weather that kept me indoors most of the day, it was a good day. (Susan—Phase 1)

Mary's comment regarding her Christian community was the only volunteer experience among the nearly 150 daily highlights mentioned by Marginalized people:

Highlight of the day: The car wash working side by side—volunteering our time. Spending quality time with other Christians.

What was so special? Everybody was around my age and all were from my church and Christians.
Anything else you'd like to mention? The call at 6:00 p.m. from [former boyfriend] asking me if I wanted to watch a movie with him. I also helped him babysit for 1 hr. too. (Mary—Phase 1)

As noted earlier, there were many times when daily highlights reported by Marginalized People were qualified in some fashion. This was especially common among Surplus People:

Highlight of the day: We got out of our apartment pretty quickly.
What was so special? It was so special because we couldn't wait to move away from our neighbours. (Diane—Phase 1)

Highlight of the day: Overall not a bad day. Most fun was with my boyfriend.
What was so special? Made me feel relaxed, happy. Didn't yell at me like family does. (Peggy—Phase 1)

Highlight of the day: When I was walking in the park.
What was so special? It gave me time to look over some things that had happened to me earlier that day.
Anything else you'd like to mention? It was a little boring. (Darlene—Phase 1)

Other statements, such as the two from Larry (an alcoholic Rover), were beautifully written, albeit downright disturbing:

Highlight of the day: Listening to songs of love and hate by Leonard Cohen.
What was so special? You may find this very strange but I take great pleasure in listening to suicidal tendencies.
Anything else you'd like to mention? Without actual partaking in the act, I do not recommend you listen to this alone unless you have failed and come to grip with your worst fears. (Larry—Phase 1)

Highlight of the day: Met a dear and trusted friend after the funeral home trip.
What was so special? It was nice to know that I am still loved and respected.
Anything else you'd like to mention? I got through the whole day without a drink or putting a needle in my arm. Those who are not busy being born are busy dying. So many times I wanted to end it. But God in his infinite wisdom chose not to take me. How will I ever pay back that debt. All I wanted was to be free but that's not the way it's turning out to be. (Larry—Phase 1)

The extreme mood swings discussed earlier as characteristic of the Lonely People are illustrated in these two consecutive daily highlights reported by Susan:

Highlight of the day: My supervisor approached me to ask to work overtime tomorrow.
What was so special? She acknowledged the fact that I already work very hard "every minute of the day."
Anything else you'd like to mention? For some reason I had an unbelievable amount of energy. It must be the water. (Susan—Phase 2)

Highlight of the day: Nothing. This day sucked the big one.
Anything else you'd like to mention? I wished today never happened. I did 3-1/2 hours over time and was told that I can't take a day off to go away for the weekend. (Susan—Phase 2)

Marginalized People often rejoiced in "little victories" such as temporary part-time jobs, stable housing, or found money:

Highlight of the day: I went for an interview with a food sampling company. I've been hired to work Thurs., Fri., Sat. But I won't be starting 'til another week.
What was so special? I was hired. (Carrie—Phase 1)

Highlight of the day: The best part was being able to put my deposit on an apartment.
What was so special? It was special because I know I have the apartment for sure now.
Anything else you'd like to mention? It's been a pretty good day. I also got a part-time babysitting job. (Diane—Phase 1)

Highlight of the day: I found a good—usable rocking chair in the garbage.
What was so special? In my life I have given rocking chairs away. It was real nice to get one back with no strings attached. (Larry—Phase 1)

Highlight of the day: I found another $5.00 today.
What was so special? It's found money, it is a lucky week for me. (Carrie—Phase 2)

Highlight of the day: That I finally got a chance to do my laundry.
What was so special? That I had clean clothes. (Keith—Phase 2)

Marginalized People rarely mentioned "creative" daily highlights. As such, these quotations from Tracy and Marcia represent exceptions:

Highlight of the day: Preparing a wonderful breakfast.
What was so special? I have not prepared anything so tasty. (Tracy—Phase 1)

Highlight of the day: I really enjoyed planting the bulbs in the garden.
What was so special? I was excited about preparing something that has the potential to be very beautiful. I am proud of the work I did. (Marcia—Phase 2)

In summary, the daily highlight question generated data that consistently corroborated other data collected in this research. A shortcoming of the data collection process, identified after-the-fact, was that the ESM questionnaires did not explicitly solicit input regarding the low point of each day. This information would have provided a valuable complement to this data on highlights of the day, and we recommend that future ESM research with unemployed populations incorporate some questions related to that issue.

Respondents' Self-Esteem and Life Satisfaction

Self-esteem and life satisfaction scores were measured using items from existing standardized scales. Self-esteem (Appendix D, Part D) was measured using 20 items derived from several sources including Rosenberg (1965) and Samdahl (1991) whereas life satisfaction was measured using Warr, Cook, and Wall's (1979) 10-item scale (Appendix D, Part E). Data were collected using a mail-back questionnaire given to respondents following their Phase 1 Follow-up Interview. Similar procedures were followed in Phase 2.

Phase 1 self-esteem scores were higher (just under 3.6 on the 5-point scale, where 5.0 indicates high self-esteem) than were life satisfaction scores (3.13 on a similar 5-point scale). In general, Connectors reported somewhat higher Phase 1 self-esteem scores than did members of other groups, but these numbers must be interpreted with caution given the small number of reporting individuals in each group (Table 40). Similarly, and subject to the same limitation, Routinizers appeared to have relatively high life satisfaction relative to other groups whereas Marginalized People reported the lowest life satisfaction scores.

Counter to our expectations, Phase 2 scores for both measures improved as self-esteem scores averaged above 3.8 and life satisfaction scores averaged above 3.4 (Table 41). Separate scores for self-esteem (Table 42) and life satisfaction (Table 43) are also reported. These increases over time might be attributable to lower response rates for Phase 2, assuming that nonrespondents and nonparticipants had lower self-esteem and life satisfaction scores than did those who remained in the study. More likely, the increases are attributable to changes in employment status for most members of the study group. Indeed, there is evidence, although it is limited due to the small number of respondents per cell (Table 43), that life satisfaction scores in particular improved among employed respondents compared with those still unemployed and (to some extent) those employed part-

Table 40 Phase 1 Self-Esteem and Life Satisfaction Mean Scores by Group and Subgroup

Group/subgroup	Self-esteem	Life satisfaction
Planners (n = 15)	3.54 (0.53)	3.27 (0.60)
Routinizers (n = 6)	3.49 (0.69)	3.15 (0.62)
Anti-Homebodies (n = 3)	3.55 (0.78)	3.30 (0.82)
Efficacy-Seekers (n = 6)	3.59 (0.23)	3.38 (0.58)
Vacationers (n = 8)	3.50 (0.85)	3.11 (0.62)
Breaking In (n = 4)	3.71 (1.00)	3.13 (0.77)
In Control (n = 4)	3.29 (0.76)	3.10 (0.56)
Connectors (n = 10)	3.76 (0.48)	3.19 (0.35)
Caregivers (n = 5)	3.74 (0.25)	3.18 (0.25)
Networkers (n = 5)	3.77 (0.67)	3.20 (0.46)
Marginalized People (n = 15)	3.59 (0.68)	2.95 (0.56)
Rovers (n = 6)	3.57 (0.68)	2.45 (0.29)
Surplus People (n = 5)	3.18 (0.58)	3.14 (0.51)
Lonely People (n = 4)	4.12 (0.52)	3.48 (0.26)
Overall Scores (N = 48)	3.59 (0.62)	3.13 (0.55)

Note. Both Self-Esteem (20 items) and Life Satisfaction (10 items) were measured on a 5-point scale where 1 = negative affect and 5 = positive affect. Standard deviations in parentheses.

Table 41 Phase 2 Self-Esteem and Life Satisfaction Mean Scores by Group and Subgroup.

Group/subgroup	Self-esteem	Life satisfaction
Planners (n = 10)	3.82 (0.54)	3.34 (0.66)
Routinizers (n = 3)	3.90 (0.65)	3.07 (0.32)
Anti-Homebodies (n = 4)	4.01 (0.51)	3.86 (0.33)
Efficacy-Seekers (n = 3)	3.48 (0.51)	2.93 (0.90)
Vacationers (n = 6)	3.83 (0.67)	3.20 (0.65)
Breaking In (n = 4)	4.01 (0.78)	3.26 (0.82)
In Control (n = 2)	3.48 (0.11)	3.10 (0.14)
Connectors (n = 10)	3.83 (0.58)	3.50 (0.61)
Caregivers (n = 5)	3.53 (0.53)	3.30 (0.69)
Networkers (n = 4)	4.21 (0.41)	3.75 (0.47)
Marginalized People (n = 10)	3.76 (0.78)	3.59 (0.91)
Rovers (n = 3)	3.30 (0.48)	2.70 (0.26)
Surplus People (n = 3)	3.18 (0.60)	3.50 (0.87)
Lonely People (n = 4)	4.54 (0.26)	4.33 (0.63)
Overall Scores (N = 35)	3.81 (0.62)	3.43 (0.71)

Note. Both Self-Esteem (20 items) and Life Satisfaction (10 items) were measured on a 5-point scale where 1 = negative affect and 5 = positive affect. Standard deviations in parentheses.

Table 42 Phase 2 Self-Esteem Mean Scores by Group and Employment Status

Group	Unemployed	Part-time	Full-time	Student
Planners	3.90 (0.64) [n = 3]	3.80 (0.60) [n = 5]	3.75 (0.57) [n = 2]	—
Vacationers	—	3.74 (0.71) [n = 3]	3.92 (0.77) [n = 3]	—
Connectors	3.93 (0.46) [n = 2]	3.77 (1.23) [n = 2]	3.40 [n = 2]	4.00 (0.49) [n = 2]
Maringalized	2.50 [n = 1]	3.60 (0.64) [n = 6]	4.48 (0.28) [n = 3]	—

Notes. Measured on a 5-point scale where 1 indicates extremely low self-esteem and 5 indicates extremely high self-esteem. Scores represent an average for 20 items. Standard deviations in parentheses.

Phase 2 employment status information for Jenny is missing.

Phase 2 employment status for respondents who completed the Phase 2 interviews, but not the Phase 2 mail-back questionnaire, include Planners—Sheila, unemployed; Jacob, part-time. Vacationers—none. Connectors—Janet, unemployed; Stacy, full-time. Marginalized People—Aaron, student; Angie, full-time; Frank, unemployed; Kim, part-time; Carolyn, unemployed.

Respondents not completing Phase 2: Joe, Kelly, Nicole, Shawn, Todd, Tom (Planners); Bruce, Matt, Donald, Jim, Lynn (Vacationers); Anita (Connector); and Christina, Darlene, Tracy (Marginalized).

Table 43 Phase 2 Life Satisfaction Mean Scores by Group and Employment Status

Group	Unemployed	Part-Time	Full-Time	Student
Planners	3.07 (0.32) [n = 3]	3.39 (0.90) [n = 5]	3.65 (0.21) [n = 2]	—
Vacationers	—	3.21 (1.00) [n = 3]	3.20 (.20) [n = 3]	—
Connectors	3.20 (0.71) [n = 2]	3.35 (0.01) [n = 2]	3.05 (0.64) [n = 2]	4.35 (0.01) [n = 2]
Marginalized	2.50 [n = 1]	3.45 (0.87) [n = 6]	4.23 (0.74) [n = 3]	—

Note. Measured on a 5-point scale where 1 indicates extremely low life satisfaction and 5 indicates extremely high life satisfaction. Scores represent an average for 10 items. Standard deviations in parentheses.

time. There was, however, no discernible pattern apparent with respect to Phase 2 employment status and self-esteem scores (Table 42).

Life satisfaction scores in the present study, for both phases, were lower than those reported by Samdahl (1991). Her 88-adult sample had a mean life satisfaction score of 3.63. Samdahl's respondents reported self-esteem scores of 3.81, a number very similar to that reported by the present sample in Phase 2. Neither sample (Samdahl or the present study) was purported to represent a larger population, so comparisons should be made with caution. However, it makes intuitive sense that the sample of unemployed adults reported lower mean life satisfaction scores than did the sample comprised largely of employed adults. The between-sample similarities in self-esteem scores are perhaps more surprising, especially for Phase 2 of the present study. Although a substantial number of respondents were employed either full-time or part-time during Phase 2, other respondents remained unemployed. Self-esteem scores for both Samdahl's research and for the present study were, however, also consistent with those reported by Pernice (1996). Pernice used the Rosenberg scale for a longitudinal study involving 77 long-term (more than 18 months) unemployed adults in New Zealand and reported subgroup self-esteem scores ranging from 3.76 to 4.15.[3]

Job Importance, Career Socialization, Leisure Boredom, Self-Definition through Leisure, and Perceived Freedom in Leisure

Another component of the Phase 1 and Phase 2 mail-back questionnaires was a battery of questions derived from five standardized scales and some items previously used by one of the present researchers. The standardized scales included Warr, Cook, and Wall's (1979) three-item scale measuring job importance; Iso-Ahola and Weissinger's (1990) five-item Leisure Boredom Scale (LBS); a three-item self-definition through leisure and a three-item perceived freedom in leisure scale developed by Neulinger and Breit (1969); and the 25-item Perceived Freedom in Leisure scale taken from the longer Leisure Diagnostic Battery (adult version) developed by Witt and Ellis (1985). To avoid confusion between the Neulinger and Breit (1969) and Witt and Ellis (1985) perceived freedom scales, the latter scale will be referred to as the Leisure Diagnostic Battery (LDB). The other items on this questionnaire included three statements related to career socialization and three statements related to family and leisure (Samdahl, 1991).

With the exception of the LDB, which appears in Appendix D, Section C, the scales described in this paragraph are included in Appendix D, Section B. (Refer to the footnote in that Appendix for placement of specific scale items.) Items were reverse coded, as appropriate, prior to analysis. Most items are reported here using a 5-point Likert response where 1 = strongly disagree (negative affect) and 5 = strongly agree (positive affect). The exception to the rule is the Iso-Ahola and Weissinger (1990) LBS, wherein low scores indicate positive affect and high scores indicate negative affect (high levels of leisure boredom). The data from the mail-back questionnaire should be interpreted with caution given the small sample and even smaller subsamples from which they were drawn; nevertheless, they provide interesting corroborative information when considered in the context of previously presented information.

Similar to the self-esteem and life satisfaction measures just discussed, these scales were analyzed at the group and subgroup levels. Table 44 includes the group-level data. It is not surprising that Marginalized People appeared to experience more leisure boredom than members of other groups. It is also noteworthy that, in contrast to scores reported by other groups, their leisure boredom apparently increased during Phase 2. Relative to the other groups, the general lack of leisure boredom reported by Planners is also congruent with expectations, but the relatively high levels of boredom reported by Vacationers ran counter to expectations. Overall, members of our sample experienced marginally more leisure boredom than did two of the three samples reported in Iso-Ahola and Weissinger's (1990) original study but considerably less boredom than did the third.[4] Descriptive scores for the Leisure Diagnostic Battery (Perceived Freedom in Leisure subscale) varied little between groups. Scores on this measure were unexpectedly high during both Phase 1 (3.72) and Phase 2 (3.85). Indeed, they appear to be at least as high as those reported by Witt and Ellis (1985) in their original work with the Adult version of the LDB.[5] By contrast, Planners and Vacationers seemed more likely to acknowledge links between self-definition and leisure than were Connectors and Marginalized People. These data are intuitive given Planners' efforts to maintain active leisure repertoires and Vacationers' general comfort levels with leisure activity. These differences were less apparent in Phase 2; at that time, Planners and Connectors seemed more likely to report high levels of perceived freedom in leisure than did Marginalized People, which was congruent with other data, but the mid- to low-level scores of Vacationers on this indicator were unexpected.

Table 44 Scores Reported by Group for Leisure Boredom, Job Involvement, Leisure Diagnostic Battery, Self-Definition in Leisure, Perceived Freedom in Leisure, Career Socialization, and Family Leisure

	N	LBS	JI	LDB	SDL	PFL	CS	FL
Full sample	50 (36)	2.19 (2.12)	3.86 (4.06)	3.72 (3.85)	2.99 (3.06)	3.52 (3.46)	2.59 (2.77)	3.18 (3.34)
Planners	15 (10)	2.01 (1.78)	3.31 (4.07)	3.66 (3.73)	3.36 (3.33*)	3.73 (3.53)	2.44 (2.47)	2.98 (3.53)
Vacationers	8 (6)	2.25 (2.10)	3.67 (3.78)	3.65 (3.83)	3.17 (3.11*)	3.50 (3.50)	2.50 (2.67)	3.13 (3.19)
Connectors	10 (8)	2.14 (1.92)	4.03 (4.00)	3.76 (3.76)	2.10 (2.54*)	3.70 (3.73)	2.77 (3.08)	3.40 (3.17*)
Marginalized	15 (10)	2.39 (2.74*)	4.38 (4.17)	3.76 (3.98)	2.76* (3.07)	3.18 (3.20)	2.76 (2.90)	3.21 (3.77)

Notes. Phase 1 numbers are followed by Phase 2 numbers (in parentheses)

• Most scales are coded such that 1 = negative affect and 5 = positive affect. The exception is the LBS wherein 1 = low leisure boredom and 5 = high leisure boredom

• Asterisk indicates standard deviations greater than 1.0

• Shaded boxes indicate that descriptive Phase 2 scores were equal to or greater than Phase 1 scores

LBS = Leisure Boredom Scale (Iso Ahola & Weissinger, 1990)
JI = Job Involvement scale (Warr, Cook, & Wall, 1979)
LDB = Leisure Diagnostic Battery (Perceived Freedom in Leisure) scale (Witt & Ellis, 1985)
SDL = Self-Definition through Leisure scale (Neulinger & Breit, 1969)
PFL = Perceived Freedom in Leisure scale (Neulinger & Breit, 1969)
CS = Socialization items (Samdahl, 1991)
FL = Family Leisure items (Samdahl, 1991)

The relatively high job importance and career socialization scores reported by Connectors and Marginalized People in comparison to those reported by Planners and Vacationers was counterintuitive. The more severe income restrictions faced by Connectors and Marginalized People may help explain the inconsistency between the interview and mail-back data. Nevertheless, it is surprising that scores from the Routinizer, Anti-Homebody, and In Control subgroups did not support our expectations on these measures. These are all subgroups for whom work was perceived as both important and closely linked to self-concept. That Connectors scored the highest level of satisfaction with respect to family leisure was consistent with expectations. However, their scores on this indicator dropped markedly in Phase 2 whereas scores for the other three groups all rose. In deference to the minimal sample size at the subgroup level, we chose not to report most subgroup mean scores. We did, however, include those for Rovers and Networkers (Table 45) in order to illustrate the divergent patterns of those subgroups. In every case where Networker scores increased from Phase 1 to Phase 2, those for Rovers decreased, and vice versa. These patterns if nothing else serve to illustrate, over time, the potentially diverse experiences of people who are unemployed. Recall, as well, that the Networkers were in many ways the most socially oriented of the ten subgroups, whereas the Rovers were arguably the least socially oriented subgroup in the study.

Perceived Constraint on Favourite Leisure and Recreation Activities

Respondents were, following completion of the ESM component of data collection, afforded an opportunity to record their favourite leisure activities and to note any perceived constraints which limited or prevented ongoing participation in those activities. This information is summarized in Table 46. Taken as a whole, it is fair to say that respondents often felt constrained from leisure participation. Indeed, constraints were noted for over 70% of the highlighted activities. There was considerable group and subgroup variability in the data, however. Anti-Homebodies stood out in several somewhat contradictory ways. First, consistent with previously analyzed data relating to their gender, life stage, and perceived lack of entitlement, they listed very few favourite leisure activities. Second, but inconsistent with their interview data, they listed no constraints on leisure participation. Networkers were the only other subgroup to report perceived constraints for fewer than half of their preferred activities; however,

Table 45 Comparison of the Networker and Rover Subgroups with Respect to Leisure Boredom, Job Involvement, Leisure Diagnostic Battery, Self-Definition in Leisure, Perceived Freedom in Leisure, Career Socialization, and Family Leisure

	N	LBS	JI	LDB	SDL	PFL	CS	FL
Networkers	5 (3)	3.68 (4.15)	4.13 (4.22)	3.78 (3.32)	2.13 (2.11)	3.40 (4.11)	2.80 (2.67)	3.53 (3.33)
Rovers	6 (3)	3.57 (3.47)	3.94 (3.44)	3.66 (4.12)	3.28 (3.00*)	3.00 (2.78)	2.28 (2.44)	3.07 (3.89)

Notes. Phase 1 numbers are followed by Phase 2 numbers (in parentheses)

• All scales are coded such that 1 = negative affect and 5 = positive affect

• Asterisk indicates standard deviations greater than 1.0

• Shaded boxes indicate that descriptive Phase 2 scores were equal to or greater than Phase 1 scores

LBS = Leisure Boredom Scale (Iso Ahola & Weissinger, 1990)

JI = Job Involvement scale (Warr, Cook, & Wall, 1979)

LDB = Leisure Diagnostic Battery (Perceived Freedom in Leisure) scale (Witt & Ellis, 1985)

SDL = Self-Definition through Leisure scale (Neulinger & Breit, 1969)

PFL = Perceived Freedom in Leisure scale (Neulinger & Breit, 1969)

CS = Socialization items (Samdahl, 1991)

FL = Family Leisure items (Samdahl, 1991)

Table 46 Phase 1 Perceived Constraints on Favourite Recreation Activities by Subgroup

	Planners			Vacationers	
Constraint	Routinizers	Anti-Homes	Efficacy-Seekers	Breaking In	In Control
Time/other obligation	Time w/ Partner Reading Nightlife Chess Weight training Reading Watch TV		Walking (3) Reading (2) Movies Play w/kids Visit friends Hobbies Running Crafts Skill updates Gardening Camping Cycling	Reading Cycling	Computer program-ming Reading Soccer Watch TV
Money	Nightlife Hockey		Dining out Crafts Gardening Camping Hobbies	Shopping Nightlife	Movies Golf
Willpower/moods	Writing Weight training Watch TV		Reading (2) Gardening Movies	Writing	Cycling
Logistics	Fishing (too far) Hockey (ice time) Soccer (no babysitter)		Camping Tea Intelligent conversation	Nightlife (no designated driver)	Parties
Weather			Walking Camping Cycling	Tennis Cycling	Tennis Cycling
Substance abuse					
Injury/fear					
Number constrained/Total activities	13/18	0/3	20/20	6/12	9/12
Modal constraint	Time	—	Time	Time/Money/Weather	Time

▼

Table 46 (continued)

Constraint	Connectors		Marginalized People		
	Caregivers	Networkers	Rovers	Surplus	Lonely
Time/ other obligation	Watch TV Play w/kids Chess w/son Swimming Movies	Sewing		Swimming Camping	Baking
Money	Dancing Swimming Family outings Visiting the beach		Reading Visiting family Time w/ friends Bingo Nightlife (2) Movies	Movies Fishing Bingo	Movies (2) Coffee w/ friends
Willpower/ moods			Reading Time w/ friends	Exercise Movies	Swimming Visiting park
Logistics		Time w/ husband (when he golfs)	Time w/ family Nightlife	Swimming (pool schedule)	Hanging out Going out w/ friends
Weather	Family outings Horseback riding Walk dogs		Walking Swimming	Walking	Cycling Walking
Substance abuse			Fishing Hunting Hockey		
Injury/ fear		Dancing		Walking	
Number con-strained/total activities	11/14	3/9	14/18	7/15	10/12
Modal Constraint	Time	Time/Injury /No companion	Money	Money	Money

much of the Networkers' leisure activity included unstructured social interaction. Breaking Ins, as expected, also reported a relatively low level of constraint; only half of all favourite leisure activities were constrained. The other seven subgroups each reported that a majority of their favourite leisure activities were constrained. Most extreme were the Efficacy-Seekers, who reported some level of constraint on each of 20 mentioned leisure activities, a level of frustration very consistent with sentiments expressed in their interview data.

The types of constraints mentioned also varied by group and subgroup. Seven broad categories of constraints are listed in Table 46. These categories capture the essence of each constraint, though not necessarily as eloquently as originally expressed by respondents. For example, Jack commented with respect to his electronics and photography hobbies, "Money and/or time (never seem to have both at same moment) are limiting factors; would like to participate more often—money main issue presently," and this was coded as both a time-related and financial constraint. Most of these seven types of constraints would be classified as intrapersonal and structural, based on Crawford, Jackson, and Godbey's (1991) widely cited leisure constraints model.

The most commonly reported constraint was related to a lack of time and obligatory activities, a type of constraint that may be intrapersonal, interpersonal, or structural depending on individual circumstance. Conventional wisdom would suggest that constraints related to time and obligation would not normally be major issues for unemployed adults, but our interview and ESM data suggest otherwise. These constraints were, consistent with their interview data, most widely reported by Efficacy-Seekers and Routinizers. Also consistent with interview data, time and obligation-related constraints were common among Caregivers and In Controls. As expected, financial constraints were also important for many respondents. Indeed, this constraint was the dominant issue for members of all three Marginalized subgroups, a finding consistent with their interview data. However, monetary constraints were not dominant for any of the other subgroups.

The constraint data, though relatively cryptic, provide useful information for agencies hoping to serve people who are unemployed. It should be noted, however, that many of the activities listed (for example, shopping, parties, and nightlife) are outside of the normal range of social service agency mandates. That is not to say that social events commonly organized by many agencies do not have many elements of those activities. Also, not all of the constraints are related to unemployment per se. For example, poor weather, pool schedules, and distance to recreation venues may be problematic for many potential participants regardless of employment status. The latter issue, distance to recreation venues (camping, fishing, swimming at the beach, and the like), suggests that regional and provincial agencies, not just municipal agencies, may have active roles to play in ameliorating many leisure constraints reported by unemployed adults.

Notes

1 Kubey and Csikszentmihalyi's primary sample comprised 107 working adults.
2 Samdahl's (1992) 18 respondents were evenly split between males and females, and ranged in age from eighteen to over fifty-five (with a median age thirty). Fourteen participants were employed full-time (including managerial, professional, and service occupations), three were employed part-time, and one was not employed during the study. Out of total 695 ESM episodes reported, 309 (44%) were considered leisure (+1, 2, 3 on the "I would call that leisure" item), 308 (44%) were not considered leisure (–1, 2, 3 on that item), and 78 (11%) were neutral. By comparison, Samdahl and Jekubovich (1993) reported that, "A total of eighty-eight volunteers participated in the study, including fifty-seven (65%) women and thirty-one (35%) men. One participant was of south Asian descent; the rest were Caucasian. The median age was forty-four years, with fifty-one (59%) between the ages of thirty and forty-five years. Fifty (57%) were married and fourteen others (17%) were living with a partner. The sample included twenty couples in which both partners participated in the study. Thirty-five participants (40%) had children living in their households.... The sample included professionals and proprietors; clerical workers and administrative assistants; loggers, mill workers, and labourers; a deputy sheriff; and several artists and authors. Fifteen (17%) were not currently employed, twenty-three (26%) held part time jobs, and forty-nine (56%) were employed full time." Of the total 3,177 ESM questionnaires collected for that study, 1,455 (46%) were leisure to some degree (+1, +2, or +3) and 1,289 were non-leisure (–1, –2, –3). Fourteen percent of the reported episodes were classified "neutral," as neither leisure nor non-leisure.
3 Pernice (1996) actually reported cumulative self-esteem scores ranging from 37.6 to 41.5 which we converted to single digits by dividing by ten, the number of items in the scale.
4 All three of Iso-Ahola and Weissinger's samples comprised undergraduate university students. For purposes of this comparison, we coded our data so that it would be consistent with that of Iso-Ahola and Weissinger (1990) wherein 1 = little leisure boredom and 5 = considerable leisure boredom. Iso-Ahola and Weissinger reported mean leisure boredom scores of 2.89, 2.10, and 2.10 respectively, whereas our respondents recorded overall leisure boredom scores of 2.19 in Phase 1 and 2.12 in Phase 2.
5 Data were collected by Baack and Witt (1985) from a sample of older adult members of the Baptist church (mean age = 70.9, no sample size reported). The overall LDB score for their sample was 3.58. Scores were higher among respondents participating in church and community recreation activities (3.94) than among those who did not participate (3.35).

5 Integrating the Present Study with the Literature

To this point we have analyzed several types of data, some of which are regularly encountered and others which are somewhat less frequently used in unemployment research. In combination, the varied data types explored here provide a unique glimpse into the daily behaviour and psychosocial well-being of a sample of unemployed adults. Given our initial concentration on the qualitative data, and congruent with generally accepted practice (Patton, 1990), we have for the most part refrained from any premature attempts to integrate our findings with the extant body of unemployment literature. However, before providing directions for future research and public policy, such integration is required in order to explore fully the varied issues and their ramifications.

Conventional wisdom asserts that unemployment is a negative state in the lives of adults. Indeed, a considerable list of negative consequences of unemployment emerges in the literature. As Hanisch (1999) noted in her review of unemployment research published between 1994 and 1998, "virtually every study … described some negative outcomes of unemployment from the perspective of the individual" (p. 195). Negative outcomes of unemployment that have been reported include increases in depression, anxiety, loneliness, social isolation, anger, and fear, and decreases in self-esteem, self-confidence, positive affect, concentration, perceptions of competence, and social identity (Hanisch, 1999; Warr, 1987). However, "simplistic identifications of work as 'good' and unemployment as 'bad' are manifestly inadequate as explanations of observed variations in the effects of unemployment on mental health" (Ezzy, 1993, p. 41), a point that has been made by many (Liem & Liem, 1990; Martella & Maass, 2000; Roberts et al., 1989; Rodriguez, 1997).

In order to explain the varied responses to the unemployed state, a variety of theoretical frameworks have been suggested. Perhaps the most well-researched among the many attempts to account for the often-deleterious effects of unemployment has been the functional model developed by Jahoda and associates (Jahoda, 1982; Jahoda, Lazarsfeld, & Zeisel, 1933/1971). This framework postulates that employment serves not only the manifest function of providing an income but also the latent functions of providing valued categories of experience and satisfying basic human needs. As Jahoda (1982) noted, "an unintended though inevitable consequence" (p. 39) of being employed are five categories of experience: time structure, participation in collective purposes, activity, the derivation of identity/status, and social contact. For the unemployed, these experiences are no longer inevitable: "While the unemployed are left to their own devices to find experiences within these categories if they can and suffer if they cannot, the employed take them for granted" (Jahoda, p. 39). Thus, by being deprived of the institutional support of employment, unemployed individuals are deprived of these "unintended though inevitable" categories of experiences and may suffer psychological deprivation as a result. The emphasis in this line of thinking is the institutional role of employment in providing these categories of experience.

It has been suggested, though, that in emphasizing the role of the institution of work, Jahoda's functionalist "deprivation" theory is unable to account for positive effects of unemployment, as the loss of the latent consequences of employment is necessarily seen as problematic (Ezzy, 1993; Fryer & Payne, 1984). That some people's mental health seems to improve following a layoff certainly suggests the need to address the possibility that other institutions may provide these categories of experience, or that the work environment itself only provided minimal access to these categories of experience and that unemployment is viewed as a relief. However, as Feather (1990) has pointed out, and as is implied in the above quotation, Jahoda's theory implicitly suggests that one should expect to find a variety of different responses to unemployment, and that some individuals may not suffer the predominantly negative effects of unemployment. This is clearly indicated in the classic Marienthal study (Jahoda et al., 1933/1971), in which fully a quarter of the families studied were described as "unbroken" and coping well with the joblessness of the husband. Indeed, other studies have shown that some individuals react positively to unemployment. This variability of experience is reflected in the body of literature produced by researchers who have aggregated unemployed people into meaningful clusters based on a number of different criteria (e.g., Hendry, Raymond, & Stewart, 1984; Jahoda et al., 1933/1971; Kilpatrick & Trew, 1985; Lobo, 1996, 1999, 2002; Wanberg & Marchese, 1994).

Fryer and Payne's (1984) agency approach, offered as a contrast to Jahoda's, views an individual as an "active social agent striving to make sense of his or her situation and acting according to reasons and intentions to pursue chosen goals" (p. 287). As such, the authors added, "given material and social freedom, individuals will create their own social institutions or seek existing ones which satisfy their social and psychological growth needs" (p. 291). This agency model provides a needed counterpoint to Jahoda's deprivation theory by suggesting that the experience of unemployment is not simply determined by the loss of the latent functions of employment but is predicated upon personal agency in the face of such deprivation. However, whereas Jahoda has been criticized for over-emphasizing the structural without due regard for the individual, the agency model has been similarly criticized for under-emphasizing structural constraints that limit possibilities for individual action.

Nevertheless, as Lobo (1999) has suggested, "Jahoda and Fryer both stress the importance of well-being of the psychological categories of experience. Jahoda stresses the importance of social institutions in facilitating access to these categories of experience, whilst Fryer points to the inhibitory influence which poverty, social arrangements and cultural practices can have on personal agency, thereby restricting access to positive categories of experience" (p. 147). The need to examine not only the role of institutional supports but also the purposive action people take in the absence of those supports is a compromise deemed acceptable to both sides of the debate (Fryer & Payne, 1984; Jahoda, 1984). That being the case, it seems fruitful to frame the following discussion in terms of these categories of experience, with the recognition that job loss may provoke other forms of loss but that, through individual agency, unemployed people may find avenues beyond paid employment to satisfy these basic needs. Thus, with reference to existing research, we will explore the nature of our participants' perceptions of and reactions to the loss of these categories of experience, and the individual efforts undertaken to compensate for their lack.

Past research has also explored other variables that moderate the relationship between unemployment and decreased well-being, largely through their impact upon the likelihood of accessing the valued categories of experience. These will be discussed with reference to our data as well. Lastly, in light of the literature and based upon our results, the potential of leisure activity and leisure environments to contribute to well-being during unemployment will be explored. This will lay the groundwork for the following chapter, which deals with implications for providers of leisure services.

Loss of Latent Functions or Categories of Experience

As has been stated above, job loss necessarily entails the loss of a major institutional provider of the five categories of experience proposed by Jahoda and her associates (Jahoda, 1982, 1984; Jahoda et al., 1933/1971). There is no doubt, based upon our data, that the loss of the latent functions of work has often been perceived as problematic and has led to psychological distress. However, within our sample there are clear differences in the extent to which a particular lack is personally important or significantly affects the likelihood that the experience of unemployment will be negative. This is best illustrated in the clusters derived through our analysis of the qualitative data: particular deficits were seen as dominant issues for some people but only of marginal significance for others, and these differences served in part as defining features of our categorizations. The following discussion will highlight these differences and illustrate how our participants have differentially perceived the loss of each category of experience. Further, in light of these differences, we shall also note instances where proactive behaviour has gained access to these categories of experiences outside of paid work and has thereby mitigated the psychological deprivation of unemployment.

Time Structure

A number of different researchers have found that unemployment is associated with decreased time structure, and that decreased time structure is related to subsequent decreased mental health (Bond & Feather, 1988; Feather & Bond, 1983; Jahoda et al., 1933/1971; Kilpatrick & Trew, 1985; Martella & Maass, 2000; Wanberg, Griffiths, & Gavin, 1997). Individuals from several of our groups voiced complaints about the loss of routine and structure, lending support to the contention that for contemporary adults such structure may be a near-universal need. Within our sample, the deleterious effects of this lack was most clearly illustrated in the Routinizers, whose dominant complaint during unemployment was the lack of structure and routine, and whose primary approach to daily life when unemployed was to attempt to replicate a work-like routine by rigorously scheduling activities. In contrast to the Routinizers, those placed within the Breaking In group seldom noted that they were troubled by a lack of routine. Their daily life was characterized by, and appreciated for, the lack of an imposed routine, as this afforded them the freedom to pursue their own desires without temporal constraint. However, it must be noted that the Routinizers and the Breaking Ins represented opposite poles with regard to the perceived importance and deprivation of time structure. The majority of our participants fell somewhere in the middle: they were cognizant of the surfeit of unstructured time on their hands and to lesser or greater degrees troubled by it, but they did not perceive being deprived of an imposed time structure as one of the dominant pitfalls of unemployment, nor did they see establishing such a structure as a necessary coping strategy.

Although the perceived importance of structure seemed related to coping efforts in this regard, it must also be noted that the ability to structure one's time in the absence of external factors is variable across individuals (Wanberg et al., 1997). Such has certainly been demonstrated within our data. The Routinizers may be contrasted with the Efficacy-Seekers in this regard. While both of these subgroups were broadly classified as Planners, and as such voiced a pre-eminent complaint about the loss of time structure, the Routinizers achieved considerably more success in compensating for this loss when left to their own devices than did the Efficacy-Seekers. That gaining access to this category of experience moderated the negative psychological consequences of unemployment is not only evident in a comparison of the qualitative assertions of the participants in each of these groups but is also borne out in the ESM data. Efficacy-Seekers scored lower on all mood-state measures than did Routinizers (Table 35), and this pattern was seen almost without exception irrespective of the time of day (Table 36), the participant's engagement in leisure (Table 37), or the social context (Table 38).

As Haworth, Chesworth, & Smith (1990) have noted, depressed mood states are associated with decreased cognitive function among the unemployed, and "impairment of both cognitive abilities and mood state would make it doubly difficult for [the unemployed] to plan and organize their lives, to behave proactively, in the very situation which calls for this" (p. 255). Thus, a vicious cycle may be set into motion depending upon one's ability to impose order and routine on oneself. Should one perceive this deficit as problematic and yet be unable to compensate, depressed moods may result. This may reduce cognitive performance, which makes it less likely that effective action can be taken, which thus reinforces the perceived negativity of unemployment. Although our data do not speak to differences in cognitive function, this underlying dynamic may help explain the repeated failure of the Efficacy-Seekers to proactively structure their daily lives, notwithstanding their desire and attempts to do so.

The issue of time structure not only relates to the actual sequence of daily events but also has implications with regard to maintaining a sense of purpose in the absence of work. Martella & Maass (2000) speculated that maintaining or imposing a structure on one's time during unemployment might be beneficial in providing a sense of purpose as well as routine, and our data largely support this idea. Maintaining a work-like time structure was often noted as an accomplishment in itself, as was avoiding behaviours that detracted from the maintenance of a work-like routine. This argument suggests that maintaining time structure during unemployment may be of dual benefit: on the one hand, it may compensate for the loss of time structure associated with loss of work; and on the other hand, it may also compensate somewhat for the goal structure inherent in work and missing during unemployment. Both time structure and goal structure moderate the relationship between unemployment and reduced psychological well-being.

(Pro)Activity and Goal Structure

Clearly, time structure and a sense of purpose are closely allied with actual behaviour during unemployment; both of these stem from what actions are performed and activities undertaken in the absence of employment. As Underlid (1996) pointed out, "virtually all studies in recent times conclude that the unemployed are generally passive" (p. 269) compared to when they were working or compared to employed individuals, a sentiment that has been oft repeated (Haworth, 1997; Warr, 1987). Warr observed that "fewer demands are made, objectives are reduced, and purposeful activity is less encouraged by the environment.... With fewer goals ... a person's experience may come to lack positive tone as well as being homogenous in its limited challenge" (p. 213). That unemployment is less encouraging of purposeful activity than work is clear, but what is also clear is that the "environment" of unemployment is not the only thing to be considered. As Fryer and Payne (1984) so amply demonstrated in their study of the proactive unemployed, not all individuals resign themselves to passivity during unemployment, and those who don't are able to maintain better psychological health. Indeed, although passivity was evident among the participants in our sample, it was certainly not a universal response to unemployment, and many reacted proactively to their situation by "actively changing or creatively reperceiving the situation to allow fulfilment of valued goals" (Fryer & Payne, p. 274).

O'Brien, Feather, and Kabanoff (1994) and Haworth and Evans (1987) suggested that activities may promote adjustment to unemployment because they afford progression toward the attainment of personal goals. Of significance here are not the activities undertaken per se, but that the activities are "proactive" by definition and promote the fulfilment of personally meaningful goals. The range of such goals that may be striven for during unemployment is limitless, but there is evidence in our data to suggest that those who were able to pursue activities that were perceived as more than mere time-fillers were at an advantage.

More will be said about the particular activities and activity contexts later, but at this point it is necessary to comment upon what was perhaps the dominant goal of the majority of our sample: finding work. Job-search activities contributed to the time structure and sense of accomplishment discussed above, but most importantly they constituted a set of activities inextricably related to a particular goal. Within our groupings of participants, the degree to which job-search activities constituted a major class of activities was clearly variable. For instance, the Planners group may be contrasted with the Vacationers; the former proactively organized their daily life with the expressed intent of securing employment, whereas the latter were more likely to take a more laissez-faire approach to their vocational future. The extent to which this difference was dispositional or generational is unclear; however, that the difference existed is indisputable, and it suggests that future research should assess the origin of such varied behavioural approaches to securing re-employment.

Some authors have suggested that such "problem-focussed" coping behaviours—explicitly intended to eliminate the stressor of being unemployed—may be variable across gender lines. Leana and Feldman (1991) found that men are more likely than women to employ such strategies, and our results support this possibility. We may contrast the experience of the Routinizers, who were perhaps the most aggressive job hunters, with that of the Networkers, who chose instead to focus their behaviour toward social interaction. That differences in their behaviour existed is without doubt, but the degree to which either set of behaviours is related to well-being during unemployment is unclear from our results. Leana and Feldman note that women are more likely than men to employ "symptom-focussed" coping, relying to a greater extent upon the social support of family and friends to help them deal with unemployment. Such affect-based coping, though, has been found to be positively associated with decreased mental health during unemployment (Waters & Moore, 2001). However, our data show that the Networkers (all women) had marginally higher mood-state scores than did the Routinizers (all men). While it is not known whether observed differences are due to the behaviours themselves or their contribution to meeting valued goals, it is possible that differences in the goal structure between the two groups accounts for this difference. The Networkers generally succeeded in accessing the social interaction they desired, while the Routinizers' job-search activities did not necessarily secure employment. Support for this assessment is evident when comparing the similar moods of Anti-Homebodies (another all-women subgroup who also had planning-oriented goal structures) with those of Routinizers.

All else being equal, though, it may be surmised that those who most aggressively acted to secure employment would be better off than those who did not, as such activity has the potential to compensate for a number of the lost functions of employment. However, "while behaviors such as self-initiated job search are certainly instrumental in obtaining a new job and structuring the day's routine, they are also activities filled with frustration and rejection" (Leana & Feldman, 1990, p. 1178). Such behaviours may be a mixed blessing; on the one hand, they afford routine and goal structure, but on the other hand, they are potentially damaging to self-conception. As Leana and Feldman have noted, then, "although problem-focused coping behaviours may ultimately be the most beneficial activities for terminated employees to engage in, for quite understandable reasons, they may also be under-utilised" (Leana & Feldman, p. 1178). Although our data do not allow a full exploration, it is possible that repeated rejection might explain the decreased prominence of job-search activities as the length of unemployment increased. For those with a fragile self-concept and limited self-confidence during unemployment, repeated fruitless attempts to find employment may cause the extinction of such behaviours and withdrawal from active job searching.

Identity and Self-Conception

Another significant category of experience lost during unemployment is one's occupational identity and status: "On becoming unemployed a person loses a socially approved role and the positive self-evaluations that go along with it" (Warr, 1987, p. 224). Sheeran and associates (Sheeran & Abraham, 1994; Sheeran & McCarthy, 1992) have found that the self-perceptions of the unemployed were indeed less positive than those of the employed, and that the unemployed believe that employed people judge them negatively. Both private and public self-esteem were negatively related to depression. The issue, though, is double-barrelled: not only are an occupational identity and status lost, but also the undesirable identity and status of "unemployed" is gained.

Our categorization scheme certainly supports the idea that the loss of a valued identity may be a problem, but it also suggests that the significance of this issue depends on other variables. As Ezzy (1993) noted, "any attempt to explain the social psychological consequences of job loss must explain the relationship of participation in the work role to the individual's more general project of the development and maintenance of the self-concept" (p. 50). With respect to this, age may be a potent contributor to the effect that job loss has upon one's self-concept. It is more likely that the occupational self-concept of those who have had lengthy employment histories is more salient to their overall self-conception than is the occupational self-concept of those who have had shorter employment histories. The difference in the degree of identity loss expressed by predominantly older groups, such as the Anti-Homebodies, and younger groups, such as either of the Vacationers subgroups, may be related to their employment histories as well as to the centrality of, or their commitment to, the employment role (Shams & Jackson, 1994).

A further contrast in this regard may be made between the Anti-Homebodies and the Caregivers. Sheeran & Abraham (1994) have provided evidence to suggest that women who find themselves in domestic roles following job loss may resent these roles after experiencing the benefits derived from working. Such has certainly been the case among the Anti-Homebodies, whose daily functioning was largely predicated upon their dissatisfaction with the homemaker role and their desire to re-enter the workforce. However, the predominantly female Caregivers group did not voice similar sentiments. Thus, one must be mindful of the prominence of occupational identity in an individual's self-schema to understand the potential variability of responses to its loss.

In a similar vein, and with respect to the issue of stigma introduced above, Kulik (2000) examined the perception of a stigma associated with unemployment among the unemployed and noted gender differences, with men perceiving the state of unemployment as more stigmatic. This difference is clearly seen in the contrast between the Routinizers and the Anti-Homebodies. Although both of these groups were broadly characterized as Planners, individuals in the former, all-male group were likely to report perceiving the stigma associated with unemployment, whereas individuals in the latter, all-female group were not. Although the perception of stigma is related directly to decreased well-being during unemployment by virtue of the negative effects it has upon self-conception, it may also have significant indirect effects, as well. In particular, the perception of stigma may come to bear negatively upon social interaction, the last of the categories of experience to be considered here.

Social Interaction

Generally speaking, social support has been found to moderate the relationships between unemployment and negative psychological consequences; however, unemployment may disrupt social networks and lead to decreased social interaction or the perception thereof (Broomhall & Winefield, 1990; Dorin, 1994; Jones, 1991; Kilpatrick & Trew, 1985; Kong, Perrucci, & Perrucci, 1993; Lobo, 1999; Rantakeisu, Starrin, & Hagquist, 1999; Reynolds & Gilbert, 1991; Schwarzer, Hahn, & Fuchs, 1994; Shams, 1993; Ullah, Banks, & Warr, 1985; Underlid, 1996). In an objective sense, simply being laid off disrupts one's social network as one's workmates are no longer a guaranteed feature of one's daily patterns of social interaction. Beyond that, though, unemployment may disrupt one's extraoccupational social network for a variety of reasons. It has been found that among the unemployed the perception of stigma or feelings of shame impact negatively upon social activities (Rantakeisu et al., 1999). As Jones (1991) noted, embarrassment about loss of status may prompt social withdrawal on the part of either the unemployed or those within his or her social network. Among those in our study who perceived unemployment as stigmatic, both sides of the social withdrawal equation were reported as reasons for decreased social interaction.

As with the other categories of experience, though, there is great variability in the degree to which the unemployed in our sample felt deprived of social interaction and suffered negative affective consequences as a result. It is clear, for example, that the individuals in the Lonely subgroup missed the social interaction previously provided by work, took measures to attempt to make up for its lack, and suffered greatly for its loss when they were unable to find social outlets. However, other groups were not greatly troubled by the loss of social contact; for instance the Rovers, as we have seen, seemed to prefer to keep their social distance. Alternately, some participants managed to access ample social outlets even while unemployed, for instance, the Networkers.

Although it does seem that social support may play a role in moderating the negative psychological consequences of unemployment, it is important to consider dispositional differences, as illustrated in the contrast between the Rovers and the Networkers. Reynolds & Gilbert (1991) suggested that "unemployment has a negative effect on psychological well-being if the environment of the unemployed person does not provide opportunities that match the needs of the autonomous or socially dependent individual.... For autonomous individuals, unemployment may threaten their ability to pursue achievement and independence. Sociotropic individuals also perceive unemployment as threatening, but in this case, because it disrupts their positive and reinforcing relationships with other people" (p. 82). Autonomous is an accurate characterization of our Rovers group, and sociotropic of the Networkers; thus our results accord nicely with the observation of these authors and highlight the importance of considering not only the categories of experience but also individual orientations toward them.

Jahoda's (1982) deprivation model asserts that no other informal or formal institution is as well suited to providing access to all the categories of experience as work. However, other institutions may compensate for the lack of particular categories of experience, and such was the case for some of our participants with respect to social interaction. Shams and Jackson (1993) noted that religious affiliation may moderate the negative effects of unemployment, and we found that organized religion was instrumental in allowing participants to access social support and to interact in social situations outside the home. In particular, the Lonely People and Networkers seemed especially prone to rely on religious institutions for needed social support, and they expressed great satisfaction that this avenue was available to them. Although this may in part have been due to the dearth of other avenues available to them, it does provide support for the contention that other social institutions beside work may afford access to valued categories of experience.

It is important to reiterate, though, that unemployment can engender a sense of social isolation. Our data certainly support the contention that a dearth of social contact may elicit more negative moods; as reported, mood states when "alone" were the lowest of all the social contexts explored. Notwithstanding one's social independence or efforts, the lack of opportunities for social contact outside the home may produce feelings of isolation; this can also have negative ramifications for one's family, often the dominant source of social support. Hill (1978) noted that job loss "reduces effective social contacts outside the home and focuses tension within the family. In turn, this reduces the support the family can give" (p. 120). It is important then to consider how these effects may be transmitted and to what effect, as familial support may act as a buffer against the psychological trauma of job loss (Leana & Feldman, 1991).

Much research has evaluated the negative effects of unemployment on family function and the results tend to indicate that joblessness is associated with increases in family stress, spousal depression, and family cohesion (e.g., Broman, 1997; Dail, 1988; Lobo & Watkins,

1995; Patton & Donohue, 2001; Targ & Perrucci, 1990; Vinokur, Price, & Caplan, 1996). Further, unemployment is related to spousal depression and more negative mood states (Liem & Liem, 1990). Liem and Liem also noted increased levels of conflict and arguing between spouses, and perceived decreased quality of communication, levels of support, marital satisfaction, and cohesion. Although our research did not explicitly address issues of family function and cohesion, that unemployment could negatively impact family life was an observation that emerged during the interviews, as did the possibility that familial support might mitigate the detrimental effects of job loss.

Our data, too, speak to an issue that has not received much attention in research on unemployment and the family: that of unemployed children at home. Of those who commented upon the familial stress that unemployment produced, perhaps the most ardent expressions came from the young adults who were still living with their parents. Concentrated for the most part in the Surplus People and Breaking In groups, these young adults often indicated increased family stress and arguments, and decreased family cohesion. It is clear that a family system may be disrupted by what happens to any of its members. Given the increasing age at which adolescents and young adults leave their family of origin, future unemployment research should attend to decrements in family function that may result from having unemployed children in the household.

As is clear in the preceding, the loss of the categories of experience previously derived from work may be problematic for some individuals during unemployment. The literature suggests, and our results largely support, the notion that accessing these categories of experience may mitigate the detrimental effects of job loss. However, it is also clear that individual differences affect the way in which the loss of these experiences will be perceived and the measures that might be taken during unemployment to make up for their lack. As we have seen, such differences may be related to demographic, social, and/or personality variables (Ezzy, 1993; Martella & Maass, 2000; Reynolds & Gilbert, 1991). Thus, overarching statements related to perceptions of the loss of these experiences, to the likelihood that compensation for their loss will be sought or achieved, or to the possibility that improved well-being will result from securing access are not tenable. Nevertheless, one may make the qualified assertion that if one perceives a particular environmental deficit, one is more likely to attempt to compensate for it and, if successful, achieve greater levels of well-being. That being said, one must be aware of the other variables that affect this causal chain. Foremost among these, and neglected to this point, is the manifest function of work—earning one's living—and the impact that it has upon the likelihood that the lost latent functions of work will be satisfactorily obtained during unemployment.

Income as Moderator

The loss of the manifest function of work has been under-emphasized relative to the degree of attention paid to the loss of latent functions (Rantakeisu et al., 1999). However, it has been argued that income acts as a moderator between being unemployed and suffering negative consequences as a result. As such, those who are more distressed by loss of income are likely to experience the other deprivations of unemployment to a greater extent (Hanisch, 1999; Shelton, 1985). As Barling (1990) suggested, perceived financial deprivation may be as potent as objective financial circumstances. There is strong evidence that associates perceived financial hardship or distress with negative psychological reactions to job loss (Barling, 1990; Leana & Feldman, 1990; Rantakeisu et al., 1999; Ullah, 1990; Vinokur et al., 1996; Waters & Moore, 2001). Indeed, it has been suggested "that financial concern is the most important factor associated with psychological distress" (Creed & Macintyre, 2001, p. 329). It is not contended that money, in and of itself, moderates the relationship, but that having adequate funds may provide greater latitude for action and may thus allow greater efforts to be taken in order to compensate for the lack of valued categories of experience. The lack of money, in this respect, may reduce the possibility of agency action, a central point made by Fryer and Payne (1984).

More will be said about the effects of financial distress on attaining valued categories of experience, but for now it suffices to note that among our groups, those whose psychological well-being indicators were lowest are frequently found in the most impoverished groups. Clearly, the Rovers and the Lonely People often fared badly while unemployed, and financial deprivation limited their range of effective action. It must be noted, though, that participants entered this study shortly after losing jobs and were receiving Unemployment Insurance money that helped reduce the financial impact of job loss. Further, relatively few participants were still unemployed during Phase 2, making long-term effects difficult to assess. In addition, our evidence of the effect of financial deprivation upon mood states is mixed as, for example, the Lonely People generally scored high on all measures. As previously noted, though, this may reflect their seeming affective bipolarity, and these results may very well have differed markedly had the scales been administered at a different time. Surplus

People's negative reaction to unemployment also seemed predicated in part on the lack of funds that limited the extent to which they were able to behave proactively during unemployment, although to a somewhat lesser extent because some of them received financial support from their parents.

In contrast to the members of these Marginalized groups, by and large Planners were more affluent and not as limited in their behavioural options. This is reflected in their greater propensity to engage in long-term planning and allied behaviours, which are associated with the benefits already described. The greatest variability in this regard is found among the Efficacy-Seekers who, perhaps not coincidentally, show the greatest variability in pre-employment income and were most likely among the Planners to report restrictions due to financial considerations.

Our results are largely in accordance with the findings of Broman and associates (Broman, 1997; Broman, Hamilton, & Hoffman, 1990) and Grant and Barling (1994) that financial strain is associated with family stress and dysfunction, indicating the often-indirect influence of many of the variables under consideration here. In this case, the lack of funds limited potentially beneficial behavioural options outside the home, thus concentrating the stress of unemployment within the family unit. In short, as was clearly articulated during the presentation of the interview data, there is evidence to suggest that the lack of money may be a problem for some unemployed individuals, and it seems likely that the negative effects stem from the limitations such a lack imposes upon opportunities for expressions of personal agency and the achievement of valued categories of experience. This leads us to consider, firstly, the effects of financial deprivation upon engagement in extradomestic activities and, secondly, the contributions to positive well-being that these activities may provide should they be financially accessible.

Activity during Unemployment

As Lobo (1996) has noted, previous research has demonstrated that "most unemployed people tend to reduce the time spent on active, out-of-home, and social activities, and increase their passive, solitary and home-based pursuits" (p. 172). Indeed, in our study over 55% of the ESM signals were received when the participant was at home, and over a third of the signals were received when alone. In light of the preceding section, it must be noted that those who perceived the greatest lack of disposable funds were least likely to be active during unemployment (Ullah, 1990; Waters & Moore, 2001). Given this, it is perhaps not surprising that remaining active during unemployment can be problematic, and less surprising still that unemployment is more negatively experienced in such instances. The Surplus People are illustrative in this regard. Deprived of the valued categories of experience provided by work, and unable to achieve such categories of experience due to shortcomings in their financial situation, Surplus People did not realize the moderating effects of activity as well as the potential social contact and the self-affirmation it provides. As a consequence, the financially constrained may be particularly vulnerable to the negative psychological outcomes of unemployment.

However, financial constraint is not the only variable that may limit activity during unemployment. As well, uncertainty about the future may dissuade individuals from engaging in or embarking upon meaningful activity. While it may be that such individuals don't have the finances to fund an ongoing endeavour, of greater importance might be the concern that they wouldn't have the opportunity to complete a project should they be offered employment (Wanberg et al., 1997). Furthermore, as noted earlier, social embarrassment may cause social withdrawal by the unemployed or members of his or her social network, which may limit the range and quality of activities available. There is some evidence to suggest that both the Rovers and the Routinizers fell victim to such withdrawal. Nevertheless, individuals may find the means to remain active while unemployed, perhaps by accessing low-cost alternatives (Lobo, 1996, 1999). For those who are able, activities that involve social interaction and are perceived as purposeful have the potential to pay mental health dividends (Fryer & Payne, 1984; Lobo & Watkins, 1995; Underlid, 1996; Winefield, Tiggemann & Winefield, 1992). As Winefield and Tiggemann (1989) suggested, "If unemployed people can be encouraged to maintain a high level of ... activities that are seen as worthwhile and that expand their social networks, then, as long as they are in good health and their financial needs are satisfied, they may be able to avoid the psychological distress that otherwise accompanies unemployment" (p. 335). This statement is certainly supported by the results of our study. Those participants with the most diverse repertoire of activity during unemployment seemed to cope most effectively with their job loss. These activities were often leisure-oriented, as is seen in the behaviour patterns of the Breaking Ins; vocationally or professionally oriented, as seen in the Anti-Homebodies; or volunteer-based, as was the case for the Networkers and Caregivers. However, in all cases the activities were consistently noted as positive features of their daily existence. In contrast, passive, solitary, and home-bound activity patterns were often associated with poor psychological well-being, as we have seen in the Surplus People.

Thus, we concur with the numerous unemployment researchers who have posited the need for activity during unemployment, as such activity seems to enable the unemployed to attain those categories of experience denied due to job loss. In addition, facilitating the attainment of positive categories of experience for the unemployed seems incumbent upon those working within the leisure services field if we are to meaningfully reach all constituents within our communities. If, as is suggested here (Tables 34 and 36) and elsewhere, leisure activity may moderate the negative impacts of unemployment for most people, then not to facilitate the leisure engagement of the unemployed by recognizing their particular needs and difficulties is a partial abdication of the field's mandate. The facilitation of leisure experience and the provision of leisure services for the unemployed will be taken up in the next chapter.

6 *Perceptions of Unemployment Agencies and Other Social Services*

To follow our foray into the unemployment literature, we return now to additional data from our own research that related to respondents' interactions with social service agencies. Data presented in this section are distinct from those previously presented. Although based in the qualitative data, the majority of these data regarding participants' perceptions and use of social services was offered during the follow-up interviews that occurred at the end of Phase 2. Consequently, due to attrition from the original sample of 60 individuals, the following analysis is limited. First, there were only 42 participants in Phase 2. Second, not all of the participants chose to comment upon their experiences accessing social services; in fact, close to 25% of the 42 Phase 2 participants offered no comments in this regard. Therefore, the following is based on the input of a little more than half (32) of the original sample. This being the case, it is unwarranted to make many claims about the differences in outlook or experience with regard to social services on a group or subgroup basis. However, based on an analysis of the comments of these 32 participants, some broad themes are evident pertaining to the nature of their experiences with the services offered by Human Resources Development Canada (HRDC), their impressions about the provision of leisure services, and their motivations and desires concerning the provision of services related to both their search for work and their desire for an adequate leisure lifestyle.

First, this chapter will detail the participants' perceptions of HRDC, their primary institutional contact. HRDC programs are accessed from a variety of facilities, including the Canada Employment Centre, which was the venue of initial contact for participants in this study. It is perhaps not surprising that many of the participants' comments concern their use of the "unemployment insurance system"; however, the participants expressed a broad range of opinions with regard to the level of service and their perceived needs. Second, we shall examine the various perspectives offered concerning HRDC's role in the provision or facilitation of leisure opportunities for the unemployed. Third, we shall look at the participants' impressions regarding the role that other social service agencies may play to maximize the leisure well-being of the unemployed, and various means through which this may be accomplished.

Interacting with Human Resources Development Canada

"The System"

Common sentiments expressed about interactions with Human Resources Development Canada (HRDC) pertained to three main issues: the difficulty of negotiating "the system," which included unanticipated delays that characterized the participants' receipt of funds; the need for personal and/or material support to facilitate the participants' search for employment; and the participants' experience with training schemes set up by HRDC. As shall be seen, by no means were all of the expressed sentiments negative; however, by and large the participants experienced a variety of frustrations that seemed to compound the negativity of their period of unemployment.

Interacting with HRDC staff and services was often described using the "red tape" metaphor, stereotypically characteristic of large bureaucratic organizations. Given the importance of HRDC as one conduit through which the participants sought employment, the perceived lack of support for individual efforts was frustrating for some. As Aaron commented during Phase 1, "If there's an idea in order to get employed, they should support that, and I think definitely then there's red tape again right there. That takes part of my day away ... if you're stuck in the system, it's really hard to get out of the system."

Although the services and support offered by HRDC were often perceived as beneficial, there seemed to be an undercurrent of resignation with respect to negotiating "the system." "The system" referred to no one in particular, as Anna commented during her Phase 2 interview: "I can't really think of anything that would have made it easier because they are now on a new computerized system where you can just walk in and the listings for jobs available are right in the computer so that seems really easy to me that you can just walk up and use them.... I can't really say that someone could have made it easier. It was just the system I guess." However, while Anna expressed a certain degree of satisfaction with having the computerized job-search database freely available, other means by which HRDC facilitates reemployment were more negatively received. Stemming in part from his failure to understand the "the system," in Phase 1 Dick expressed his frustration with both the process and also the outcome of his association with a particular job-search agency:

> I've been involved with a couple of government organizations and I've never gotten one positive response from one employer, and with one agency I was involved in about 45 different companies that I sent resumes to. This government agency assured me that "This is the way to go," and then I found out that this government agency was just a broker for a government agency and that this broker got money from me being signed up, thousands of dollars because I signed my name. I never heard from one single employer.... I feel real disappointed that the government and these private agencies are just like vultures, sitting there wanting to feed on your misfortunes.

Although Dick's frustrations with the particular agency he had been involved with were by no means indicative of the level of frustrations others felt with the services offered by HRDC or allied governmental units, certain elements of the participants' interactions were more universally experienced as frustrating. In particular, the length of time that it took to access or to receive services was problematic for many, as was their relative ignorance about the process and the seeming lack of personnel who may have provided some indication of what to expect. As Melanie pointed out in Phase 2, "They don't have enough monitors on." A consequence of the perceived lack of personnel was that certain information of importance to the participants was not offered. Jenny suggested, "I think if they had told you it takes that long for somebody to get back to you, [it] might have eased the waiting time."

The issue of "time" was of relevance to most, not only with respect to the length of time that one might have to endure prior to being contacted by a potential employer, but also with respect to the length of time it typically took to receive their Unemployment Insurance cheques. Given that financial issues were at the forefront for many, the time lag between filing for Unemployment Insurance and receiving the first payment was often troubling. During the Phase 2 interview, Harry noted that he "found that it was kinda rough and rocky; like uh when you file for unemployment it takes 6–8 weeks, sometimes more." Kim voiced a similar sentiment: "The only thing I found with that is you had to leave a long time before you actually received the cheque. Although I got four or five cheques all at one time because it takes a long time I guess to process it...." The pleasure at having received a number of cheques at one time notwithstanding, the financial strain experienced while waiting seemed to compound the distress for many of the less financially solvent participants.

In addition to the length of time preceding the receipt of financial assistance, participants in the study noted other areas of financial burden that could potentially be ameliorated by HRDC. In particular, costs incurred as a direct result of searching for a job were often perceived as reasonably under the purview of HRDC. For instance, in Phase 1 Dick commented, "I have to take my food money that I get to buy stamps and envelopes. If I could hand in a receipt to show that I've purchased these stamps, and have the government reimburse me for that, that would be much better for me." Kim, as well, felt that HRDC could have helped cover direct costs associated with job searching. In Phase 2 she suggested, "I think they could have provided childcare ... but they wouldn't supply childcare for you to go look for work, which I don't think is really fair because how are you supposed to get out to work? You can't ... very well take a two-year-old, three-year-old at an interview." Thus, HRDC was seen as having a role to play not only in facilitating job-search activities and distributing Unemployment Insurance benefits, but also in providing needed ancillary services and a means through which the unemployed may be reimbursed for job-search expenses. The notion of subsidies will be broached again later, but at this point it suffices to point out that, perhaps not surprisingly, economic issues were at the forefront for many, and it was felt that HRDC's role might be expanded to meet the varied needs of the unemployed beyond what "the system" currently allows.

However, while not all participants were entirely satisfied with the range of services offered, neither were participants entirely dissatisfied with "the system." Jeffrey pointed out during his Phase 2 interview, "There's so many people using it. It doesn't work for me, but that doesn't mean it has to change." Thus, while an ideal might be imagined, there was also an acknowledgement on the part of some of the participants that the existing arrangement of services might, indeed, meet the needs of a certain portion of the unemployed population. As Jeffrey noted, the number of people accessing the services offered by HRDC may make universal satisfaction impossible, and the inability of HRDC to satisfy everyone may not indicate a need for change. That said, the issue of communication was seen as especially problematic, and many of the participants commented that this is one area where improvements are necessary.

Need for Information

As may be inferred, the broad system that seeks to help the unemployed find employment was perceived as very complicated, especially for the uninitiated. In Phase 2, Robert captured the sentiments expressed by many of the participants about the need for assistance when navigating through HRDC:

> With, um, them tightening up on unemployment, the process has become incredibly complex. I wouldn't want to just go into it blind anymore.... There's an incredible line-up of people waiting while they check over your form. Why? Because a lot of people don't know how to fill out the form—you just give them the form [and are] told to fill it out. That's wrong.
>
> It's a really an information society nowadays, there's, there's all sorts of, of opportunities out there, but unless you have the information to, uh, to know where to go, how to go about getting the opportunities and realizing the potential, you might as well have nothing. My personal opinion is that they need to hire more people.... And I mean, I'm not saying that the, the people doing it aren't doing a good job, but they're just swamped.

Participants often noted that they were not receiving desired information from HRDC due to a variety of reasons. As Donna stated during Phase 2, "They don't seem to tell you what services or what is out there—the message isn't getting out." She suggested that this information might be effectively disseminated via printed material: "I'd like to know what my options are at the beginning—what's available, like a directory or something." Peggy expressed a similar thought: "I think if they advertise it more ... sent out fliers. Or as soon you apply for unemployment that you get like, ah, a small mail package saying you can try this type of program, different activities." Mary expressed a need for more information about resources that could help her during her job search activities: "By having easier access to knowing where you can get free computer, where you can use the computer free.... And where you can get free photocopies and where you can get free service on how to do your resume over and how do you, like just lots of things there's ways of doing things, there's money out there, but you don't know there's money out there."

Participants not only expressed their desire for information received through static channels, but also suggested that greater personal service/counselling would have been helpful as they attempted to negotiate the system and cope with their unemployment. In Phase 2, Andrea suggested, "It would have been easier if I would have had a counsellor to help me. Like I didn't have an employment counsellor, or ... anyone that ah ... I don't know there just didn't seem to be a lot of interest." While Andrea wanted one-on-one counselling, Heather felt that a more informal setting accessible by many people over the course of the day might have sufficed. During Phase 2, she suggested,

"I don't know, a drop-in, a drop-in centre, not so much where you have to show up every single day or whatever but even just a drop-in centre to tell people that don't know how to do it." Mary, as well, argued for the need for personal intervention, and added that increased motivation and access to information might have resulted from having someone counsel her during unemployment:

> If I hadda had someone professional that could say, "You're way off base." Or, or, or someone that would, that would, friendly but firmly push me to, you know, and help me, you know.... And ah, work with me to, to get a job and that, and even after, to follow up, to make sure that, you know, you, you know what it's like when you first start a job. Um, that would've made a huge difference to me.... But I needed a lot of help, but I wasn't getting it and it's like, and I didn't know who to ask or whatever.

Paul, however, did access the kind of employment counselling that others described as necessary and his impressions of the experience were not positive. During Phase 2, he described one such counselling session: "I ask him [a] real question, does he have job or not? He [gave] me ... advice, but it was useless. He told me, 'You can be [a] plant manager, you can earn at least $40,000 a year,' but when I ask him, 'Do you have any jobs for $6 per hour,' he says, 'I cannot help you I am just [a counsellor].' So, thanks ... ah, that kind of advice we don't need."

In short, a very common complaint voiced about the services of HRDC was that desired information was difficult to obtain, and that the needed personal and material means through which it might have been distributed were lacking. Given the perceived complexity of the system, many participants felt that their efforts to find a job were not adequately facilitated by the HRDC due to lack of information, and they felt that greater efforts should be made to ensure that job-seekers are informed in a timely manner about the options available to them. However, many of the unemployed participants in the study did manage to become aware of some of the opportunities furnished by HRDC, and one area of particular salience was the variety of training programs offered.

Training

As mentioned, notwithstanding the fact that many of the participants found it difficult to access information or advice about re-employment programs, many were made aware and did participate in training schemes offered through HRDC. Reactions to such offerings were varied and seemed to depend on the participants' level of need for the services offered. Indeed, some participants were aware that programs existed but chose not to participate as they felt that little benefit would accrue to them by doing so. As Kim pointed out during Phase 2, "They were pretty good actually... like they have training courses and things like that. 'Cause I already had the training, it was just getting a job." Joanne was also familiar with HRDC's services but noted that, with the exception of the employment opportunities database, they were of little use: "Like you can sort of go and look through the computers. But if you already have skills any other things they offer aren't really useful.... Um, so other than just looking at the jobs that are available, that was really the only thing I found there that, that was of any use." Aaron, however, did participate in a particular job-search training program and was less than pleased with both the program and the limited range of options available. As he noted in Phase 2, "They should offer employment training, especially retraining a lot more in-depth. Like they offer a couple of uh, programs like Path to Employment and stuff, and it's garbage.... You know, they need a program where you're subsidized on a wage as well as put on the job training where you have the option of being hired later on." Although Aaron perceived no direct benefits from the job-search training program in which he participated, others mentioned that participation in such programs might produce indirect benefits. In Phase 2, Taryn suggested that there might be psychological benefits to participating in these programs: "Looking back on it now, I think I would have gotten something out of those jobs [career assessment workshops], maybe not so much in terms of getting myself... but making my life feel more meaningful because I'm doing something. You know, I'm working towards a goal and I think that's the biggest thing... I think that's the hardest thing for people ... when they're unemployed they'll take anything they can get. But, 9 times out of 10 they don't find something they absolutely enjoy."

For many participants, HRDC was simply a conduit through which their Unemployment Insurance compensation flowed. As such, their interest in program information, counselling services, or job-search training was limited, and thus these elements of HRDC's services did not weigh in their evaluation. Such a perspective was illustrated by Barb in her Phase 2 interview: "To be honest with you, I find the service excellent. Everybody was really nice.... And before I knew it, I had money coming. So I found the system really good to be honest with you. I had no problems at all." Although pleased that "everyone was really nice," Barb's real satisfaction stemmed from the timely receipt of compensation. However, there were others who were satisfied with the personal attention they received and the advice provided by HRDC staff. As Melanie stated in Phase 2, "All the times I went there I had good experiences from them." Jenny's comments during Phase 2 were similar: "I did find the interview that they gave um, at the unemployment office helpful. It did make me feel better in that she did recommend people look for jobs in the fields that they're qualified for. The fields of interests instead of trying to take anything because like all things you wouldn't stay."

As can be seen, there were a variety of divergent opinions expressed about the services provided by HRDC. However, based on the responses of the participants in this study, it appears as though more participants were dissatisfied with the service they received than were wholly satisfied. Due in large measure to a perceived lack of information and personal support, many felt that improvements were necessary to increase the chances that those who access HRDC might find work, indeed, to increase the chances that those individuals would even be able to navigate the system successfully. Whether due to a personnel shortage or the ineffective distribution of information, many participants in the study opined that HRDC was falling short of their expectations, and with some exceptions participants asserted that more could be done to help them reintegrate themselves into the workforce.

Leisure Facilitation and Provision

In addition to being queried about the services HRDC provided in order to assist them to secure employment, participants in the study were also asked about the roles that HRDC might assume to optimize individual leisure functioning and overall well-being. With respect to facilitating positive leisure engagement, defraying transportation expenses was seen as an acceptable role for HRDC without overstepping their primary mission—to help the unemployed find work. As Shelly noted during the Phase 2 interview, "If UIC could support a bus pass ... I would think, yeah, something that could help get them motivated in some way to do something." Aaron made a similar comment on the roles HRDC may play to improve the lot of children as well as their unemployed parents:

> Giving you passes to local health clubs, or to theatres or, especially if you have kids and take, you know you give them a little bit ... they should, you know, give you free bus passes and stuff like that. Like Edmonton you get a free bus pass, or monthly they give you a pass to a health club. The bus thing would be a lot, a lot more easier.... If you can get around you can probably make, find different forms of leisure, like goin' to the parks and whatever.

Notwithstanding some participants' assertions that HRDC might play a role to improve the leisure lifestyles of the unemployed and their families, the majority of the participants who commented upon this issue were strongly opposed to expanding HRDC's involvement. Many felt that it was beyond HRDC's mandate; as Les rhetorically asked during Phase 2, "Doesn't the government want you to kind of concentrate on you finding a job instead of on their leisure? Instead of them providing a recreation a facility for you?" Others felt that leisure participation was at cross-purposes to finding a job, as Anna noted in Phase 2: "I can't see them doing that; they don't want to encourage people to stay unemployed. So no, I can't really see that." Bob more fully articulated a common objection to HRDC becoming involved in facilitating unemployed leisure participation: "I don't think it should be done. I think training programs should be done, but recreation? I think that may encourage people not to, like why, they should be teaching them or helping unemployed people get back into the job force not to have us spend spare time playing racquetball or whatever." Diane, as well, expressed a similar sentiment during her Phase 2 interview: "I don't know because I don't think it's up to them really to do it ... I think their responsibilities lie more on, um, helping people find work or, helping people understand their problems — why they can't work or something. And there's lots of programs out there like that so I don't really think that's important at all ... as far as UIC goes your, your job is to go looking for a job. It isn't supposed to be out there, uh, playing Frisbee in the park on a nice afternoon or something like that."

As Diane stated, a common sentiment was that one's primary activity during unemployment should be actively seeking work. Many of the participants felt that, by facilitating leisure engagement, HRDC might jeopardize this primary focus and, further, that HRDC might perceive the unemployed who access such services as not wholly committed to re-employment. As Susan explained, "I don't know because the employment office itself is there to, you know, offer employment. And I don't see them mixing the two ... I mean if they start setting up, like community activities or sports or something, I think that they might feel that the people who are unemployed aren't participating in the actual look, ah work, the actual hunt for employment as much as they are participating in these activities." Steven echoed this point during his Phase 2 interview, and commented: "If you're on unemployment insurance, welfare, they basically expect you to be spending a longer time looking for work. And I can't imagine them saying, you know, 'Make sure you spend 2–3 hours a day doing some recreational activity.'"

Still others felt that the government, through the services and programs set up through HRDC, were already adequately providing for the needs of the unemployed, and that any further service provision on their part is both unnecessary and unwarranted. Angie, during her Phase 2 interview, clearly expressed this point of view:

> I don't think that the government should be babysittin' anyone on UIC. Personally, you know, they're already givin' them money. I don't think they should be allocating more cash for them to have leisure time because that's what it's gonna take. It's gonna take money to give someone leisure time, or to set up programs or do studies or whatever. I think anyone who's already takin' government money has got enough.

Angie's lack of support for this was not just based on a belief that leisure services were beyond the purview of HRDC; she expressed an opinion that unemployed individuals should not be concerned about their leisure: "Personally I don't think this is a large problem.... As far as I'm concerned if you're unemployed and you're getting UIC, and you don't have a whole lot of time for leisure activities, well that's too bad. You know, get yourself a job and get yourself better."

As is clear, strong negative sentiments were expressed about HRDC becoming involved in either facilitating or providing for leisure participation. Most participants felt that an expansion of HRDC's mandate to include leisure as an aspect of their service is unwarranted, even though a minority voiced their belief that there might be a small role for HRDC to play by subsidizing transportation or leisure facilities membership. Based on the preponderance of comments made by participants in the study, it seems safe to assert that any expansion of HRDC's role was perceived as an undesirable dilution of their service mandate.

This negative reaction stems not only from the perceived incongruity with HRDC's primary mandate to assist individuals in finding work but it also reflects the sentiment of some that leisure provision for the unemployed is adequate. Specifically, it was felt that other governmental units, more appropriate to the task, already meet the needs of those of limited means. As Barb noted in Phase 2: "And that [unemployment] did not affect me in any way. It didn't. So it depends on your lifestyle. What type of lifestyle you were accustomed and you've been living before you became unemployed. I think they have a lot of things, like Kitchener Parks & Rec. They have a lot of things I know going on at the schools, that you just, you know, you can go." Kim furthered this sentiment, suggesting, "Like the recreation is there,

there's all kinds of things you can do." Larry, as well, during his Phase 2 interview, commented that special provision for the unemployed is unnecessary: "Does Kitchener Recreation say here, we're gonna give x amount of hours of ice time for unemployed people to come, to have a family skate? Well, they have to have free family skates now, that's not an issue." Paul, in line with Larry, noted that government intervention might not be strictly necessary, but added to the comment by noting an added benefit of leisure participation: "If someone really wants and cares about himself, he can walk or swim or run, something like that. Maybe you … you … you can set up something like public games or something just that people don't feel that they are alone." Paul's comment above suggests that the government may have a role to play in order to mitigate the potential isolation by providing leisure services. In contrast, Jeffrey suggested that governmental intervention might not be necessary, but that personal support and recreation provision might find its genesis within one's community: "In a sense it boils down to the community, how much the community cares … people who are interested in doing the same thing."

As described above, many felt that recreation for the unemployed was specifically not under the purview of HRDC or was, more generally, adequately covered by other government agencies. However, the notion that government did have a role to play to safeguard all citizens' access to leisure opportunity did come to the fore. Some participants commented upon the potential for leisure participation to influence positively their primary goal, securing work, and noted that facilitation thereof could reasonably fall under the auspices of HRDC. As Bob suggested in Phase 2, "So I think that there is a scope to develop programs that help people get back into the work force … you know, exercise your body so that you exercise your mind so that you are more keen to go and look for a job." During the Phase 2 interview, Robert, as well, noted that HRDC's primary mission and the facilitation of leisure were not necessarily mutually exclusive. Robert offered an analogy to the correctional system, and forwarded the opinion: "Whether you're confined in uh, a prison or confined in an apartment house…. They're all the same and what works in one system would work in the other, I'd have to say."

Although both Bob and Robert alluded to the psychological benefits of leisure participation and to its potential for improving morale and thus the success of job-searching, theirs was the minority view. The majority of participants who chose to comment upon leisure provision strongly felt that HRDC should concentrate exclusively upon their aim to reintegrate the unemployed into the workforce, leaving it to other governmental agencies and community institutions to attend to the particular leisure constraints of those who are unemployed.

Other Governmental and Community Resources

Lack of Awareness

As mentioned, participants in the study indicated that participation in leisure was beneficial. However, once again, a common complaint pertained to the lack of communication about any special allowances for people of limited financial means. As Mary succinctly stated, "I wasn't aware that there was anything." Joanne, too, commented, "I suppose I don't really know what's already out there or if there really is anything out there." Clearly, a desire to participate in recreational activities will not translate into actual participation unless there is an awareness of the community offerings available. Again echoing sentiments expressed with regard to the services offered by HRDC, during Phase 2 Robert noted, "I wasn't aware that anything was there. It's available, but it's a job just in itself to get the information."

The lack of communication about services offered in the community severely limited the options that the participants perceived were open to them. In Phase 2 Susan offered a suggestion that might help militate against ignorance about community services: "Um, if there was a community paper that listed all kinds of things that could be done that was just for that. Um, or like a newsletter kinda thing, maybe that would bring more attention." Lack of awareness of community recreational services limited many participants' attempts to engage in active recreation, which, as discussed in earlier sections, contributed to their negative perceptions about being without work. Thus, not only did they seem to lack knowledge about the services that HRDC provided that might have helped them secure work, but participants also seemed to lack information about services that could have made their daily experience during unemployment better.

Subsidies

Given that many of the participants were of limited means, the most strongly voiced opinion was their desire for subsidies at the community level to afford them the opportunities that they perceived were closed to them. During Phase 2, Andrea expressed the lack of awareness typical of many of the participants, and also the desire for subsidized participation: "They could offer some things like, um, like free, like swimming and stuff. I don't know if the Y offers anything or not. Does the Y offer anything?" Suggestions about the means through which such allowances might be made varied among the participants; during her Phase 2 interview Stephanie offered one possibility: "Just like I mentioned before, some kind of a little card, I'm unemployed or this is my unemployment card or something like that that you could kind of show at the door." In Phase 2, Heather stated: "Even if they could just give you a discount or, or um, or even open the community centres and have free um, basketball or volleyball or social get-togethers or whatever for the unemployed." In addition, it was noted that the children of those currently without work were similarly disadvantaged; indeed, many noted that children were at an even greater disadvantage. Melanie commented during Phase 2, "There should be something that's more free. I do believe the government agencies could do more in the field of recreation for people that's unemployed and especially like one parent raising a kid thing. That's always hard." Susan concurred, and added during Phase 2:

> I find children who are, I guess, where parents are on welfare, they live a more inactive, or less … involved. There's only so much money that welfare gives you and you have to pay your rent and your bills. There's not much money left over for like, you know, hockey or sports, or you know, all these little things that most kids participate in. So, if there was some kind of involvement in that case, aimed at children, to, ah, give them a more enriched childhood, then I'd go, sure, that'd be great.

In short, many felt that there should be special allowances made for the unemployed so they could participate in community-based recreation. However, notwithstanding the potential benefits to be derived should subsidies be available, it was noted that some people may not use subsidies because of the perceived stigma. As discussed earlier, some participants in the study felt that a stigma existed simply from being unemployed; to approach a leisure agency looking for special treatment would potentially exacerbate that stigma. Donna captured many of the issues related to recreation provision for the unemployed, including the issue of being stigmatized, during her Phase 2 interview:

> There's a lot of agencies out there but people don't know it and especially if people that are knocked down by unemployment and feel embarrassed or something—they're not gonna ask for help, and they're not gonna readily say, "Hey I need help," because they're embarrassed about it sometimes, or ashamed of it especially depending on their upbringing. If you thought that you worked and you

gave to society and that was your image, and then you lose that, especially if somebody is a breadwinner in the family whether it be Mom or Dad—they're not gonna readily go out cause for them it's like failure, admitting it, so you have to let them know that "Hey, I know that you're unemployed and you have three kids and they're interested in sports. Did you know that Kitchener Parks has subsidy if you qualify? It's confidential." Not a lot of people know that they'll help them out, so that their kids don't have to suffer for their misfortune, you know what I mean?

Jenny, as well, commented upon the difficulty of asking for or receiving a subsidy. During Phase 2, she noted,

So if you can pay your way even to a smallest amount, it does save face to some degree. And I know organizations say, "Well just come on in and say…" you know? But that's a really hard thing to swallow, walk in and say….You ask this person and this person goes and gets this person and in the meantime about five people know you're going in there for fee assistance, and then if people walking in see you and they know that you're standing there, and that you know. And it becomes very blatant why you're there and I find that very degrading and I won't do it for that very reason.

As Jenny mentioned, the degradation of receiving assistance may be enough to curtail active membership at a leisure organization. However, she offered a suggestion that she would have found helpful: "Now I think if they had allowed me to pay per month and maybe at a little reduced rate, I would have probably taken it [health club membership] back up again but you have to pay for the whole year or six months. And that's a lot of money to dish out at one time." Others also suggested alternate measures that could be taken so that individuals can participate and also maintain their dignity. One suggestion was to allow unemployed individuals to participate as volunteers. As Alison commented during Phase 2, "So I think any other program just for unemployment, like possibly volunteer there or possibly work there so giving people opportunity to have fun and chance to meet people [to], you know, cheer them up." Voluntary activity was felt to have the potential to occupy her time with pleasurable activity, a point which was also mentioned by Taryn in Phase 2:

I think, um, if they wanted to help people, especially during a time when, especially during the recession when a lot of people are unemployed, not turn around and try to sell them, like "Oh, you join us you'll have a job," but more a case of you finding yourself with free time on your hands and you want something that you'll get a lot of pleasure out of and you have meaningful … being a volunteer … give you something to do. Which I think is usually the biggest, the biggest thing for anyone.

In addition to occupying one's time in a pleasurable manner, such activity was felt to be one avenue wherein unemployed individuals might achieve some sense of meaning in their lives. Robert spoke of this during Phase 2: "It actually gets people back out and socialising, interactive with the community as a whole, uh, to a large extent I'd have to say that, uh, without that interaction there's, there's not much. I mean, we become a disjointed society."

Opportunities to participate in the wider community to the fullest extent possible were seen as valuable to both individual and society. However, participants anticipated difficulties inherent in subsidization or other measures to promote leisure participation, including the "red tape" that would have to be overcome to put such measures into practice. Stacy in Phase 2 said, "Of course, you get into the red tape. 'Cause a lot of recreational facilities, when you get subsides, you have to go in and give them a why. You have to go in and apply for a subsidy. And, then you get into the red tape." Thus, notwithstanding the presumed benefits of active participation, subsidized participation was thought to entail particular difficulties. Whether through the exacerbation of existing stigma, or through the bureaucratic hurdles that would need to be overcome, it was suggested that subsidies exclusive to unemployed individuals, while perhaps well intentioned, might still be problematic.

7 Leisure Services Planning and Policy

Discussion near the end of chapter 6, though focussed on HRDC and employment-specific agencies, provides a segue into the potential role of leisure service agencies in serving unemployed citizens and their dependents. Data presented to this point suggest that our respondents' life satisfaction was low and that they were generally dissatisfied with their ability to plan and control their daily schedules. Although "forced" free time was abundant for most, respondents reported far less perceived leisure than did employed adults surveyed in earlier research. Still, most individuals in the present study reported higher mood states in leisure than in nonleisure contexts. There were clearly group and subgroup differences with respect to leisure preferences, but social-based programs and opportunities seemed to be important for many members of the sample. Likewise, fitness programs and volunteer opportunities appealed to members of some groups and subgroups. Taken together, these findings imply that organized recreation opportunities may mitigate several negative aspects of unemployment including feelings of isolation, decline in physical health, and perceived contributions to society.[1] We therefore suggest that leisure service agencies should do a better job serving this segment of society.

We should clarify that our goal is not to promote levels of recreation participation for the unemployed that surpass that of employed adults, thereby making a recreational utopia of unemployment. Nor do we mean to imply that leisure should, or is even able to, replace work for people who are unemployed. However, we do favour policies that may allow equivalent levels of participation between the employed and the unemployed so that the beneficial mental health consequences of recreation may be realized by all.

This chapter deals with mechanisms through which such benefits may be realized. First, our attention shall turn to practices at the municipal level with a view to outlining potential areas for improvement and possible partnerships at the local level. In pursuing this discussion, special attention will be paid to those components of the marketing mix which seem to be rather universally under-emphasized—if not ignored—when considering unemployed individuals. In order to flesh out this analysis, concrete examples will be offered, based upon the categorization scheme developed in this study. It is worth stating, however, that not all local responses may be necessary or indeed even appropriate given the diversity of participants' experiences with unemployment. Subsequently, our attention will turn to actions that might be taken at the provincial and federal levels to facilitate positive leisure engagement and foster improved well-being among unemployed citizens.

Local Government: Standard Practice

Nearly every survey of leisure service agencies will reveal that subsidized recreation opportunities are ubiquitous. However, the literature suggests that subsidized leisure programs are generally underutilized in the sense that participation rates among the subsidized population still lag in comparison to the unsubsidized population. This study may provide information that can begin to eliminate the imbalance between the number of people potentially available and the number who actually participate in subsidized recreation programs.

As previously noted, our sample showed a general lack of awareness regarding available organized recreation programs and the processes of negotiating social service bureaucracies in order to receive available benefits. Equally, if not more, important was the "lack of entitlement" expressed by many members of the present sample. In Appendix L we provide current fee-subsidy policies from three agencies (two public, one not-for-profit) serving the municipalities from which our sample was drawn. The policy statements that appear in Appendix L, though well intentioned, thoroughly written, and arguably "state-of-the-art," are inadequate for reaching short-term unemployed citizens for several reasons.

Traditional "ask and you shall receive" strategies are unlikely to be successful in reaching the people described in this research. One major problem is that they focus primarily, if not exclusively, on the pricing component of recreation. Marketing theorists have long pointed out that there are four components of the market mix—price (cost), distribution (convenience), promotion (communication), and program development and delivery (customer value)—and they should not be considered in isolation (Crompton & Lamb, 1986; Howard & Crompton, 1980). Data collected for this research suggest that, in addition to greater specificity with respect to segmentation efforts, agencies must be sensitive to, and be willing to manipulate, all components of the marketing mix and the assumptions upon which they rest. Second, the policies, consistent with North American leisure service delivery strategies for low-income people, place the onus on the afflicted individual to seek information and assistance (Appendix L). Such policies may exacerbate perceptions of stigma and therefore not be used by some potential participants; in addition, they represent an added hurdle to be overcome by those confident enough to seek such assistance. Service delivery philosophy and marketing mix issues, therefore, will be addressed in turn in this section of the book. Though presented singularly, it is important to understand that they are often interrelated; seldom will attention to one aspect of service delivery adequately address long-range challenges. Integrated policies are necessary in order to affect meaningful change.

Market Segmentation

Unemployed adults in Canada are currently served with programs specifically tailored to their needs by government-sponsored career counselling, job training, and job-placement activities offered through HRDC. Although it was not a central question in the present research (indeed social service agencies were not surveyed), no evidence was gathered that would suggest that unemployed adults were considered a distinct market segment by other social service agencies, especially those which directly provide recreation and leisure services. If considered at all, unemployed adults and their families are normally served through pricing strategies designed to increase program access among the general population of low-income citizens. Building on past research (e.g. Havitz & Spigner, 1993; Pesavento Raymond & Kelly, 1991; Reid 1988, 1990), this study provides evidence that many unemployed adults and their dependants would benefit from more concentrated attention from North American leisure and social service agencies. We recommend that leisure service providers broadly defined, but those operating in the public and not-for-profit sectors especially, begin treating unemployed adults as a meaningful market segment.

Although it is important to recognize that unemployed adults are distinct in many ways from other low-income groups, indeed many are not even low-income per se, it is essential to consider other bases for segmenting the unemployed population. With the exception of similarities in life circumstance related to recent job loss, respondents in this study were diverse with respect to social, demographic, attitudinal, behavioural, and geographic characteristics in spite of the inherent limitations of an admittedly non-random sample. The 4 groups and 10 subgroups described herein provide ample evidence of this diversity. Thus, where possible, groups and/or subgroups from the present study are discussed in subsequent sections for the purpose of illustrating intergroup differences and the potential utility and appropriateness of various institutional practices at the local level. Though these groups are somewhat unique to this sample and other communities might find similar but not identical segments within their populations, the diversity of this sample effectively substantiates the points below.

The Marketing Mix and Municipal Action

Most recreation programming occurs at the local level. As noted above, the four separate components of the marketing mix have not received equal attention by those who program for unemployed constituents; indeed, there has been near-exclusive attention paid to pricing issues. In what follows, each of the four components shall be discussed with special reference made, where appropriate, to our categorization scheme.

Price and Cost-Related Issues

Although ability to pay may be a critical issue among unemployed adults and their families, data from this study suggest that financial needs vary widely among unemployed populations. Some respondents in the present study faced dire financial straits, whereas others were comfortable or only marginally uncomfortable. Financial need may be mitigated by the marital or partnered status of unemployed adults, the number of dependants under their care, and the housing arrangements in which they live. Unemployed adults who are supported by parents or living with roommates, such as many Breaking Ins, often got by with fewer financial resources than were necessary for individuals without such support. This was also true for Anti-Homebodies, who were all partnered and reasonably comfortable financially even while unemployed. Many Rovers and In Controls expressed financial need, but they also enjoyed relative autonomy from family-imposed routines, expectations, and social pressures.

However, the Rovers would likely be more price-sensitive than In-Controls with respect to recreation programs because Rovers did not find recreation as intrinsically rewarding. Indeed, the In Controls, along with the Breaking Ins and the Anti-Homebodies, were the exceptions within our sample; the majority of the other groups' members would almost certainly benefit from well-designed price discount policies.

How might agencies better serve unemployed adults in need of financial subsidies? In many current policies intended to mitigate financial hardship (see Appendix L), the onus is on potential participants to seek out assistance, a practice so commonplace as to raise little attention or debate among social and leisure service professionals. It is not surprising that strategies of this type are largely unsuccessful. Consider, for example, the difference between an unemployed 40 year old and a retired 62 year old seeking fee assistance at a public sector recreation facility. The unemployed adult must complete an entire set of paperwork to document financial need. In contrast, the retiree need only produce a valid photo ID such as a driver's license to gain a significant price discount. In fact, all adults aged 55 and over are eligible for substantial "Golden Age" discounts averaging 40% at City of Waterloo facilities (Appendix L). These subsidies are available regardless of whether the participant is a fixed-income pensioner, a financially secure full professor, or a wealthy corporate CEO. In addition, children and other special-need groups are normally granted a similar fee reduction as a matter of course.

This commonly held double standard of accountability is widespread in North America, yet it exists largely without justification. Our study revealed no evidence of overt work-avoidance among people in our sample, nor was there widespread evidence that people were abusing privileges, financial or otherwise, that accrue as a result of their unemployment. Indeed, the Breaking-Ins were unique among the 10 subgroups in repeatedly expressing sentiments that their unemployed lifestyle was acceptable; all other subgroups expressed a strong and immediate preference for employment. These sentiments, however, seem unrelated to the availability of government subsidies. Thus, our data suggest that there is little rationale for the invasive paperwork unemployed people must complete to prove their financial need.

By contrast, we report sufficient data related to mood states, life satisfaction, family conflict, and the like to document a real need for the social, physical, and psychological benefits available from various forms of recreation participation. The fact that recreation may better equip unemployed adults to cope with day-to-day life without a job, and may actually assist them in gaining meaningful employment, makes a strong argument for "automatic" price discounts in the public and not-for-profit sectors for short-term unemployed people and their dependants. Program and price subsidies should be made available to family members including children and partners as well as the unemployed adults themselves. In our study, the Caregivers would have had a reduced psychological burden if their dependants had been able to continue the recreation and social support programs they had enjoyed while the Caregiver was employed. Subsidies for dependants would also be important to subgroups such as the Networkers and Lonely People. It is not coincidental that women disproportionately expressed frustration about the deprivation faced by their dependants.

Although the single most important change in the status quo with respect to price subsidies for unemployed adults stems from the application and distribution process described above, privacy concerns are also paramount. As noted, entitlement issues (or more accurately the perceptions of lack of entitlement to leisure) were apparent for many respondents in this study, and these may be exacerbated by overt subsidy arrangements. Price subsidies, therefore, should not be public in the sense that other participants (or, indeed, even front-line service providers) can readily identify unemployed participants on the basis of policy-related actions. Some level of anonymity is important both to avoid stigmatizing unemployed adults and their families and to avoid "waving red flags" in the faces of community members who don't believe that unemployed people should be granted special allowances. Routinizers, for example, were meticulous in maintaining fitness regimens, but might have benefited considerably from discretely supplied fee subsidies because most were under moderate to severe income pressure and were especially sensitive to the social stigma associated with joblessness.

Distribution and Convenience-Related Issues

Perhaps the most complex and profound issues related to leisure service delivery for unemployed adults and their dependants are questions of distribution. With respect to leisure service delivery, distribution questions include the following: Who should offer the programs? How many programs should be offered? When should programs be offered? At what locations and venues should programs be offered? Based on respondents' comments, HRDC and other employment-related agencies seem to have no role in the direct provision of leisure services. We concur with this assessment. It is clear that leisure programming falls outside HRDC's mission, and it is unlikely, especially in times when unemployment rates are high, that such agencies would have sufficient staff resources to assume responsibilities in addition to those already within their purview. In addition, employment-related agencies lack necessary programming expertise, facilities, and staff to unilaterally mount recreation programs.

Nevertheless, there seems to be ample opportunity for HRDC and other employment-related agencies to broker recreation programs. This is possible for several reasons. HRDC establishes ongoing relationships with a large number of unemployed adults; as such, it is ideally situated to serve as a clearinghouse for recreation program information supplied by any number of agencies or businesses and to provide assistance with respect to fee relief applications. HRDC offices may also serve as a potential site for leisure education programs. Supporting Havitz and Spigner (1993), we found no evidence that local recreation and leisure service delivery agencies are working directly and co-operatively with HRDC or other employment-related agencies. This seems to be an obvious match, but one that is rarely made in North America. By contrast, it is quite common for municipal recreation agencies to work with youth serving agencies, school districts, and older adult service providers in order to ensure that those populations are served. Establishing a working relationship with unemployment agencies would complement those existing efforts.

The proposed interagency relationships could be relatively passive or avowedly aggressive in construction. For example, a passive role might involve HRDC simply serving as a clearinghouse for information. Program-related brochures could be stocked at Human Resources Development Centres, and these centres could provide information or computer terminals where unemployed adults who are accessing other resources could seek information about recreation and social service programs as well. It is worth remembering, though, that many participants expressed frustration that HRDC seemed unable to disseminate information directly related to their mandate. Caution is urged, then, as it is unlikely that such co-operative efforts would be possible without the infusion of additional agency material and human resources.

A more aggressive role for HRDC might extend the information broker role just described to include provision of transit passes to recreation sites or, for that matter, to job-search sites, churches, service clubs, schools, and so forth. These passes could be used by the unemployed adults and/or their dependants. Taking the role one step further, HRDC could provide income-related information to recreation agencies on behalf of clients, thus eliminating the need for unemployed adults to "beg" for program access for themselves or for their dependants. Alternately, the interagency relationship could be reversed, and recreation staff could regularly gather, with appropriate permission, client information from HRDC or simply drop off appropriate numbers of fee-discount passes to HRDC for dispersion at their discretion. This latter solution almost certainly is preferred because it would eliminate potential bureaucratic restrictions on the release of privileged client information to a, albeit well-intentioned, third party. Businesses that lay off employees could presumably share this role, thereby reducing reliance solely on actions taken by HRDC. It seems, however, that this type of program better suits the mission of HRDC, for it would likely be more effective in notifying eligible recipients of program opportunities than would cash-strapped, downsizing, or failing businesses.

One promising role for HRDC would involve working with an appropriate municipal recreation agency to develop a co-operative program wherein a leisure diagnostic and/or leisure education program could be implemented for unemployed adults and their dependants. This program could work in conjunction with career counselling already offered through HRDC, as suggested by McDaniels (1989) within his Career = Work + Leisure formulation. Furthermore, such programs could function in concert with the other options listed above in order to ensure that recreation opportunities are readily available to those in need. Efforts such as these need not be imposed from the "top-down" but could develop through "grass-roots" organizing as well. Community development approaches, wherein professional staff serve in reflective, communitarian capacities that facilitate individuals' self-determination, seem ideally suited to provide the best balance between individual and collective. This approach, Pedlar (1996) argued, is particularly appropriate for people who are socially and economically disadvantaged.

Although intuitively appealing, strategies that use unemployed adults to "fill slow times" at recreation centres will likely be unsuccessful in reaching most of our subgroups. For example, mid-morning, when many recreation facilities are underused, is often touted as an ideal time for people who are unemployed. Like people who are employed, however, many unemployed adults have relatively full daily schedules. Our data suggest that Planners, for example, might avoid morning programs because the morning is their job-search time. Others, like Breaking Ins, probably wouldn't use morning programs either because, as both interview and ESM data suggest, they were often still in bed. Data on mood-state by time-of-day (Table 37) provided additional insight into the effectiveness of morning recreation programs. Surplus People, Lonely People, and In Controls may well be most receptive to, and benefit from, recreation programming made available in morning hours. However, morning recreation programming should be avoided for Planners and Connectors, including all five subgroups comprising these categories, because these people's mood states were more depressed during leisure than nonleisure activity in the morning. The Rover subgroup of the Marginalized People also shared this characteristic. As such, it seems likely that many people in these groups would view organized morning recreation programming with distaste. It would not make sense to provide morning leisure activities to people who would get little out of those activities at this time of day.

To the extent that unemployed adults live in certain geographic neighbourhoods, municipalities may find it expedient to establish accessible and appropriate facilities and programs in anticipation of unemployment in those areas. Having such resources in place might offer a level of protection against the deleterious effects of localized unemployment that arises during an economic slowdown in a particular sector (manufacturing, high tech, etc.) or as a result of the closure of a facility (plant, office, warehouse, etc.) which might disproportionately affect citizens in those neighbourhoods. Of course, periods of generalized economic downturn increase the importance of these programs throughout the community and not just in targeted neighbourhoods.

It may also make sense to locate recreation programs in close proximity to other social service agencies that provide services for unemployed adults and their families. In this study, transportation was a frequent problem for many respondents. This finding is consistent with literature emphasizing the importance of convenience issues for relatively unresponsive markets and for people being enticed to try new things. Alternately, and as suggested by some participants, social service agencies might co-operate with local transit authorities by, for instance, facilitating the provision of transit passes or permitting public transportation at reduced rates. In line with the double-standard issue explored above, we suggest that such allowances be pre-emptively offered by the agency and that the burden of securing this allowance not be left to the unemployed individual (for example, by requiring extensive personal financial information).

Data collected for this study do not suggest the need for a plethora of recreation programs uniquely designed for unemployed adults. To the contrary, there were strong and oft-repeated sentiments that unemployed adults simply wanted existing programs to be accessible to the extent that they were when they were employed. Programs that are available at a wide variety of times and locations will likely be accessible to both employed and unemployed citizens; however, issues like pricing concerns, awareness, and entitlement still need to be adequately addressed if these programs are to be fully utilized by the unemployed.

Promotion and Communication-Related Issues

The absence of timely and relevant information was, as previously noted, the most commonly raised complaint among respondents. If effort is made to improve communication through HRDC, allied social service agencies, and/or recreation agencies and businesses, this promotional information should be presented in verbal as well as written form in order to reach adults with differing literacy competencies. Statistics Canada (2001) reports that over 20% of adults living in Canada have major literacy limitations, and another 25% have minor to moderate limitations. Together, these two groups comprise nearly half of the adult population in Canada.

Many of these literacy issues can be traced to language barriers, suggesting the importance of communicating in languages other than English. For example, local media have reported that high schools in Waterloo Region, the area in which data for the present study were drawn, currently serve a collective student body with over 60 first languages (Johnson Tew, Havitz, & McCarville, 1999). Although ethnic diversity was limited in the current sample, unemployed adults are generally drawn from recent immigrant populations in disproportionate numbers. Seasonal leisure services brochures from Waterloo Region municipal agencies are currently available only in English. While the translation and production of brochures into 60 different languages is clearly impractical, it may be possible to select and publish in a couple of languages most prevalent in the local community. In addition, it would seem very feasible to recruit volunteers fluent in languages common to the community to meet and counsel (face-to-face, by telephone, or by audio recording) individuals who cannot read, understand, or successfully navigate English language brochures that promote recreation programs. In our study, Surplus People, Rovers, and Networkers are the three subgroups who faced the most imposing literacy and language-based constraints to participation.

Promotion is essentially an exercise in communication (Crompton & Lamb, 1986). It is generally accepted that agency-based communication tasks include at least four purposes: to inform, to educate, to persuade, and to remind. Municipal recreation agencies are advised to incorporate, as appropriate, all four of these communication tasks into promotional efforts (Johnson Tew et al., 1999). However, promotion to unemployed adults may be especially challenging. The data presented here with respect to mood states, life satisfaction, feelings of isolation, and degree of frustration with daily routines, in conjunction with oft-repeated statements regarding lack-of-entitlement, indicate that unemployed adults are not readily receptive to communication about recreation programs.

The middle two tasks of communication—education and persuasion—are paramount in this regard. Johnson Tew et al.'s (1999) and Johnson Tew and Havitz's (2002) research indicated that little agency-based promotion stresses benefits of recreation to citizens in general, let alone those who are unemployed. It is important to develop and effectively articulate benefits of recreation that are specific to unemployed populations and their dependants. Rovers and Surplus People appear to be especially challenging subgroups with respect to this issue, in part because their limited social networks prevent them from receiving much word-of-mouth information. In addition, Efficacy-Seekers commonly spoke about "lack of entitlement" issues; dispelling this notion must be part of any persuasive communication to that group.

It is clear that communicating with unemployed populations raises particular challenges for municipal and not-for-profit recreation agencies. Although political and economic reality may dictate the continued use of English brochures, we believe that this form of communication will not be wholly effective for this population, particularly when messages about recreation programs are buried deep in descriptive promotional material. Non-English brochures, verbal communication, and messages that address the tasks of education and persuasion will be necessary if these agencies are to effectively promote their recreation programs to a broader cross-section of unemployed citizens.

Program Development and Delivery, and Customer Value Issues

Data collected in this research suggest that the development of recreation programs specifically for unemployed adults, with very few exceptions, is not desired, necessary, or even appropriate. Integration with existing programs is much preferred since it parallels recreation access participants may have had prior to becoming unemployed and provides the same opportunities that are available to other citizens in the community. Access to the full range of existing programs allows unemployed individuals the freedom to participate at the desired skill level and with individuals of their own choosing. Having made that point, programs specifically for unemployed adults which address issues of "a lack of entitlement" and "wasting time" are important first steps in programming for this population. As previously noted, counselling that integrates career education with leisure education would ideally suit this purpose. Attending to such issues as a perceived lack of entitlement, which may forestall active efforts to find meaningful recreation outlets, could allow unemployed adults to more fully explore available recreation programs as well as possible price discounts for those programs.

Having noted the manner in which marketing mix elements may apply to the provision of leisure services to the unemployed, we now turn more specifically to potentially appropriate program offerings based upon the group and subgroup breakdown developed within this study.

Participant Categorization: Implications for Local Service Providers

Based upon the preceding analysis, the following generalizations about potentially appropriate and beneficial leisure programs for each of our groups and the related subgroups have been drawn from the interview and ESM data:

Planners

Routinizers especially value physical activities and fitness programs for the discipline and regimentation that they provide. Programs with a predominantly social orientation are a tougher sell to these people since issues surrounding stigmatizaion are paramount and may cause social withdrawal. Price subsidy will be necessary for Routinizers, especially over the long term. Anti-Homebodies value opportunities that allow them to escape the home environment and socialize with other adults. Program opportunities for dependants are also important. Money is not the major issue for this subgroup. Efficacy-Seekers have an especially difficult time reconciling any need for recreation with their current jobless status; subsequently, they experience considerable guilt in leisure contexts. There is evidence that fitness-related and social programs may be especially valuable for members of this group, provided they can be persuaded to enroll.

Vacationers

Breaking Ins consistently reported watching too much television and tended toward passive lifestyles. Fitness programs would probably be appropriate but would be a difficult sell unless they provided the social interaction that is both valued and sought by this subgroup. In Controls were prone to volunteer, suggesting that social service organizations may find it fruitful to recruit among this segment. Emphasis on skill usage and the social aspects of volunteering may be successful, as the social networks of In Controls were relatively diffuse and inaccessible. Vacationers were adept at getting by on limited budgets, suggesting that fee subsidies would not be a significant issue for members of this group.

Connectors

Program access for dependent children is the dominant theme among Caregivers. Many members of this group would welcome programmed opportunities for improving self-esteem or providing a social respite from caregiving duties. Fee subsidies will be an important issue as very few Caregivers had means of financial support beyond their unemployment insurance. Networkers already participated in many voluntary activities, especially those connected with church and their children. To the extent that voluntary and organized religious agencies and organizations co-operate with employment-related agencies, this group is likely to be well served. Beyond those two contexts, however, fee support may often be a key issue for ensuring long-term recreation participation. Fitness activities comprise a smaller part of Connectors' leisure repertoires in comparison to other groups. Promotion of this type of activity to Connectors would likely be challenging at best.

Marginalized People

Solitary, loosely scheduled fitness activities would generally be well received by Rovers. Social activity, though needed, must be presented on a laissez-faire rather than a regimented basis. Rovers seem unlikely to buy into programs emphasizing "happy party games," nor are they likely to sign up for programs that require up-front long-term commitment. Fee support was not as big an issue for this subgroup in comparison to other Marginalized People since Rovers tended to be rather self-sufficient. Nevertheless, monetary constraints were apparent. Surplus People, though not highly educated, were favourably disposed to adult education programming. Fee support will be a big issue for them. Many Surplus People were fitness drop-outs or were struggling to maintain regular participation patterns, but would likely pick up such activities if properly supported, especially financially. Due to their interactions with various health professions, resulting from a variety of psychological and somatic complaints, medical support agencies are also likely to be important in effectively communicating to Surplus People the importance of continued physical and social activity. Lonely People craved social contact, especially with significant others. Their preferred leisure venues—movies and shopping—are provided most often in commercial sector contexts, creating a major challenge for social service agencies wishing to serve this group. As was the case with Surplus People, medical support agencies are also likely to be important communication conduits for the Lonely subgroup. Lastly, fee support will be important for Lonely People.

As is clear, segmenting the "unemployed market" by bases beyond demographic characteristics yields far greater insights into potential approaches for marketing and programming. The above discussion offers unique suggestions for reaching and effectively serving each of these subgroups of people; however, we understand that recreation centre directors lack specific knowledge about which subgroups are predominant in the local community. Our point is not to encourage isolated efforts that target one subgroup; rather, we emphasize the need for variety when serving this population—variety in times of day, variety in types of programs, variety in modes of communication. Using a mix of approaches and strategies as described above will best capture and serve this diverse population of unemployed individuals.

Provincial or Territorial, and Federal Action

In addition to the largely local-level action that has been described, there are efforts that may be taken at the provincial and federal levels in order to facilitate the provision of adequate recreation services to unemployed individuals. In Canada, the framework for provincial, territorial, and federal involvement in recreation provision was laid out in the *National Recreation Statement* of 1987 (Interprovincial Sport and Recreation Council, 1987), a document that details the responsibilities assumed by each level of government, and that provides a mechanism for co-operative efforts. Indeed, it is acknowledged that "the resources and the co-operation of all jurisdictions, as well as a wide variety of private and community agencies, are required to meet the recreation needs of all citizens" (Interprovincial Sport and Recreation Council, p. 6). Although neither provincial nor federal levels of government are charged with direct responsibility for providing leisure services or programs, each has assumed a role with respect to co-ordinating, financing, and facilitating recreation provision at the municipal level.

A primary responsibility assumed by the provinces and territories is spelled out in section 2.2.4 of the *National Recreation Statement* (Interprovincial Sport and Recreation Council, 1987, p. 8), which suggests that each province and territory should "observe and analyse recreation trends and issues ..., to alert municipalities to these trends and issues ... and to introduce, where necessary, new, broad provincial/territorial policies and legislation." Clearly, a trend identified through previous research into the experience of unemployment— and reinforced through the results of this study—is the often dismal leisure lifestyle of unemployed individuals and their correspondingly limited quality of life. It seems incumbent upon those at the provincial and territorial level of government to adequately address this persistent trend, and to develop policies that prevent unemployed people from suffering the dearth of leisure opportunity and engagement that has been often noted. Furthermore, it is imperative that provincial and territorial governments co-ordinate their efforts with municipal agencies so that any policies enacted have the possibility of succeeding at the local level.

Support for such collaborative initiatives is provided in the *National Recreation Statement* which declares that each province and territory should provide resources to municipalities such as "incentive grants ... that assist with the training of full-time, part-time and volunteer leaders, and that encourage new, supportive consulting services" (Interprovincial Sport and Recreation Council, 1987, p. 9). As has been pointed out, many unemployed individuals in our sample contend with two prominent issues in relation to leisure: a lack of information about community services and amenities, and the feeling that they are not entitled to leisure or recreation during a period of joblessness. Both of these problems may be alleviated to some extent through the establishment of leisure education programs, which would ideally be established at the municipal level with the financial and technical support of the provincial or territorial government. While certainly not a panacea for the range of hurdles unemployed individuals have to overcome, this represents a reasonable starting point for improving attitudes toward leisure, knowledge about leisure opportunities, and, consequently, the quality of life of unemployed people.

Although primary responsibility for the co-ordination and distribution of leisure services lies within the provincial or territorial and municipal governments, there is still a role for the federal government to play. Particularly with respect to policies supporting the creation of new initiatives to assist unemployed people in maintaining an adequate leisure lifestyle, the federal government is well suited to facilitating information exchange and co-ordinating efforts undertaken by other governmental units. One major role of the federal government is "developing and circulating nationally ... resource materials which will encourage individuals to participate in recreation activities" (Interprovincial Sport and Recreation Council, 1987, p. 12). Thus, both provincial, territorial, and federal agencies seem to have a role to play in the leisure education of unemployed people. Since federal co-operation with the provinces and territories is an avowed goal of the *National Recreation Statement*, if governments were to follow their own mandate in this respect, effective interventions that improve the lives of the unemployed seem quite plausible. Specifically, should the federal government seriously pursue "increased opportunities to work co-operatively in establishing ... initiatives for joint projects and activities" (Interprovincial Sport and Recreation Council, p. 13), it would be taking an important step toward improving the lot of unemployed Canadians.

We have pointed out a number of times in the preceding pages that the primary institutional contact for many of the unemployed is the Human Resources Development Centre (local job centres, or *centres d'emploi* in Quebec). It seems natural that such centres play at least some role as a conduit for recreation-related information; leisure counselling and education would effectively complement existing career counselling services offered through the HRDC. Thus, in line with the federal responsibilities outlined in the *National Recreation Statement*, there seems to be room for local job centres to initiate relationships with federal departments such as the HRDC in order to establish programs at the local level.

Although co-operative endeavours between municipal, provincial, and federal agencies would be a good start, there are some institutional barriers that may militate against the development of such arrangements. Leisure is seemingly anathema to those whose primary responsibility is to help unemployed individuals find new work. Any co-operative effort would have to contend with an established culture within HRDC that affords no room for activities that aren't work related. Indeed, as a condition for collecting Employment Insurance (EI), unemployed individuals must remain constantly willing to work and be actively seeking work. That is, the HRDC mandates that re-employment-related activities—or at very least availability for work—

be vigilantly maintained lest one's entitlements be reduced. If some-one collecting EI spent a Tuesday in August hiking through a park with his or her child, that fact must be communicated to the HRDC on a bi-weekly work report; subsequently, his or her EI cheque would be reduced to reflect the less-than-total willingness and availability to work during each day. So, while it would be ideal if the HRDC were persuaded to broaden its horizons through advocacy on behalf of fed-eral agencies responsible for recreation, such change would not be easily accomplished or even possible in the short term.

Several other problems may discourage meaningful collaboration between recreation agencies and non-recreation-related government agencies at the federal level. While the "mechanism for co-operation" discussed in the *National Recreation Statement* provides a frame-work for how the many government units fit together (Interprovin-cial Sport and Recreation Council, 1987), there is no inducement to develop relationships beyond the existing network of government agencies that are directly responsible for recreation. Compounding this problem is the recent abdication by the federal government of any serious consideration of recreation in favour of an increased emphasis upon sport. Though the *Canadian Sport Policy* avowedly "builds on the National Recreation Statement" (Sport Canada, 2002, p. 3), in fact it appears to tear down many of the significant elements fostering recreational activities that don't involve sports. Thus, given the federal government's increased emphasis on sport to the exclusion of other recreation opportunities, there would seem to be little hope that collaborative endeavours will be undertaken to increase the leisure well-being and the quality of life of unemployed people. A first step would be to have the federal government reinvolve itself in recreation. Were the federal government to produce a companion vol-ume to the *Canadian Sport Policy* that specifically details federal responsibility in the domain of recreation, it would provide a stronger framework for action. Without such a framework, the federal govern-ment seems only minimally willing and almost wholly unable to pro-mote recreation among Canadians regardless of whatever employment status.

Conclusion

In the preceding section we have tried to link many of the findings of this study and previous research with existing approaches to facilitat-ing leisure opportunities for people who are unemployed. We have noted that recreation provision for this population is rather inadequate: while issues related to accessibility and cost have been given some attention, greater consideration to each element of the marketing mix is required if real gains are to be made. Furthermore, while provincial, territorial, and federal government agencies have assumed roles in the recreation delivery system, each has fallen short with respect to meeting the needs of unemployed individuals. The existing piecemeal approaches are not enough; what is required is greater collaboration between all levels of government and greater attention to the recreation needs of all Canadians, each of whom has an equal right to leisure opportunities.

In this vein, agencies such as HRDC, whose primary responsibilities do not include recreation, may be reluctant to enlarge their mandate. However, given the interrelationship between leisure and other domains of life such as work and family, this seems narrow-minded. As we have seen, what unemployed individuals do for leisure has serious repercussions for their physical and psychological well-being, and this directly affects their willingness and ability to engage in work-related activities. It seems reasonable to suggest that agencies involved in the re-employment of unemployed individuals at the very least should not stand in the way of the pursuit of leisure opportunity, and, at best, should take special pains to ensure that people who are unemployed have the required resources, skills, and attitudes to pursue and engage in leisure pursuits.

In short, it is high time that serious attention be paid to the means and mechanisms by which leisure opportunity is made available to the unemployed. Leisure activity is not at cross purposes with the goal of securing gainful employment; indeed, it may very well facilitate that process. When policy-makers and practitioners recognize this fact and adjust their operations accordingly, and a greater number of unemployed people have access to and an appreciation of leisure, society in general will benefit.

Note

1 It is important to note here that members of this sample did not necessarily view leisure and recreation as synonymous. The ESM questionnaire included items related to both recreation and leisure. Recreation was measured as categorical data (a particular episode was either recreation or was something else) whereas leisure was measured, as noted earlier, on an interval scale where one pole was designated as definitely not leisure and the other was definitely leisure. Glover (1998) analyzed this section of the data and concluded, "not surprisingly, recreational activities were perceived to be more

leisurely than nonrecreational activities" (p. 3). However, some gender-based differences were apparent. Women were more likely than men to blur the distinctions between leisure and recreation. The bottom line of this analysis is that it may be problematic to assume that organized recreation programming will be received by unemployed adults in the same manner as unstructured or, for that matter, structured leisure activity.

8 Summary, Conclusion, and Future Directions

O ver the course of this book, we have covered a fair amount of ground—both conceptually and methodologically. Through an examination of interview transcripts from five dozen people, we developed a categorization scheme that vividly depicted several distinct "segments" of the unemployed population. From our initial four-group breakdown that categorized respondents on the basis of their dominant perceptions of, or reactions to, unemployment, to the subsequent refinement of these groups into two or three distinct subgroups apiece, the qualitative portion of this study provided ample evidence of the diversity of experiences for people who are unemployed. Our discussion highlights the heuristic as well as practical benefits of understanding that this population is composed of a number of relatively distinct "market segments." In addition, analysis of the quantitative data provided by mail-back questionnaires and Experience Sampling provided further insight into the experiences of unemployed individuals. Although the ESM and mail-back data for the most part confirmed our original analysis, these data occasionally provided evidence contrary to some conclusions we had reached on the basis of the qualitative data and, as such, were invaluable additions to our understanding of the meanings and experiences inherent in unemployment. In addition, by allowing a detailed look at the contextually and temporally bound emotional states of our participants, we were able to derive a more complete picture of the moment-by-moment experience of currently jobless individuals.

That said, in the foregoing chapters we have taken care to avoid suggesting that the groups and subgroups identified in this study are necessarily found in other communities and situations. We do, however, believe that populations of unemployed adults are heterogeneous with respect to demographic, attitudinal, and behavioural circumstance. In that sense, our participants are not unlike what might be found in other community contexts. Thus, we feel it is of value to revisit and highlight some of the more salient findings of this study.

The preceding chapters have documented the negative characteristics of unemployment, including financial constraints, lack of structure, social isolation, reduced self- esteem, and stigma. One might expect that recreation and leisure, if financially accessible, could ameliorate these negative experiences associated with being unemployed. However, the ESM portion of the study revealed that these unemployed participants were often homebound, were often engaged in tasks related to home and family, were often alone or not interacting even if others were present, often had low mood states, and were often in contexts distinctly described as "not leisure." Again, the caveat must be made that such overarching generalizations do not apply to all individuals in this study, let alone to all unemployed people. However, these results seem, for the most part, to corroborate the interview results and, when taken with a grain of salt, seem to represent majority opinion about the experience of joblessness.

Several reasons account for the relative dearth of activity beyond the home environment, and the dearth of leisure activity in particular. First, many of our participants' options were limited by either financial constraint or an unwillingness to spend money on leisure opportunities. The latter was certainly a matter of personal priority, but for a number of our participants infrequent leisure participation stemmed from a lack of a sense of entitlement to leisure while unemployed. Furthermore, even when willing, many participants expressed difficulty accessing available and affordable leisure opportunities. They lacked information concerning recreation offerings in the community and, even when aware of leisure services, were unaware of low-income subsidies for recreation or felt that the process required to access these subsidies was potentially belittling or stigmatizing. As a result, many participants tended to withdraw from, or avoid, leisure and social situations.

It bears repeating that these conclusions do not apply to all participants in this study. However, the relative degree to which each was expressed helped us understand the similarities among individuals' experiences and, as such, helped us consolidate our understanding of many of the common threads of unemployment—common threads which were interwoven within each of our groups and subgroups. With that in mind, we suggest that these factors not be overlooked in future research in this area. Our sample was diverse with respect to gender, age, education, and pre- and post-unemployment family income, and that diversity was reflected in their varied responses to unemployment. We recommend that these issues be explored in future academic research and be taken in to consideration by social and leisure service agencies wishing to work with people who are unemployed. In addition, ethnicity, race, and religion represent key variables that could influence people's experience in unemployment, but the relative homogeneity of our sample prevented us from fully exploring those factors. Nevertheless, though sociodemographic data represent an important starting point, by themselves they are insufficient for understanding the diversity of experiences in unemployment.

Behavioural data provided an important basis for understanding the unemployed lives of these participants. Behavioural data are relatively easy to collect using ESM, for example, or other established research methods such as time diaries. As shown here, ESM provided a glimpse of the types of activities engaged in and the associated social contexts and moods of the participants. In addition, the "walk me through a typical day" question from the interview also provided invaluable information about when individuals typically slept, when they awoke, how they structured their day, how they got around, and what types and amounts of volunteer, family support, and household activity were common. Much of the most valuable data used in developing our group and subgroup categorization were collected in response to the "typical day" line of questioning. The ESM data provided important evidence to corroborate the findings of those interviews.

Attitudinal measures are also important to segmentation efforts, yet are often the most difficult data to access. In this study we collected attitudinal data using a variety of methods. The semi-structured interview allowed interviewers to gather attitudinal information in conjunction with the behavioural data just discussed. For example, it was important to know how respondents felt about their daily routines, leisure activities and constraints, time for themselves, contact with others, and so forth. The standardized scales for self-esteem, life satisfaction, leisure boredom, and perceived freedom in leisure that we used in our mail-back questionnaire provided additional attitudinal data. These scales have been widely used in a variety of contexts and remain available for future use. It seems possible, as well, that reliable and valid scaling could be developed for other salient attitudes related to unemployment. For example, items related to daily planning and perceptions of stigmatization seem relatively straightforward to compile and test, and would be useful additions to the quantitative data reported here. Such measures would likely assist social service agencies in segmentation efforts but, like all such scaling, would require ongoing vigilance and periodic updates in order to achieve desirable levels of validity for use with people who are unemployed.

It is important to point out that any study of leisure and unemployment aims to understand a complex and often moving target. Furthermore, unlike other segments of society commonly served by social service and leisure service agencies, such as older adults, youth, and children, the number of unemployed adults is seldom predictable, especially in the mid- to long-range future. Indeed, unemployment rates were high when this study was undertaken, dropped for several years, and then rose significantly as the book neared completion. The unpredictable nature of both the source and scope of unemployment makes service planning and efforts at service provision difficult. Compounding this inherent difficulty is the fact that service requirements will generally be greatest at times when agency resources are at their lowest, because high unemployment will often result in lower tax revenues for various government agencies. Although property tax revenues, the major source of revenue for local government agencies, may remain reasonably stable during times of economic downturn, income tax and sales tax revenues, mainstays of provincial and federal budgets, often diminish to a greater extent. Circuitously, then, local government agencies often feel the pinch as transfer payments are reduced. It seems prudent, therefore, to finance programming efforts for people who are unemployed in much the same manner as unemployment benefits themselves are funded. Money must be set aside in good times in anticipation that resources will be available when times are bad. It is beyond the scope of this study, however, to propose specific measures that might make this possible, and we leave it for future policy-makers to contemplate the means to implement such safeguards.

Concluding Thoughts

As noted many times in this study, the diverse nature of experience among people who are unemployed greatly complicates program planning and delivery. We believe that our look into the daily lives of five dozen unemployed adults, through the application of a diverse set of methods, will move the literature forward in several ways. First, our use of multiple methodologies expands the means for studying people who are unemployed. Each method produced rich insights into a different facet of their lives, and together these methods formed an important framework for triangulating and testing our emerging understanding. It is our hope that similar multi-method approaches will be used in future research in this field.

In addition, by categorizing participants into groups and subgroups based on similarities in their experience of unemployment, we effectively performed market segmentation as is done in analyses of other consumer populations. This exercise led to a more complex understanding of how best to serve these diverse groups. Our suggestions for developing, marketing, and managing policies and services for unemployed adults is a new contribution to both research on unemployment and literature on leisure services. We believe that understanding and respecting diversity among any group of people is a necessary prerequisite if we are to design services that truly meet their desires and needs. It is our hope that this research will encourage further study of issues related to unemployment and leisure, and that the accumulated evidence will both encourage and empower leisure service professionals to act in a more proactive manner with respect to their unemployed constituents.

Phase 1 Initial Interview Guide

ID#: _____

Interviewer: _____

Initial Interview Schedule—Unemployed

I would like to tape record our conversation to help me remember what you have to say, but I'll do so only with your permission. Is it alright with you if I turn on the tape recorder? We will turn it off if you begin to feel uncomfortable. [*Turn on tape recorder.*]

Just for the record, is it okay to be taping this interview?

Part I: Introduction

Could you start us off by telling me a little bit about yourself?
Who is [*name*] _____ ? What should we know about you?

Probes

    Do you live alone? Are there any children in your household?
    What are their ages?
    Is your husband/wife/partner employed? Doing what?
    How long have you lived in the Kitchener–Waterloo area?
    Do you have other family living near here?
    Does this feel like "home" to you?
    Do you feel like you have a strong social network of friends?
    Do most of them live in the Kitchener–Waterloo area?

Part II: Employment History

I understand that you are currently unemployed. Where had you been working? What did you do there?

Probes

    Was that a pretty good job for you?
    Had you worked there very long? [*If less than 12 months at that job determine if there was another period of unemployment in past 12 months*]

Becoming Unemployed
Tell me about losing your job. What happened?

Probes
How much notice did you have that you might be losing your job?
I know you miss the income. Is there anything else that you miss because you no longer have that job?
What do you think will happen next? Do you have your eye on another job yet?
Had anything like this ever happened to you before? Have you been unemployed before?

Social Stigma and Relationships
Do you feel that being unemployed has affected your relationships with your family?

Probes
Have things changed negatively or positively? Could you describe how?
Has being unemployed affected your relationships with your friends?

Probes
How? Why?
Do you still see friends from work? What is that like? What do you do when you see them?

Part III: Daily Routine

I'd like to know what a typical day is like for you now. Could you take me through one of your days, from the time you get up until you go to bed at night. For example, tell me about yesterday. [Note: *make it a weekday.*]

Probes
What time did you get up?
What did you do then?

[Note: *Do not introduce or name a specific activity in your questions; ask generic probes and let them define activities.*]

Is that a pretty typical day for you right now?

Changes
Compare the day you just described to a day from your life a few weeks or months ago, before you lost your job. How have your days changed?

Probes
How do you feel about these changes? Things you don't like?

Special Events
Are there special events that you regularly look forward to during the day or the week?
What are they? What is special about that—what happens that makes you like it?

Part IV: Recreation

Back before you knew you were going to lose your job, what did you do in your free time?

Probes

Did you do that often? Was it important to you? Why did you do that?
Are there certain types of things you like to do in your free time?

Probes

What do you like about them? Why do you think you do them?
Has your free time changed very much because of your unemployment? How? Why?

Probes

[*For* "given up" *activities*]: Why don't you still do that?
[*For* "new" *activities*]: Why do you think you didn't do that before?
Do you spend your free time with the same people as you did before becoming unemployed?

Probes

[*For* "No"] Who do spend time with now? Why do you think you don't see some of your other friends? How do you feel about this change?
[*For* "Yes"] How is it being with these friends? Are they unemployed too?
Do you intentionally plan times or activities just for yourself, like time for hobbies or sports, or just leisure time for yourself?

Probes

[*If* "Yes"]: What do you do?
[*If* "No"]: Why not?
Are there regular activities that you like to do, like a ball team or a club?

Part V: Other

When you look back on it, what will have been the worst thing about being unemployed right now?

When you become employed again, is there anything about this time right now that you will regret having to give up? Will there be anything hard about going back to work?

Do you know many other people who are unemployed right now?

Is there anything else I should know in order to understand your daily life right now?

Part VI: Demographics

The following section asks questions which will provide information that will allow us to describe participants as a group. Please understand that all responses will remain confidential. You may choose not to answer any individual question.

From the categories on this card [*show card*] would you tell me the letter that indicates your:

Your age

Your education

Approximate household income before you became unemployed

Racial/Ethnic background

Date: _____ Time signaled: _____ Time filled out: _____

1. Where were you at the time of the signal?

   ☐ at home
   ☐ at a friend's house
   ☐ at work or school
   ☐ at recreation site
   ☐ in a store or office
   ☐ other: _____

2. Briefly, describe that situation in a few words: _____

3. Was the *main* thing you were doing:

   ☐ family/home related
   ☐ personal care
   ☐ employment related
   ☐ recreation
   ☐ other types of tasks
   ☐ other: _____

4. How *involved* were you in what you were doing:

   ☐ entirely; I wasn't paying attention to anything else at that time
   ☐ mostly; but I was putting some attention to other things too
   ☐ only partially; my mind was on other things at the same time

5. Was there a time limit, so that you had to do something else soon?

   ☐ no; I didn't feel any pressure of time
   ☐ partially; I knew I had to do some other things in a while
   ☐ very much; I was monitoring the clock because of other commitments

6. Who was with you? (*Check as many as apply*)

   ☐ no one
   ☐ my spouse/partner
   ☐ child(ren)

6. (*continued*)
   ☐ friend/relative(s)
   ☐ other adults _____
   ☐ pet(s)

7. Were you talking, listening, or otherwise interacting with anyone?
   ☐ no
   ☐ yes, primarily task related; formal
   ☐ yes, social but somewhat formal
   ☐ yes, casual or intimate

8. Think about how you were *feeling* at the time of the signal, and indicate below:

I was *feeling*:

Happy	1	2	3	4	5	Unhappy
Bored	1	2	3	4	5	Involved
Relaxed	1	2	3	4	5	Anxious
Irritable	1	2	3	4	5	Good-humoured

9. Think about *what was happening* at the time you were beeped. For each of the following statements, circle the response that best describes that situation.

	Strongly Disagree						Strongly Agree
I was doing that because I felt I should or ought to do it	−3	−2	−1	0	1	2	3
I liked what I was doing	−3	−2	−1	0	1	2	3
I was concerned about what others thought of me	−3	−2	−1	0	1	2	3
That is something that interests me a lot	−3	−2	−1	0	1	2	3
I was fulfilling some of my responsibilities	−3	−2	−1	0	1	2	3
I was really enjoying doing that	−3	−2	−1	0	1	2	3
I was doing that because it was expected of me	−3	−2	−1	0	1	2	3
I am confident that was the right activity for me to be doing right now	−3	−2	−1	0	1	2	3
I would call that leisure	−3	−2	−1	0	1	2	3
I was aware of how I appeared to others	−3	−2	−1	0	1	2	3
My doing that gives a glimpse of the type of person I really am	−3	−2	−1	0	1	2	3

▼

9. (*continued*)

	Strongly Disagree						Strongly Agree
I had expected to be doing that about this time today	−3	−2	−1	0	1	2	3
I was interested in making a good impression on others	−3	−2	−1	0	1	2	3
I feel good about myself right now	−3	−2	−1	0	1	2	3
I will be annoyed if that proves to be a poor use of my time	−3	−2	−1	0	1	2	3

What else would you like to mention about this situation: _____

Fill this out at the end of the day:

11. Of everything that happened today, what was the one situation that was the best part of the day for you?

12. What was so special about that situation?

13. Is there anything else you want to mention about today?

Phase 1 Follow-up Interview Guide

ID#: _____

Interviewer: _____

Follow-up interview schedule

Collect the pager and the ESM booklet

[*Briefly talk with them about the ESM process and how things went during the week. Write a brief summary of their comments in your field notes.*]

Get permission to tape the following section:

I would like to tape record our conversation to help me remember what you have to say, but I'll do so only with your permission. Is it alright with you if I turn on the tape recorder? We will turn it off at any time if you begin to feel uncomfortable. [*Turn on tape recorder.*]

Just for the record, is it okay to be taping this interview?

Part I: Involvement with Leisure and Nonleisure Activities

Think back to the situations when you were beeped in the past week. Can you name one situation, more than any of the others, that you considered leisure?

[*Help them find the situation in the booklet. Check to confirm that they checked a "3" for that situation on the "I would call that leisure" question. If they did not check a "3" for that question, find another question that meets the criteria. Record their comments about the chosen situation along with the date and time in your field notes.*]

Think back to the situations when you were beeped in the past week. Can you name one situation, more than any of the others, that you considered *not* to be leisure?

[*Help them find the situation in the booklet. Check to confirm that they checked a "−3" for that situation on the "I would call that leisure"*

question. If they did not check a "−3" for that question, find another
question that meets the criteria. Record their comments about the chosen
situaiton along with the date and time in your field notes.]

Part II: Mail Back Questionnaire

[*Give respondents a copy of the mail-back questionnaire (and postage-
paid envelope). Remind them that completion of the questionnaire will
be the last task associated with Phase 1. Remind them that the Phase 1
prize drawings will occur in July and that they will be notified regardless
of whether they win. Encourage them to stick with us in Phase 2, which
will begin in late August/early September. Thank them for their help!*]

Daily Activities Study

Dear Participant # _____ :

Thank you for your participation in this study. Completing this question-naire is our final request at this time. The questions within this booklet ask about your work, your leisure, and your outlook on life. Your answers will provide important opinions that will help us interpret the information from the beeper study. Many sections of this questionnaire contain items used by other researchers. Even though some questions may seem similar, please answer each question as carefully as you can.

The ID number at the top of this page will help us match your answers here with the information you provided during the beeper study and inter-view. Your name will never be associated with this information, and all of your answers are completely confidential. A postage-paid envelope has been provided so that you can mail back the completed questionnaire. Please return the completed questionnaire in the next day or two.

When we receive the questionnaire, your name will be entered again into the grand prize drawing, increasing your chances of winning one of our prizes. That drawing is simply one way we can show our appreciation for the help you have offered by participating in this study. Thank you again for your prompt return of this questionnaire.

Sincerely,

Mark E. Havitz, Ph.D.
Department of Recreation and Leisure Studies
University of Waterloo
Telephone: 885-1211, Ext. 3013

And your interviewer, _____

Part A

Please indicate, in the spaces provided, the three leisure activities that you feel are most important to you. Place the most important activity in the first space, the next most important in the second space, and the activity deemed next important in the third space. Also, please indicate how often you participate in each activity.

Most Important Leisure Activities

Activity 1 _____ _____ times per month

Activity 2 _____ _____ times per month

Activity 3 _____ _____ times per month

What factors (if any) limit your participation in those activities? Do you participate as often as you like? If not, why not?

Activity 1 _____

Activity 2 _____

Activity 3 _____

Where do you most often participate in those activities?

Activity 1 _____

Activity 2 _____

Activity 3 _____

Part B

The following questions ask about various aspects of your life. Please read each statement and indicate the extent to which you agree or disagree. Circle "1" if you **strongly disagree** with the statement; circle "5" if you **strongly agree**; or circle one of the other numbers if your answer is somewhere between those extremes.

	Strongly Disagree				Strongly Agree
Having a job is very important to me	1	2	3	4	5
Even if I had a great deal of money, I would want to work anyway	1	2	3	4	5
I often have more things to do than I have time for	1	2	3	4	5
My job is the most important part of who I am	1	2	3	4	5
I am at my best when I am with my family	1	2	3	4	5
I soon get bored when I have no work to do	1	2	3	4	5
Little of my free time is actually leisure	1	2	3	4	5
My family often takes up just too much time	1	2	3	4	5

▼

Part B *(continued)*

	Strongly Disagree				Strongly Agree
It would be hard for me to move into a different line of work	1	2	3	4	5
You'd get a more accurate impression of me by observing me in my free time than other times	1	2	3	4	5
In my leisure, I often want to do something but I don't know what to do	1	2	3	4	5
I spend too much of my free time sleeping	1	2	3	4	5
My family and my leisure are one and the same	1	2	3	4	5
During my leisure, I almost always have something to do	1	2	3	4	5
My leisure activities are more satisfying than my job or other aspects of my life	1	2	3	4	5
During my leisure, I usually become highly involved in what I am doing	1	2	3	4	5
My leisure is boring	1	2	3	4	5
I often find myself just "killing time"	1	2	3	4	5
My work often feels like leisure to me	1	2	3	4	5
I express myself better in my free-time activities than at home or in my job	1	2	3	4	5

Notes related to Section B [These notes were not included on the original questionnaire.]:

Items 1, 2, and 6 are from Warr, Cook, and Wall's (1979) job importance scale.

Items 3, 7, and 18 are from Neulinger and Breit's (1969) perceived freedom in leisure scale.

Items 10, 15, and 20 are from Neulinger and Breit's (1969) self-definition through leisure scale.

Items 4, 9, and 19 are from Samdahl's (1991) career socialization scale.

Items 5, 8, and 13 are from Samdahl's (1991) family and leisure scale.

Items 11, 12, 14, 16, and 17 are from Iso-Ahola and Weissinger's (1990) Leisure Boredom Scale.

Part C

The following questions ask about your recreation. Please read each statement and indicate the extent to which you agree or disagree with it. Circle "1" if you **strongly disagree** with the statement; circle "5" if you **strongly agree**; or circle one of the other numbers if your answer is somewhere between those extremes.

	Strongly Disagree				Strongly Agree
My recreation activities help me feel important	1	2	3	4	5
I know many recreation activities that are fun to do	1	2	3	4	5
I can do things to improve the skills of the of the people I do recreation activities	1	2	3	4	5
I have the skills to do the recreation activities in which I want to participate	1	2	3	4	5
Sometimes during a recreation activity there are short periods when the activity is going so well that I feel I can do anything	1	2	3	4	5
It is easy for me to choose a recreation activity in which to participate	1	2	3	4	5
I can do things during recreation activities that will make other people like me more	1	2	3	4	5
My recreation activities enable me to get to know other people	1	2	3	4	5
I can make a recreation activity as enjoyable as I want it to be	1	2	3	4	5
I can do things during a recreation activity that will enable everyone to have more fun	1	2	3	4	5
I usually decide with whom I do recreation activities	1	2	3	4	5
I'm good at recreation activities I do with other people	1	2	3	4	5
I am good at almost all the recreation activities I do	1	2	3	4	5
I'm able to be creative during my recreation activities	1	2	3	4	5
I can enable other people to have fun during recreation activities	1	2	3	4	5
During my recreation activities, there are often moments when I feel really involved in what I'm doing	1	2	3	4	5
I can usually persuade people to do recreation activities with me, even if they don't want to	1	2	3	4	5
I can make almost any activity fun for me to do	1	2	3	4	5
I participate in recreation activities which help me to make new friends	1	2	3	4	5

▼

Part C (*continued*)

	Strongly Disagree				Strongly Agree
I can make good things happen when I do recreation activities	1	2	3	4	5
When participating in recreation activities, there are times I really feel in control of what I am doing	1	2	3	4	5
I can do things to make other people enjoy doing activities with me	1	2	3	4	5
When I feel restless, I can do recreation activities that will help me to calm down	1	2	3	4	5
Sometimes when I do recreation activities I get excited about what I am doing	1	2	3	4	5
I usually have a good time when I do recreation activities	1	2	3	4	5

Source: Witt and Ellis's (1985) leisure diagnostic battery

Part D

The following questions ask about how you feel about yourself. Please read each statement and indicate the extent to which you agree or disagree with it. Circle "1" if you **strongly disagree**; circle "5" if you **strongly agree**; or circle one of the other numbers if your answer is somewhere between those extremes.

	Strongly Disagree				Strongly Agree
I take a positive attitude towards myself	1	2	3	4	5
I find myself often wishing I were someone else	1	2	3	4	5
I don't feel that I have much to be proud of	1	2	3	4	5
Most people I know seem to like me	1	2	3	4	5
Basically, I like myself	1	2	3	4	5
I am able to do things as well as most people	1	2	3	4	5
I wish I could have more respect for myself	1	2	3	4	5
I feel that I have a number of good qualities	1	2	3	4	5
I wish my life had turned out differently	1	2	3	4	5
On the whole, I am pretty satisfied with myself	1	2	3	4	5
I certainly feel useless at times	1	2	3	4	5
I get upset too easily	1	2	3	4	5
I'm typically fun to be with	1	2	3	4	5
I typically feel in control of what happens around me	1	2	3	4	5
I feel that I'm a person of worth, at least on an equal basis with others	1	2	3	4	5
At times I think I'm no good at all	1	2	3	4	5
I often get discouraged at what I am doing	1	2	3	4	5

▼

Part D (*continued*)

	Strongly Disagree				Strongly Agree
There isn't much about myself I would change	1	2	3	4	5
I wish I were more confident	1	2	3	4	5
Overall, I'm pretty happy with myself right now	1	2	3	4	5

Sources: Rosenberg (1965); Samdahl (1991)

Part E

The following questions ask you to consider some aspects of your life at the present moment. Please indicate how satisfied you are with each of the following.

How satisfied are you with:	Very Dissatisfied				Very Satisfied
Having a job is very important to me	1	2	3	4	5
Your standard of living; the things you can buy and do	1	2	3	4	5
The house and neighborhood that you live in	1	2	3	4	5
Your present state of health	1	2	3	4	5
Your work and the responsibilities in your life	1	2	3	4	5
What you are accomplishing in life	1	2	3	4	5
What the future seems to hold for you	1	2	3	4	5
Your family life	1	2	3	4	5
Your social life	1	2	3	4	5
The way you spend your free time	1	2	3	4	5
Taking everything together, your life as a whole these days	1	2	3	4	5

Source: Warr, Cook, and Wall's (1979) life satisfaction scale

We are extremely grateful for your willingness to volunteer for this study. Your time and your answers have been very valuable to us. Thank you very much! Please return this questionnaire using the postage-paid envelope we provided.

Phase 2 Initial and Follow-up Interview Guides

ID#: _____

Interviewer: _____

Phase 2 Interview Schedule—Unemployed

I would like to tape record our conversation to help me remember what you have to say, but I'll do so only with your permission. Is it all right with you if I turn on the tape recorder? We will turn it off if you begin to feel uncomfortable. [*Turn on tape recorder.*]

Just for the record, is it okay to be taping this interview?

Part I: Introduction

The last time we interviewed you we asked you a little bit about yourself. Has anything important changed in your family or living arrangements during the past couple months?

Probes

Try to assess if the family situation is the same

Are there still children in your household?

Is your husband/wife/partner still employed? Doing what?

Part II: Employment History

Last time you told us about your last job and how you came to be laid off. Have you found work during these past months, since our last interview?

Probes

[*If found work*] How long were you unemployed? How did you hear about this new job?

For you, is it as good as your last job? Why or why not?

Probes

[*If still unemployed*] Tell me a bit about how you feel. What is it like for you to be unemployed right now?

Last time I asked if you missed anything about your old job and you said _____ . Thinking back on it, do you still miss that? Do you miss anything else?

Social Stigma and Relationships
Do you feel that being unemployed has affected your relationships with your family?

Probes
Have things changed negatively or positively? Could you describe how?
Has being unemployed affected your relationships with your friends? How? Why?
Do you still see friends from work? What is that like? What do you do when you see them?

Part III: Daily Routine
I'd like to know what a typical day is like for you now. Could you take me through one of your days, from the time you get up until you go to bed at night? For example, tell me about yesterday. [Note: *make it a weekday.*]

Probes
What time did you get up? What did you do then?

[Note: *Do not introduce or name a specific activity in your questions; ask generic probes and let them define activities.*]

Is that a pretty typical day for you right now?

Changes
Compare the day you just described to a day from your life the last time we talked, just after you lost your job. Have your days changed?

Probes
How do you feel about these changes?
Are there things about your current routine that you like better? Things you don't like?

Special Events
Are there special events that you regularly look forward to during the day or the week? What are they? What is special about that—what happens that makes you like it?

[*If employed now*]
When you became employed again, was there anything that was hard to give up about having been unemployed? Anything you miss about that period?

Part IV: Recreation
Last time we spoke you told me that your favourite activities were
_____ . Do you still do those things?

What do you do now in your free time? What's fun, or what kind of recreation do you like?

Probes
> What do you like about them? Why do you think you do them? Has your free time changed since we last talked? How? Why?

Probes
> [*For* "given up" *activities*]: Why don't you still do that?
> [*For* "new" *activities*]: Why do you think you didn't do that before?

Do you spend your free time with the same people as you did before becoming unemployed? How about when you were first unemployed?

Probes
> [*For* "No"] Who do spend time with now? Why do you think you don't see some of your other friends? How do you feel about this change?
> [*For* "Yes"] How is it being with these friends? Are they unemployed too?

> Do you intentionally plan times or activities just for yourself, like time for hobbies or sports, or just leisure time for yourself?

Probes
> [*If* "Yes"]: What do you do?
> [*If* "No"]: Why not?

> Are there regularly scheduled activities that you like to do, like a ball team or a club?

Enduring Involvement Questionnaires:

I would like to read some questions about four (three) activities that were mentioned in your "beeper booklet." I will read a series of statements and ask that you respond with the appropriate number from this card. A "3" means you agree completely, "0" means you neither agree nor disagree, and "-3" means you completely disagree. *Please don't* feel that you have to recall anything about a specific situation, we are just interested in the way you usually feel about these activities. Some of the statements may seem a little strange for the activity in question. All we ask is for your best response. [*Allow them to check not applicable for individual items.*]

[*Read the four (or three) enduring involvement questionnaires.*]

Part V: Other

When you look back on it, what will have been the worst thing about being unemployed right now?

When you become employed again (assuming they are planning to work again), is there anything about this time right now that you will regret having to give up? Will there be anything hard about going back to work?

Do you know many other people who are unemployed right now?

From this chart [*show card*] would you tell me the letter of your net (take-home) *monthly household* income right now?

Is there anything else I should know in order to understand your daily life right now?

Follow-Up Interview Schedule

Collect the pager and the ESM booklet

[*Briefly talk with them about the ESM process and how things went during the week. Write a brief summary of their comments in your field notes.*]

Part I: Transition To Unemployment

We are interested in what you can tell us about that period when you were first unemployed. I know it was hard for you. During those first few weeks, was there anything that might have made things easier for you? What could have been done?

Probes

What about filing for unemployment—was that smooth for you?
What about the services at the unemployment centre—how could that process be improved?

As you know, we are particularly interested in what happens to people's recreation and leisure interests when they become unemployed. What are your insights on this? How do you think recreation changes after unemployment?

Do you think recreation and leisure are important for people who are unemployed? Why or why not?

Is there anything that you think could be done by business, government, and/or non-profit agencies to make recreation more readily available for people who are unemployed? Are there activities in which you might participate? How could those things be brought about?

Anything else about any of these topics that you would like to share?

Part II: Mail-Back Questionnaire

[*Give respondents a copy of the mail-back questionnaire (and postage-paid envelope). Remind them that completion of the questionnaire will be the last task associated with Phase 2. Remind them that the Phase 2 prize drawings will occur in November and that they will be notified regardless of whether they win.*]

Appendix F

Detailed Description of Qualitative Data Analysis

A qualitative analysis was undertaken to find themes of similar experiences among the participants, primarily based on information they shared during interviews in Phase 1 of the study. Phase 2 material was, at times, included to supplement information collected during Phase 1. This qualitative analysis was an integral part of the study, for it led to a categorization that shaped subsequent analysis and discussion. As is typical with qualitative analysis, these themes were extracted through extensive, systematic examination of the data. In this study, two researchers independently performed that analysis and then met to discuss their findings, eventually coming to agreement on a classification scheme that best captured similarities and differences among these participants. Their analyses are described below.

Mark's Independent Analysis

Preliminary Data Assessment

Although I had done a fair amount of transcribing for this project and had worked on several preliminary analyses, my concentrated efforts to "get to know" each individual participant began by reading each full transcript twice. This process took several weeks. During the second reading of the full transcripts, I developed summary notes wherein key words and phrases, occasionally supported by short quotes, were compiled to form a basic sketch of each participant. These sketches ranged in length from a minimum of 3 to 5 typewritten lines to a maximum of 2 dozen lines, and averaged 12 to 15 lines per individual.

Descriptive analyses of the data, done for our unpublished ministry report and other preliminary work (e.g., Samdahl and Havitz, 1996; Havitz, Samdahl, and Whyte, 1996), also informed this stage of the research. However, as predicted, our early attempts at univariate analyses (e.g., isolating individual independent or dependent variables such as age, gender, or Phase 2 employment status) generally led to frustration as the analyses consistently failed to capture shared meaning with respect to the experiences of the broad group of participants. Nevertheless, numerous sensitizing concepts were revealed in the literature and in these preliminary analyses, many of which proved useful in subsequent analyses. Sensitizing concepts included living arrangement (not partnered, partner employed, partner unemployed), extended family support, presence of parents, presence of young children in household, presence of older children in household, degree of daily and weekly routine including job search, leisure, family-related activity, friendship network support, care giving, presence of pets in the household, self-esteem, depression, pressure to find work, guilt, relocation/move, substance abuse, financial pressure/lack of money, boredom, perceived contribution to family and society, age and life stage, gender, race/ethnicity, Phase 2 employment status, and education level. Some concepts, such as perceived financial pressure, were ubiquitous to the point of providing little information to differentiate between individual respondents (although degree of perceived financial pressure varied to some extent). Others, such as family conflict and substance abuse, seemed particularly important to some individuals but were non-issues for others. I was especially mindful of Strauss' (1987) suggestions regarding conditions specified by respondents (as a result of, because of, and so forth), interactions or lack thereof with other people, respondent strategies and tactics (such as job searching first thing in the morning), and perceived consequences and outcomes as expressed by respondents.

Categorization of Participants

My academic training in marketing led me, at this point, to consider a departure from traditional methods for analyzing this type of data. Rather than probing the extent to which various variables and sub-themes manifested themselves in the entire sample, I sought to focus first at the individual level and develop "market segments." Crompton and Lamb (1986), in their social services marketing text, note that "a marketing oriented agency aims at 'specific somebodies,' that is, targeted groups of people ... [and] recognises that different client groups have different wants which may justify the development of different services" (p. 14). Though these were obviously not markets in the traditional private-sector sense of the word (I had no intention of selling them anything), I was interested in isolating distinct experiential sub-worlds among this sample of recently unemployed people and, after in-depth analyses were completed, offering potential suggestions for allowing various social service agencies to better understand, access, and work with people comprising these sub-worlds.

I started with a single individual, read her "summary," and, occasionally referring to the full transcript for specific detail, placed the summary on the floor in front of me. At this point I recorded the dominant theme comprising this person's experience as I interpreted it through my repeated reading of the interview transcript. Then I picked up the summary for a second individual, repeated the process for him or her, and so forth. If a particular person fit into an existing pile, he/she was placed there. If not, a new pile and accompanying major theme was created. By the end of the day, I had created seven groups comprising the following people:

Caregivers:	Andrea, Alison, Pauline, Janet, Donna, Heather
Footloose people:	Jeffrey, Marianne, Lynn, Marcia, Taryn, Shawn
Surplus people:	Carrie, Steven, Peggy, Tracy, Christina, Larry, Darlene, Diane, Mary

Discrimination-
based: Melanie, Joe, Paul, Nicole, Dick, Dale, Harry

Planners: Kelly, Anna, Stephanie, David, Stacy, Sheila, Jenny, Todd, Jack, Jacob

Generation X: Joanne, Bob, Susan, Donald, Bruce, Jim

Independent
personalities: Frank, Kim, Angie, Keith, Walter

The next morning I read through summaries, once again referring from time to time to full transcripts, for the 13 heretofore unplaced individuals and added 8 of them to one of the various categories. No new groups were created at this point; however, 5 respondents were still not placed, either because I felt that they didn't fit into one of the groups or because information was lacking.

Added to footloose category: Jeanne, Aaron
Added to surplus people: Carolyn
Added to planners category: Jackie, Shelly
Added to Generation X category: Tom, Les
Added to the independent personality category: Robert
Not placed after two rounds [*lack of information*]: Kevin, Gerry
Not placed after two rounds [*lack of fit*]:   Matt, Anita, Barb

Description of Categories

The caregiver group included 6 women, mostly middle-aged. The dominant theme was their commitment to various dependants, which superseded perceived personal needs. The footloose group comprised 8 respondents. Most were younger and geographically ungrounded, either because they had moved in the past year or because they planned to move in the near future. Few considered Kitchener–Waterloo their home, and they were largely detached from their social networks and/or favourite places. The 6 members of the independent personality group were also geographically and socially ungrounded, but differed from the footloose group in that they didn't seem to particularly miss those connections. In contrast to the footloose group, the independent personalities seemed to be "running from" instead of "moving toward." The 10 surplus people, although similar to the remainder of the sample in that their job losses were relatively recent following some established work history, seemed characteristic of people chronically or permanently unemployed. They consistently emphasized a sense of drifting, wasted days, and frequently mentioned frustration and depression. Such sentiments were common to the entire sample but were most pronounced among this group. The 12 respondents who placed special emphasis on the maintenance of daily and weekly routine were classified as planners. Planning traits were variously manifested in the form of extensive regimented job search, maintenance of fitness regimens, and regular contact with social networks including friends, family, and/or former co-workers. The Generation X group included 8, mostly younger, respondents. They generally had career and/or hobby aspirations of a high technology nature, and they consistently expressed a willingness to relocate as necessary. Finally, 7 respondents, though disparate with respect to most sociodemographic indicators, shared important experiences related to some form of cultural transition, ageism, racism, sexism, or discrimination of some form. Please refer to the left-hand columns of Table 47 (pages 226–28) for my complete initial categorization of individual participants.

The short descriptions in the preceding paragraph were derived from a detailed 65-page narrative developed to formally present a rich representation of each group. As suggested by Wolcott (1990), I began writing fairly early in the process with the intent of thinking things through as the narrative progressed. I tried to include my biases and assumptions in the text as a matter of record. Although the groups held together well under this increased scrutiny (no respondents were moved to other groups), several individuals from each group generally shared important characteristics with people in other groups. These nuances were duly noted and were presented at the concluding section of each group narrative.

I recognized that this analysis, though sincerely undertaken and not without some validity, would not likely survive rigorous academic scrutiny and could not stand alone as the basis from which additional analyses and triangulation with other data were to be based. My original co-researcher, Diane, was not available at this point primarily due to some new and unanticipated work-related commitments. Hence I recruited, late in 1999, a doctoral candidate who possessed considerable background related to both qualitative data analysis, and to the work/leisure interface, and invited him to join the research team. Peter was instructed to conduct a secondary data analysis. Though he was apprised of the existence of my earlier work, he and I agreed that it would be preferable for him to steer clear of it until such time as his own independent analyses were complete.

Table 47
Pre-Negotiation Categorization of Participants by Mark's Categories and by Peter's Categories

Name	Mark's category	Peter's category	Name	Peter's category	Mark's category
Matt	Not placed	TV pals	Paul	Not placed	Cultural transition
Alison	Caregiver	Anti-homebody	Keith	Not placed	Libertarian
Janet	Caregiver	Anti-homebody	Carolyn	Not placed	Surplus
Heather	Caregiver	Lonely	Alison	Anti-homebody	Caregiver
Andrea	Caregiver	Slippery slope	Janet	Anti-homebody	Caregiver
Donna	Caregiver	Slippery slope	Barb	Anti-homebody	Not placed
Pauline	Caregiver	Vacationer	Anna	Anti-homebody	Planner
Paul	Cultural transition	Not placed	Jack	Anti-homebody	Planner
Harry	Cultural transition	Limited freeloaders	Shelly	Anti-homebody	Planner
Melanie	Cultural transition	Networker	Frank	Insecure stigmatics	Libertarian
Nicole	Cultural transition	Data not available	Robert	Insecure stigmatics	Libertarian
Joe	Cultural transition	Self-evaluators	Larry	Insecure stigmatics	Surplus
Dale	Cultural transition	Slippery slope	Steven	Insecure stigmatics	Surplus
Dick	Cultural transition	Structuralist (almost)	Harry	Limited freeloaders	Cultural transition
Marcia	Footloose	Lonely	Joanne	Limited freeloaders	Gen X
Marianne	Footloose	Limited data	Les	Limited freeloaders	Gen X
Jeffrey	Footloose	Self-evaluators	Tracy	Limited freeloaders	Surplus
Jeanne	Footloose	Slippery slope	Heather	Lonely	Caregiver
Taryn	Footloose	Slippery slope (close)	Marcia	Lonely	Footloose
Aaron	Footloose	Structuralist	Susan	Lonely	Gen X
Shawn	Footloose	Structuralist (almost)	Mary	Lonely	Surplus

▶

Name		
Jim	Not eligible	Gen X
Melanie	Networker	Cultural transition
Anita	Networker	Not placed
Jenny	Networker	Planner
Stacy	Networker	Planner
Stephanie	Networker	Planner
Nicole	Data not available	Cultural transition
Marianne	Limited data	Footloose
Todd	Data not available	Planner
Darlene	Data not available	Surplus
Joe	Self-evaluators	Cultural transition
Jeffrey	Self-evaluators	Footloose
Kelly	Self-evaluators	Planner
Andrea	Slippery slope	Caregiver
Donna	Slippery slope	Caregiver
Dale	Slippery slope	Cultural transition
Jeanne	Slippery slope	Footloose
David	Slippery slope	Planner
Jackie	Slippery slope	Planner
Sheila	Slippery slope	Planner
Taryn	Slippery slope (close)	Footloose
Peggy	Slippery slope (close)	Surplus
Aaron	Structuralist	Footloose
Tom	Structuralist	Gen X
Jacob	Structuralist	Planner

Name		
Lynn	Footloose	Vacationer
Joanne	Gen X	Limited freeloaders
Les	Gen X	Limited freeloaders
Susan	Gen X	Lonely
Jim	Gen X	Not eligible
Tom	Gen X	Structuralist
Bob	Gen X	Vacationer
Bruce	Gen X	Vacationer
Donald	Gen X	Vacationer
Keith	Libertarian	Not placed
Frank	Libertarian	Insecure stigmatics
Robert	Libertarian	Insecure stigmatics
Angie	Libertarian	TV pals
Kim	Libertarian	TV pals
Walter	Libertarian	Vacationer
Barb	Not placed	Anti-homebody
Anita	Not placed	Networkers
Anna	Planner	Anti-homebody
Jack	Planner	Anti-homebody
Shelly	Planner	Anti-homebody
Jenny	Planner	Networker
Stacy	Planner	Networker
Stephanie	Planner	Networker
Todd	Planner	Data not available
Kelly	Planner	Self-evaluators

Table 47 (*continued*)

Name	Mark's category	Peter's category
David	Planner	Slippery slope
Jackie	Planner	Slippery slope
Sheila	Planner	Slippery slope
Jacob	Planner	Structuralist
Larry	Surplus	Insecure stigmatics
Steven	Surplus	Insecure stigmatics
Tracy	Surplus	Limited freeloaders
Mary	Surplus	Lonely
Carolyn	Surplus	Not placed
Darlene	Surplus	Data not available
Peggy	Surplus	Slippery slope (close)
Carrie	Surplus	TV pals
Christina	Surplus	TV Pals
Diane	Surplus	TV Pals

Name	Peter's category	Mark's category
Dick	Structuralist (almost)	Cultural transition
Shawn	Structuralist (almost)	Footloose
Matt	TV Pals	Not placed
Angie	TV Pals	Libertarian
Kim	TV Pals	Libertarian
Carrie	TV pals	Surplus
Christina	TV Pals	Surplus
Diane	TV Pals	Surplus
Pauline	Vacationer	Caregiver
Lynn	Vacationer	Footloose
Bob	Vacationer	Gen X
Bruce	Vacationer	Gen X
Donald	Vacationer	Gen X
Walter	Vacationer	Libertarian

Peter's Independent Analysis

Preliminary Data Assessment

As the data to be analyzed had been collected by a team of research assistants not including me, the initial task was one to familiarize myself with the participants in the study without attempting to organize the data in any way or effecting any analysis. Having received hard copies of all the interview transcripts, the first task undertaken was reading each in order to get a general sense of the participants and their life situations, and to gain a certain familiarity with the issues that they were facing in their day-to-day lives. One outcome of this process was the determination that four of the transcripts (those for Darlene, Marianne, Nicole, and Todd) were of sufficiently poor quality that I was initially uncomfortable assigning them to any particular group. Reasons for the poor data quality stemmed primarily from technical difficulties that arose from the use of a microcassette recorder during the interviews, including inefficient voice activation, inability to register soft voices, and the occasional, unintentional tape stoppage. As well, based on the interview data, I concluded that one participant (Jim) should not have been included in the sample as he didn't meet the criteria for inclusion; specifically, he was a part-time university student who was concurrently working part-time. The technical problems and the inappropriateness of one individual led to my exclusion of five participants from my ensuing analysis.

Data Treatment and Coding, Part 1

After this initial familiarization period, the second task was to import all of the data from the original text files into QSR Nud*ist, a computer program used to do qualitative analysis. As the majority of participants were interviewed more than once, all of the data for each participant was collated within QSR Nud*ist; thus, each participant was thereafter represented at a single "node." Each of these nodes, containing Phase 1 and Phase 2 interviews plus their associated follow-up interviews, was systematically read and subdivided along objective dimensions generally in line with the interview schedule, including such factors as daily routine, leisure behaviour, and social support and relationships, as well as along more subjective dimensions pertaining to the participants' perceptions and experience of unemployment. Following the coding of the data for half of the sample, there were seven broad categories, each including a wide array of impressions as well as reported behaviours. At this point, due to my impression that there were a number of common themes represented within each node, I decided to shift the level of analysis from the individual and concentrate on drawing out individual themes within each particular node.

The most varied categories, in terms of the diversity of the data represented therein, had been labelled "impressions of unemployment" and "relationships," and included both positive and negative statements from the participants spanning a variety of situational and interpersonal contexts, although other categories similarly entailed a number of distinct issues. To take "experience of unemployment" as an example, all of the data coded at this node was reread and subsequently divided along positive and negative dimensions. Following this, the "impressions of unemployment–negative" and "impressions of unemployment–positive" sub-categories were reread in order to draw out the particular elements of the unemployment experience that were perceived and reported by participants as contributing to or indicative of each. Within the negative category, for example, such factors as lack of money, boredom, lack of purpose, isolation, and decreased sense of self-worth emerged as contributing to the overall negativity of unemployment. In contrast, such factors as decreased stress, increased opportunity for social interaction, and increased energy emerged as positive aspects of being unemployed. Where appropriate, this process was repeated within the other broad categories such that at the end of the process the data represented at each "parent node" were distributed throughout a number of subordinate nodes which specified the exact nature of the issue expressed.

Throughout this process, two other tasks gained increasing importance. The first was an evaluation of the importance of each particular sub-node or theme within the broad context of the entire sample of participants. For example, although a node was created for both decreased sense of self-worth as well as increased opportunity for social interaction, the prevalence and significance of expressions relating to the former considerably outweighed those of the latter within the sample thus far analyzed. The second task was to maintain an ongoing chronicle of emerging ideas about the interrelationship of many of the ideas expressed. For the most part, these ideas were recorded as memos at particular sub-nodes so that, when reorienting myself to the data after time away, conceptual linkages between that node and others would be immediately evident. More general thoughts and impressions were maintained separately within a journal and, occasionally, appended as notes to specific transcripts.

Categorization of Participants

Once the significance of each particular theme had been assessed within the context of the first half of the sample analyzed, I turned my attention to evaluating the significance of each of these themes within the experience of each participant. To aid in this process, I constructed a grid in which the vertical axis denoted each participant and the horizontal axis all of the possible themes that might be represented within any given individual's data. Following a thorough review of each participant's coded data, within each cell of this grid a score was placed that signified the importance of this theme for each participant, both within the context of his or her experience and relative to the other participants. These heuristic scores, ranging from zero (theme not represented within the data or pronounced unimportant) to three (repeated mention of the theme and its significance) meant little in themselves in terms of understanding their potential interrelationships within the context of individual experience. However, the completed grid was helpful as I attempted to refine my understanding of the dominant issues expressed by each participant and to orient my thinking about broad similarities that existed between participants.

Based upon my readings of each participant's data and the superficial similarities evident within the grid, broad groupings were derived that reflected similarities of experience along a number of dimensions. Most significant to the placement of participants within a particular group at this stage were the participants' perceptions of the importance of financial constraint, boredom, isolation, and feelings of non-contribution to society-at-large. The majority of these themes were evident within all of the groups; however, each group was differentiated based on the relative level of each within the context of the individuals' lived experience. Five broad groups were formed, with a further three groups that were closely allied with one of these five but that were clearly different based upon the presence or predominance of a particular issue or issues. A description of each of these groups, a summary description of each participant, and the rationale for the inclusion of each of the participants in a particular group were written at this point. Accompanying notes described subtle differences of experience to be explored further following a review of the remainder of the data.

Data Coding, Part 2

Following the placement of the first half of the sample of participants into relatively homogenous groups based on their reported experience, the remainder of the participants' data was coded in a similar fashion, with one major exception. Given the specificity of the subnodes created during the first part of the analysis, data was not coded at the parent node but was placed directly into the appropriate subnode, for example "leisure behaviour–sense of entitlement–weak." Naturally, as further issues came to light, specific nodes were created to hold the relevant data. In the majority of cases these were easily integrated into the node framework that had been developed to this point and, where appropriate, existing nodes were modified or subdivided in order to accommodate the new data and remain a consistent repository of similar experiences or perceptions expressed by the participants.

After coding the remainder of the data, summaries of each of the 27 unplaced participants were written, and they were each provisionally placed within one of the extant groups. At this time, a more rigorous evaluation of each of these groups was undertaken in order to articulate more fully the commonalities of experience and life-situation that were the basis for the formation of these groups. Similarities of affective, behavioural, and sociodemographic characteristics of the participants within each group were noted, as was the perceived significance of each within the context of explaining each participant's experience of unemployment. Due to the integration of the second half of the sample and the insights gained during the process of evaluating their data, it became clear that the original groups were less tenable than originally thought, primarily due to their overemphasis upon subjective experience and underemphasis of other salient factors such as family composition, stage in the family life cycle, and occupational orientation. Nevertheless, the original groupings provided an adequate grounding for the purposes of reconceptualizing the nature of the groupings and the conceptual linkages between groups.

In order to effect the regrouping of the participants and to allow for a greater number of relevant subjective and objective variables to differentiate the groups, each group was split into even smaller, yet more homogenous, groups. To better visualize the similarities that existed between as well as within groups, all of the transcripts, notes and summaries amassed thus far were arranged within a physical space spanning approximately 200 square feet. Based on similarities noted between participants originally placed within different groups, and other explanatory dimensions that came to light, various recombinations were evaluated over a period of two weeks. The result of this process was the abandonment of the original groups and the emergence of a different set of ten groups where similarities existed among the participants along a greater number of dimensions. It must be noted that although none of the original groups was kept, the dimensions that originally formed the basis for their formation remained operative within the context of the new groups and, as such, there was much overlap between the new groups and the old. That is to say that participants placed within any particular group originally were more than likely to be found with a number of their original group members in the new grouping scheme. At the end of this process, three of the participants were not adequately described by the new groups and were left unplaced. For my complete categorization of individual participants, please refer to the right-hand columns of Table 47.

Description of Peter's Categories

The ten groups that were eventually formed through this process were "Anti-Homebodies ," "Insecure Stigmatics," "Limited Freeloaders," "Lonely," "Networkers," "Self-evaluators," "Slippery slope," "Structuralists," "TV pals," and "Vacationers." The Anti-Homebody group included five women and one man, predominantly between the ages of 30 and 50 years. The dominant theme for these six was their sense that being at home was not an adequate use of their skills and not a good substitute for the rewards achieved at work. Consequently, their reaction was one of concerted effort and planning in order to escape from the perceived confinement of home, often through retraining for employment. The four Insecure Stigmatics were men aged between 30 and 50, each of whom was worried about his employment prospects and what the future might hold. In addition, each perceived that he was stigmatized from diverse sources, and this limited his behaviour somewhat, particularly with respect to engaging in social situations. The four Limited Freeloaders were between 20 and 29 years old, and all of them lived with their parents. They all perceived that they were financially constrained and that this constraint limited their opportunities for satisfying leisure engagements. Because their survival needs were financially supported though, the Limited Freeloaders typically assumed a laissez-faire approach to securing employment. The Lonely group included four women, three of whom were in their 20s and one in her 40s. Each of these women felt keenly that she was cut off from opportunities for social interaction due to not having a workplace, and felt very isolated while unemployed. They typically had few local and available friends, and consequently pined for social contact. The Networkers group, as well, was made up exclusively of women, and their ages ranged from 30 to 50. These women felt that a lack of money was a constraint that limited their social interaction; nevertheless, they attempted to satisfy their longing for personal interaction by a near-exclusive focus on engaging in social leisure. The three Self-Evaluators were young adults in their 20s, and the dominant reaction to their period of unemployment was one of self-reflection and self-analysis. They generally derived a sense of purpose and belonging through their leisure activities, and used opportunities for leisure engagement to connect with "something larger" than themselves. The seven individuals on the "Slippery Slope" varied greatly in terms of age, pre-unemployment income, and education, but each had in common the sense of not being able to find any routine or structure and, as a result, found his or her physical, emotional, and mental state deteriorating as time passed. In contrast, the five Structuralists devoted a great deal of energy to maintaining a routine in their lives, and the structure that they maintained helped them to feel a sense of accomplishment that they were lacking due to being unemployed. The TV pals shared many characteristics with those on the slippery slope and perceived a general worsening of their condition as time passed. Of significance, though, was their predilection to use television viewing to compensate for many of the negative features they perceived in their lives, including a lack of social interaction, too much time on their hands, and too few things to do that might keep them productively engaged. Lastly, the six Vacationers were all single, young adults who, while occasionally financially limited, perceived their unemployment to be akin to a vacation; none was overly concerned with being unemployed or worried that they would not secure employment before their situation became less tenable.

Reconciliation (Meeting of the Minds)

Following the preliminary groupings effected by both parties involved in the data analysis, the task to be accomplished was arriving at a consensus about the dimensions that would differentiate groups and about the inclusion of each participant within a particular group. This process spanned approximately one month, in which 10 working days were in joint data analysis. The stages through which we went in order to arrive at the final groupings and their associated descriptions and make-up included an initial day-long interchange during which we described our independent analyses and a further four days during which we explored common ground within each of our analyses and reorganized the grouping of the participants. During the four days following the initial regrouping of the participants, we returned to the data to articulate more fully the issues involved and the defining dimensions of each group. During this process, data for three participants (Darlene, Nicole, and Todd) was recovered based on the retranscription from the original interview tapes. This additional information allayed Peter's reticence and allowed their placement within the developing groups. We were, however, unable to recover sufficient data for Marianne, and she was excluded from subsequent consideration and analysis. A reanalysis of Jim's data indicated that he did qualify for the study and should remain within the sample of participants. Lastly, we spent a day re-evaluating the legitimacy of one of our groups and finalizing the placement of previously unplaced participants.

Our initial "meeting of the minds" had two broad objectives. First, each of us described the groups that had emerged from each of our analyses; second we each provided a rationale for the inclusion of the participants in each particular group. It was most important to articulate the commonalities among participants in each particular group and to describe the dimensions of experience that seemed to make each group a cohesive unit. During this process there was occasional disagreement about the salience of particular experiences, perceptions, and social situations within the lives of particular participants, but there was general agreement with regard to the overall issues that were represented within the data. However, given the different emphases each of us gave to various issues, we were forced to acknowledge that various factors might come to adversely affect the joint analysis that was to follow.

Of primary importance was the danger that the ideas, attitudes, and conceptualizations about unemployment that we had derived in our independent analysis would become entrenched and severely constrain any meaningful dialogue and negotiation of the conceptual organization of the participants. In addition, we acknowledged the potential for problems to arise due to the existing power differential: Mark is a well-published, tenured professor whereas Peter, while more experienced with qualitative data analyses, was a young academic in the process of completing a doctoral degree. Closely allied with this, we noted that divergent academic experiences, research orientations, and skills might constrain our ability to reach a meaningful consensus if we failed to remain vigilant about seeing how each perspective might complement the other. Because we discussed these issues, sensitizing ourselves to the potential problems that might ensue, the process that followed was not plagued by the pitfalls that we foresaw, and the ultimate categorization of participants and group descriptions reflect in equal measure the analytic input of us both.

The result of this initial meeting was the decision, after we had each described our groups and the participants within them, to assess what overlap might be found within our categorizations of the participants. The result was the creation of a table with each of the participants listed vertically, and the categories into which they each fell within both Peter's and Mark's scheme (Table 47). This table was sorted on the basis of both Mark's categories and Peter's categories in order to evaluate where each of the participants from a particular group was distributed among the conceptual grouping of the other researcher. Following the production of this table, we set about in earnest to discover the common ground between both our groupings and our assessments of individual participants.

As may be seen, there were five smaller subsets of participants that each contained three participants that were placed together in both Mark's and Peter's typologies. A further eight pairs of individuals had also been placed in the same groups by both Mark and Peter, for a total of 31 participants for whom there appeared to be a certain degree of agreement. Although the conceptual groupings differed, it was felt that, since each of these pairs or sets of individuals were grouped together within both typologies, they were a logical place to begin a negotiated reconceptualization of the way in which participants might be most appropriately grouped. Given that over half of the total sample indicated at least some measure of agreement, we were encouraged that an emergent reconceptualization of the groups was indeed possible and would be stronger for the incorporation of both perspectives.

Based upon a closer review of the participants placed in these "seed groups," however, a great deal of consternation arose from our attempts to articulate why, exactly, these particular sets of individuals should form the foundation for a new grouping scheme. For example, we asked ourselves why such a group as "networker/planner" should form the basis of a larger group to emerge with the placement of further participants. What characteristics, life experiences, and subjective perceptions are both common to all and generally of equal significance? What subordinate issues are also operative? What differences exist, and do these indicate a general or only a specific dissimilarity? We spent two days attempting to answer these and other questions through a return to the individuals' data and through the integration of each of our perspectives into a general sketch of each of the "seed groups." Ultimately, agreement was reached about the commonalities inherent within each of the groups, including sociodemographic and dispositional characteristics, as well as similarities along both social and geographic dimensions. A thumbnail sketch of each group was written, and the remainder of the participants was placed within each of the newly formed groups. At this point, we acknowledged that, as the process unfolded, replacement of certain individuals was likely, as was the potential for one or more of our existing groups to be recombined, redefined, or abandoned. Following this stage in the process, two of the participants were not placed into any of the groups.

Having established a new set of 10 groups, we returned to the data to move beyond the broad sketch of each of the groups. We spent four days reassessing each individual's data and extracting the full range of issues each expressed about his or her experience of unemployment. This process had two aims: to re-evaluate the placement of each participant and to develop more explicit descriptions of each group. During this process we developed exhaustive lists of each of the issues represented within each participant's data and, following lengthy discussions, reached consensus concerning the significance of particular issues expressed and the prevalence of specific subordinate issues that served to differentiate the groups. As expected, there was some replacement of participants as well as refining and redefining of our original groups. Following the analysis of each group and a comfortable level of agreement concise, yet thorough group descriptions were written.

The majority of the groups satisfactorily captured the essence of each of its participants' experience while also accommodating slight deviations from the norm. However, one group that was seemingly functional at the outset was deemed, after further reflection, to be insufficiently unique to stand on its own based upon certain dissimilarities among its participants. We decided to dismantle this group and participants' data were again re-evaluated. Of the seven participants, six were reassigned to other groups while the seventh was rejected from further analysis as we acknowledged that the data were too limited to draw firm conclusions from and to allow reasonable comparisons with other participants.

After we had completed grouping the participants and writing group summaries, we sought to more adequately conceptualize the relationships that existed between the groups. As a part of this process, we clearly articulated the dominant features that discriminated between groups and, as a result, developed more precise group names to more accurately reflect the common bonds that existed within each group. Similarly, the refined organization of our groups into broad groups and subcategories allowed the recognition of particular commonalities that existed between groups. In all, the participants were grouped into four broad categories that included a total of ten sub-categories. After exclusions due to limited data, a total of 59 participants were distributed among these 10 categories.

The participants within each group were not entirely alike; indeed, they showed a fair amount of diversity in their experience of unemployment and their life situations. However, although there is some within-group variability, we believe that the categorization scheme developed captures the essence of the experience of unemployment for the majority of participants while acknowledging the uniqueness of each individual's situation and perceptions.

Appendix G

Where Were Respondents When Signalled?
(by Subgroup)

| | Planners | | | Vacationers | | Connectors | | Marginalized | | |
	Routin-izer %	Anti-homebody %	Efficacy-seeker %	Breaking In %	In control %	Care-giver %	Net-worker %	Rover %	Surplus People %	Lonely People %
Home	64	64	55	62	56	47	59	55	64	40
Work/School	4	8	15	7	20	14	5	9	5	22
Store/Office	9	4	3	6	6	6	6	5	6	7
Friend's house	4	2	5	6	3	4	8	11	4	6
Recreation site	6	6	3	5	4	8	3	3	5	3
Other	14	17	18	14	10	21	18	17	16	22

$\chi^2 = 283.50$, df $= 15$, p $< .001$
Total ESM (N $= 4,415$)

238 | Appendix H

Appendix H

What Was the Main Thing Respondents Were Doing When Signalled? (by Subgroup)

| | Planners | | | Vacationers | | Connectors | | Marginalized | | |
	Routin-izer %	Anti-homebody %	Efficacy-seeker %	Breaking In %	In control %	Care-giver %	Net-worker %	Rover %	Surplus People %	Lonely People %
Family/home related	35	49	18	14	7	30	27	25	25	20
Employment related	13	13	20	11	28	12	8	18	10	19
Other tasks	13	18	28	11	19	26	30	11	23	18
Personal care	18	7	13	30	24	12	12	21	16	15
Recreation related	21	21	21	34	22	20	24	26	26	28

$\chi^2 = 535.95$, df = 45, p < .001
Total ESM (N = 4,415)

Appendix I

How Task Involved Were Respondents?
Did Respondents Perceive a Time Limit? (by Subgroup)

	Planners			Vacationers		Connectors		Marginalized		
	Routin-izer %	Anti-homebody %	Efficacy-seeker %	Breaking In %	In control %	Care-giver %	Net-worker %	Rover %	Surplus People %	Lonely People %
Task involvement										
Entirely	43	48	33	43	41	59	56	51	44	41
Mostly	43	42	46	47	39	35	36	25	44	41
Partially	14	10	21	10	20	6	8	24	12	18
Time pressure										
No time limit	48	41	44	68	56	68	64	65	58	53
Some time pressure	35	41	42	27	37	25	27	28	31	31
Lots of time pressure	17	18	14	5	7	7	9	7	11	16

Task involvement $\chi^2 = 111.77$, df = 18, p < .001
Time pressure $\chi^2 = 175.76$, df = 18, p < .001
Total ESM (N = 4,415)

Appendix J

Who Were Respondents With? (by Subgroup)

	Planners			Vacationers		Connectors		Marginalized		
	Routin-izer %	Anti-homebody %	Efficacy-seeker %	Breaking In %	In control %	Care-giver %	Net-worker %	Rover %	Surplus People %	Lonely People %
Presence of others										
Alone	31	31	36	46	59	34	42	35	38	25
Partner	36	32	20	8	6	11	17	13	25	46
Friend	18	12	21	33	17	25	18	21	33	22
Other adults	15	10	22	26	26	26	17	30	15	19
Children	18	50	17	2	1	26	21	15	1	8
Pets	16	8	19	6	1	14	15	20	10	6
Level of interaction										
No	51	39	50	56	54	41	52	49	43	34
Yes (task related/formal)	12	11	10	6	14	9	17	10	13	8
Yes (social/formal)	13	6	5	3	11	10	13	12	21	6
Yes (casual/intimate)	25	44	35	35	21	40	18	29	23	52

Percentages do not add to 100. Respondents were instructed to check as many categories as applied. Presence of others: No statistical test. Level of interaction: $\chi^2 = 264.12$, df = 27, $p < .001$ Total ESM (N = 4,415)

Appendix K

Mood States (by Subgroup)

	Planners			Vacationers		Connectors		Marginalized		
	Routin-izer %	Anti-homebody %	Efficacy-seeker %	Breaking In %	In control %	Care-giver %	Net-worker %	Rover %	Surplus People %	Lonely People %
Bored ± Involved	3.68 (.96)	4.08 (.80)	3.63 (.90)	3.75 (.91)	3.50 (.90)	4.19 (.96)	3.88 (.94)	3.64 (1.06)	3.20 (1.28)	4.21 (1.05)
Unhappy ± Happy	3.71 (.84)	3.54 (.78)	3.39 (.91)	3.81 (.83)	3.42 (.87)	3.57 (1.44)	3.79 (.93)	3.58 (.97)	3.78 (1.21)	4.34 (.83)
Irritable ± Good humour	3.63 (.96)	3.60 (.80)	3.49 (.78)	3.73 (.83)	3.53 (.74)	3.91 (1.09)	3.82 (.93)	3.59 (1.00)	3.36 (1.22)	4.26 (.89)
Anxious ± Relaxed	3.57 (.99)	3.17 (.86)	3.40 (1.00)	3.47 (1.08)	3.54 (.93)	3.50 (1.46)	3.56 (1.26)	3.45 (1.08)	3.29 (1.34)	4.15 (1.00)

Where 1.00 = negative mood state and 5.00 = positive mood state. Standard deviations are reported in parentheses.

$F = 24.88$, df = 9, $p < .001$

Total ESM (N = 4,415)

Appendix L

Price Subsidy Messages

Price Subsidy Message from the City of Kitchener Community Services Department.

Fee Assistance (Leisure Access Card)

The Community Services Department (CSD) is committed to providing subsidy to Kitchener residents who cannot afford to pay for programs that we directly offer. Approved applicants receive a Leisure Access card that allows them to register for programs at a discounted rate. This card is only valid for programs offered by CSD—it is not valid for programs offered by our affiliated sport groups and neighbourhood associations. The majority of these groups, however, do have their own fee subsidy program in place and you are encouraged to contact them directly. Applications will be assessed on a basic needs test on income availability, based on the latest Statistics Canada Income levels. If you are on social assistance, you will be asked to attach to the application form, a supporting letter from your case worker or a copy of your most recent statement. Applications for fee assistance can be picked up at all City of Kitchener community centres, swimming pools, senior centres and the 7th floor of City Hall. Applications are accepted at any time, however, please apply at least two weeks in advance of registration to allow time for processing of your application—you must register for programs via the regular registration process. For more information, please call 741-2382, or TDD/TTY 741-2385.

Source: *Leisure*, Winter 2001/02, p. 2. City of Kitchener Community Services.

Price Subsidy Message from the City of Waterloo Recreation and Leisure Services Department.

Payment Assistance

is available to Waterloo residents participating in our programs. For information on payment assistance, please speak with the Administration receptionist when registering. Payment Assistance may be in the form of deferred payment or partial subsidy. Any other registration questions? 886-1177.

Source: *2001 Fall Leisure*, p. 62. City of Waterloo Recreation and Leisure Services.

Price Subsidy Message from the YMCA of Kitchener-Waterloo.

Is it possible to join the YMCA for free?

We expect everyone to make a financial contribution to their membership. No one is denied access due to an inability to pay. Some may decide however, that they are not willing to make any commitment and do not join on that basis.

How does the YMCA determine how much I pay?

We trust that you understand better than anyone your financial capabilities and the commitment you are making to the YMCA. We ask for half the fee or more, but we will come to a financial agreement that is acceptable to both the YMCA and yourself. Your fee will be determined based on your needs and financial capabilities.

What is expected of me if I receive membership assistance?

All information provided by you will be kept confidential. We expect the same confidentiality from you. A YMCA membership also requires a commitment of making your payments on time.

If I feel I qualify, how do I apply for membership assistance?

Individuals or families interested in applying should visit the member service desk to receive a tour of the facility and membership information.

- Fill out the application form completely. Incomplete forms slow the process. Feel free to ask for assistance from the YMCA staff.
- Attach proof of gross (before taxes) family income, including wages, spousal income, family allowance, EI (UIC), WCB, pension support and any other sources.
- Attach proof of monthly expenses such as rent, mortgage, utilities, cable, phone, etc.
- It takes approximately ten days to process your application. It is your responsibility to call the YMCA to find out if your application has been approved.
- Applications may be submitted in an envelope to the attention of the assistance coordinator. Please ensure that all documentation is enclosed.

Source: YMCA Membership Assistance brochure (2001).

References

Baack, S., & Witt, P.A. (1985). *Predictors of perceived freedom in leisure of Baptist church members.* Unpublished manuscript, Denton, TX: North Texas State University.

Barling, J. (1990). *Employment, stress, and family functioning.* New York: Wiley.

Bond, M.J., & Feather, N.T. (1988). Some correlates of structure and purpose in the use of time. *Journal of Personality and Social Psychology, 55*, 321–29.

Brenner, H. (1984). *Estimating the effects of economic change on national health and social well-being.* Washington, DC: United States Government Printing Office.

Broman, C.L. (1997). Families, unemployment, and well-being. In R.J. Taylor, J.S. Jackson, and L.M. Chatters (Eds.), *Family life in black America* (pp. 157–66). Thousand Oaks, CA: Sage.

Broman, C.L., Hamilton, V.L., & Hoffman, W.S. (1990). Unemployment and its effects on families: Evidence from a plant closing study. *American Journal of Community Psychology, 18*(5), 643–59.

Broomhall, H.S., & Winefield, A.H. (1990). A comparison of the affective well-being of young and middle-aged unemployed men matched for length of unemployment. *British Journal of Medical Psychology, 63*(1), 43–52.

Crawford, D.W., Jackson, E.L., & Godbey, G. (1991). A hierarchical model of leisure constraints. *Leisure Sciences, 13*, 309–20.

Creed, P.A. & Macintyre, S.R. (2001). The relative effects of deprivation of the latent and manifest benefits of employment on the well-being of unemployed people. *Journal of Occupational Health Psychology, 6*(4), 324–31.

Crompton, J.L. & Lamb, C.W. (1986). *Marketing government and social services.* New York: Wiley.

Dail, P.W. (1988). Unemployment and family stress. *Public Welfare, 46*(1), 30–34.

Dorin, C. (1994). The psycho-social effects of unemployment. *The Social Worker/Le Travailleur social, 62*(1), 9–12.

Ezzy, D. (1993). Unemployment and mental health: A critical review. *Social Science & Medicine, 37*(1), 41–52.

Feather, N.T., (1990). *The psychological impact of unemployment.* New York: Springer-Verlag.

Feather, N.T., & Bond, M.J. (1983). Time structure and purposeful activity among employed and unemployed university graduates. *Journal of Occupational Psychology 56*, 241–54.

Fryer, D. & Payne, R. (1984). Proactive behaviour in unemployment findings and implications. *Leisure Studies, 3*, 273–95.

Glover, T.D. (1998). *Is recreational activity leisure? If so, for whom?* Unpublished manuscript, Waterloo, ON: University of Waterloo.

Glyptis, S. (1989). *Leisure and unemployment.* Philadelphia: Open University Press.

Grant, S., & Barling, J. (1994). Linking unemployment experiences, depressive symptoms, and marital functioning: A mediational model. In G.P. Keita & J.J. Hurrell Jr. (Eds.), *Job stress in a changing workforce: Investigating gender, diversity, and family issues* (pp. 311–27). Washington, DC: American Psychological Association.

Hanisch, K. (1999). Job loss and unemployment research from 1994 to 1998: A review and recommendations for research and intervention. *Journal of Vocational Behavior, 55*(2), 188–220.

Havitz, M.E., Samdahl, D.M., & Whyte, L.B. (1996, May). Employment status and daily activities: Involvement and moods associated with leisure and non-leisure situations. In D. Dawson (Ed.), *Proceedings of the 8th Canadian Congress on Leisure Research* (pp. 103–106). Ottawa: University of Ottawa Press.

Havitz, M.E., & Spigner, C. (1993). Unemployment, health, and leisure: The role of park and recreation services. *Trends, 30*(4), 31–36.

Haworth, J.T. (1997). *Work, leisure, and well-being.* New York: Routledge.

Haworth, J.T., Chesworth, P., & Smith, P. (1990). Cognitive difficulties in samples of unemployed, middle-aged men. *Leisure Studies, 9*(3), 253–57.

Haworth, J.T., & Evans, S.T. (1987). Meaningful activity and unemployment. In D. Fryer & P. Ullah (Eds.), *Unemployed people: Social and psychological perspectives.* Philadelphia: Open University Press.

Hendry, L.B., Raymond, M., & Stewart, C. (1984). Unemployment, school and leisure: An adolescent study. *Leisure Studies, 3*, 175–87.

Hill, J. (1978). The psychological impact of unemployment. *New Society, 43*(798), 118–20.

Howard, D.R., & Crompton, J.L. (1980). *Financing, managing and marketing recreation and park resources.* Dubuque, IA: Wm. C. Brown.

Interprovincial Sport and Recreation Council. (1987). *National recreation statement.* Ottawa: Fitness Canada.

Iso-Ahola, S.E., & Weissinger, E. (1990). Perceptions of boredom in leisure: Conceptualization, reliability and validity of the Leisure Boredom Scale. *Journal of Leisure Research, 22*, 1–17.

Jahoda, M. (1982) *Employment and unemployment: A social psychological analysis.* Cambridge: Cambridge University Press.

Jahoda, M. (1984). Social institutions and human needs: A comment on Fryer and Payne. *Leisure Studies, 3*, 297–99.

Jahoda, M., Lazarsfeld, P.F., & Zeisel, H. (1971). *Marienthal: The sociography of an unemployed community* (T. Elsaesser, M. Jahoda, P.F. Lazarsfeld, J. Reginall, & H. Zeisel, Trans.). Chicago: Aldine/Atherton. (Original work published 1933).

Johnson Tew, C.P., & Havitz, M.E. (2002). Improving our communication: A comparison of four promotion techniques. *Journal of Park and Recreation Administration, 20*(1), 76–97.

Johnson Tew, C.P., Havitz, M.E., & McCarville, R.E. (1999). Origins of municipal programming decisions: A challenge to conventional wisdom. *Journal of Park and Recreation Administration, 17*(1), 1–20.

Jones, L.P. (1991). Unemployment: The effect on social networks, depression, and reemployment opportunities. *Journal of Social Service Research, 15*(1–2), 1–22.

Kilpatrick, R., & Trew, K. (1985). Life-styles and psychological well-being among unemployed men in Northern Ireland. *Journal of Occupational Psychology, 58*, 207–16.

Kong, F., Perrucci, C.C., & Perrucci, R. (1993). The impact of unemployment and economic stress on social support. *Community Mental Health Journal, 29*(3), 205–21.

Kubey, R., & Csikszentmihalyi, M. (1990). *Television and the quality of life: How viewing shapes everyday experience*. Hillsdale, NJ: Lawrence Erlbaum Associates.

Kulik, L. (2000). Jobless men and women: A comparative analysis of job search intensity, attitudes toward unemployment and related responses. *Journal of Occupational & Organizational Psychology, 73*(4), 487–500.

Leana, C.R., & Feldman, D.C. (1990). Individual responses to job loss: Empirical findings from two field studies. *Human Relations, 43*(11), 1155–1181.

Leana, C.R., & Feldman, D.C. (1991). Gender differences in responses to unemployment. *Journal of Vocational Behavior, 38*(1), 65–77.

Liem, J.H., & Liem, G.R. (1990). Understanding the individual and family effects of unemployment. In J. Eckenrode and S. Gore (Eds.), *Stress between work and family* (pp. 175–204). New York: Plenum.

Lobo, F. (1996). The effects of late career unemployment on lifestyle. *Loisir et societe/Society and leisure, 19*(1), 169–99.

Lobo, F. (1999). Young people and unemployment: Does job loss diminish involvement in leisure? *Loisir et societe/Society and Leisure, 22*(1), 145–70.

Lobo, F. (2002). *Leisure, family and lifestyle: Unemployed young people*. New Delhi: Rawat Publications.

Lobo, F., & Watkins, G. (1995). Late career unemployment in the 1990s: Its impact on the family. *Journal of Family Studies, 1*, 103–13.

Martella, D., & Maass, A. (2000). Unemployment and life satisfaction: The moderating role of time structure and collectivism. *Journal of Applied Social Psychology, 30*(5), 1095–108.

McDaniels, C. (1989). *The changing workplace*. San Francisco: Jossey-Bass.

Neulinger, J., & Breit, M. (1969). Attitude dimensions of leisure. *Journal of Leisure Research, 1*, 255–61.

O'Brien, G.E., Feather, N.T., & Kabanoff, B. (1994). Quality of activities and the adjustment of unemployed youth. *Australian Journal of Psychology, 46*(1), 29–34.

Patton, M.Q. (1990). *Qualitative evaluation and research methods* (2nd ed.). Newbury Park, CA: Sage.

Patton, W., & Donohue, R. (2001). Effects on the family of a family member being long term unemployed. *Journal of Applied Health Behaviour, 3*(1), 31–39.

Pedlar, A. (1996). Community development: What does it mean for recreation and leisure? *Journal of Applied Recreation Research, 21*(1), 5–23.

Pernice, R. (1996). Methodological issues in unemployment research: Quantitative and/or qualitative approaches? *Journal of Occupational & Organizational Psychology, 69*(4), 339–49.

Pesavento Raymond, L.C. (1984). The effects of unemployment on the leisure behavior of unemployed steelworkers. *World Leisure and Recreation, 26*(6), 61–64.

Pesavento Raymond, L.C., & Havitz, M.E. (1995). Validation of the impact of recreation for the unemployed. *Illinois Parks and Recreation, 26*(3), 43–45.

Pesavento Raymond, L.C., & Kelly, J.R. (1991). Leisure activity patterns of young unemployed inner-city women. *World Leisure and Recreation, 33*, 23–26.

Rantakeisu, U., Starrin, B., & Hagquist, C. (1999). Financial hardship and shame: A tentative model to understand the social and health effects of unemployment. *British Journal of Social Work, 29*(6), 877–901.

Reid, D.G. (1988). The needs of the unemployed and the ability of the unemployed to respond. *Society and Leisure, 11*, 117–27.

Reid, D.G. (1990). Leisure and recreation as an instrument for maintaining life quality during unemployment. *Leisurability, 17*(1), 3–11.

Reid, D.G. (1995). *Work and leisure in the 21st century: From production to citizenship*. Toronto: Wall & Emerson.

Reynolds, S., & Gilbert, P. (1991). Psychological impact of unemployment: Interactive effects of vulnerability and protective factors on depression. *Journal of Counseling Psychology, 38*(1), 76–84.

Roberts, K., Lamb, K.L., Dench, S., & Brodie, D.A. (1989). Leisure patterns, health status and employment status. *Leisure Studies, 8*, 229–35.

Rodriguez, Y. (1997). Learned helplessness or expectancy-value? A psychological model for describing the experiences of different categories of unemployed people. *Journal of Adolescence, 20*(3), 321–32.

Rosenberg, M. (1965). *Society and the adolescent self-image*. Princeton, NJ: Princeton University Press.

Samdahl, D.M. (1991). *Leisure and gender: An exploration of the patterns of freedom and obligation in the daily lives of men and women*. Unpublished manuscript, Athens, GA: University of Georgia.

Samdahl, D.M. (1992). Leisure in our lives: Exploring the common leisure occasion. *Journal of Leisure Research, 24*, 19–32.

Samdahl, D.M., & Havitz, M.E. (1996, May). Assessing validity in leisure measurement: Comparisons across time, comparisons across method. In D. Dawson (Ed.), *Proceedings of the 8th Canadian Congress on Leisure Research* (pp. 237–40). Ottawa: University of Ottawa Press.

Samdahl, D.M., & Jekubovich, N.J. (1993). Patterns and characteristics of adult daily leisure. *Loisir et societe/Society and Leisure, 16*, 129–49.

Schwarzer, R., Hahn, A., & Fuchs, R. (1994). Unemployment, social resources, and mental and physical health: A three-wave study on men and women in a stressful life transition. In G.P. Keita and J.J. Hurrell, Jr. (Eds.), *Job stress in a changing workforce: Investigating gender, diversity, and family issues* (pp. 75–87). Washington, DC: American Psychological Association.

Shams, M. (1993). Social support and psychological well-being among unemployed British Asian men. *Social Behavior & Personality, 21*(3), 175–86.

Shams, M., & Jackson, P.R. (1993). Religiosity as a predictor of well-being and moderator of the psychological impact of unemployment. *British Journal of Medical Psychology, 66*(4), 341–52.

Shams, M. & Jackson, P.R. (1994). The impact of unemployment on the psychological well-being of British Asians. *Psychological Medicine, 24*(2), 347–55.

Sheeran, P., & Abraham, C. (1994). Unemployment and self-conception: A symbolic interactionist analysis. *Journal of Community & Applied Social Psychology, 4*(2), 115–29.

Sheeran, P., & McCarthy, E. (1992). Social structure, self-conception and well-being: An examination of four models with unemployed people. *Journal of Applied Social Psychology, 22*(2), 117–33.

Shelton, B. (1985). The social and psychological impact of unemployment. *Journal of Employment Counseling, 22*, 18–22.

Smit, P., & Reid, D.G. (1990). Intervention in community leisure service systems. *Journal of Applied Recreation Research, 15*, 146–58.

Spigner, C., & Havitz, M.E. (1992). Health, recreation, and the unemployed: An interactive model. *International Quarterly of Community Health Education, 13*(8), 31–45.

Sport Canada. (2002). *The Canadian sport policy*. Retrieved April 30, 2003, from < http://www.pch.gc.ca/progs/sc/pol/pcs-csp/index_e.cfm >.

Statistics Canada. (2001). *International Adult Literacy Survey*. Retrieved January 11, 2002, from < http://www.statcan.ca/english/freepub/89-572-XIE/89-572-XIE.pdf >.

Strauss, A.L. (1987). *Qualitative analysis for social scientists*. Cambridge, UK: Cambridge University Press.

Targ, D.B., & Perrucci, C.C. (1990). Plant closings, unemployment and families. *Marriage & Family Review, 15*(3–4), 131–45.

Ullah, P. (1990). The association between income, financial strain and psychological well-being among unemployed youths. *Journal of Occupational Psychology, 63*(4), 317–30.

Ullah, P., Banks, M.H., and Warr, P.B. (1985). Social support, social pressures and psychological distress during unemployment. *Psychological Medicine, 15*, 283–95.

Underlid, K. (1996). Activity during unemployment and mental health. *Scandinavian Journal of Psychology, 37*(3), 269–81.

Vinokur, A.D., Price, R.H., & Caplan, R.D. (1996). Hard times and hurtful partners: How financial strain affects depression and relationship satisfaction of unemployed persons and their spouses. *Journal of Personality & Social Psychology, 71*(1), 166–79.

Wanberg, C.R., Griffiths, R.F., & Gavin, M.B. (1997). Time structure and unemployment: A longitudinal investigation. *Journal of Occupational & Organizational Psychology, 70*(1), 75–95.

Wanberg, C.R., & Marchese, M.C. (1994). Heterogeneity in the unemployment experience: A cluster analytic investigation. *Journal of Applied Social Psychology, 24*(6), 473–88.

Warr, P. (1987). *Work, unemployment and mental health.* New York: Oxford.

Warr, P., Cook, J., & Wall, T. (1979). Scales for the measurement of some work attitudes and aspects of psychological well-being. *Journal of Occupational Psychology, 52*(2), 129–48

Waters, L.E., & Moore, K.A. (2001). Coping with economic deprivation during unemployment. *Journal of Economic Psychology. Special Issue, 22*(4), 461–82.

Winefield, A.H., & Tiggemann, M. (1989). Unemployment duration and affective well-being in the young. *Journal of Occupational Psychology, 62*(4), 327–36.

Winefield, A.H., Tiggemann, M., & Winefield, H.R. (1992). Spare time use and psychological well-being in employed and unemployed young people. *Journal of Occupational & Organizational Psychology, 65*(4), 307–13.

Witt, P.A., & Ellis, G.D. (1985). Development of a short form to assess perceived freedom in leisure. *Journal of Leisure Research, 17*, 225–33.

Wolcott, H.F. (1990). *Writing up qualitative research.* Thousand Oaks, CA: Sage.

Author Index

Abraham, C., 152-53

Banks, M.H., 154
Barling, J., 157-58
Bond, M.J., 148
Breit, M., 136, 138, 140, 214
Brenner, H., 3
Brodie, D.A., 2, 145
Broman, C.L., 155, 158
Broomhall, H.S., 154

Caplan, R.D., 156-57
Chesworth, P., 1, 149
Cook, J., 133, 136, 138, 140, 214
Crawford, D.W., 143
Creed, P.A., 3, 157
Crompton, J.L., 179, 186, 223
Csikszentmihalyi, M., 98, 144

Dail, P.W., 155
Dench, S., 2, 145
Donohue, R., 156
Dorin, C., 154

Ellis, G.D., 136-38, 140
Evans, S.T., 150
Ezzy, D., 145-46, 153, 156

Feather, N.T., 146, 148, 150
Feldman, D.C., 151, 155, 157
Fryer, D., 146-47, 150, 157, 159
Fuchs, R., 154

Gavin, M.B., 148-49, 158
Gilbert, P., 154, 156
Glover, T.D., 194
Glyptis, S., 1
Godbey, G., 143
Grant, S., 158
Griffiths, R.F., 148-49, 158

Hagquist, C., 154, 157
Hahn, A., 154
Hamilton, V.L., 158
Hanisch, K., 145, 157

Havitz, M.E., 1, 3, 179, 183, 186-87, 222
Haworth, J.T., 1, 149-50
Hendry, L.B., 146
Hill, J., 155
Hoffman, W.S., 158
Howard, D.R., 179

Interprovincial Sport and Recreation
   Council, 190-93
Iso-Ahola, S.E., 136-38, 140, 144, 214

Jackson, E.L., 143
Jackson, P.R., 153, 155
Jahoda, M., 146-48, 155
Jekubovich, N.J., 105, 144
Johnson Tew, C.P., 186-87
Jones, L.P., 154

Kabanoff, B., 150
Kelly, J.R., 1, 3, 179
Kilpatrick, R., 146, 148, 154
Kitchener Community Services, 242
Kong, F., 154
Kubey, R., 98, 144
Kulik, L., 153

Lamb, C.W., 179, 186, 223
Lamb, K.L., 2, 145
Lazarsfeld, P. F., 146
Leana, C.R., 151, 155, 157
Liem, G.R., 145, 156
Liem, J.H., 145, 156
Lobo, F., 1, 3, 146-47, 154-55, 158-59

Maass, A., 145, 148-49, 156
Macintyre, S.R., 3, 157
Marchese, M.C., 146
Martella, D., 145, 148-49, 156
McCarthy, E., 152
McCarville, R.E., 186-87
McDaniel, S.C., 184
Moore, K.A., 151, 157-58

Neulinger, J., 136, 138, 140, 214
O'Brien, G.E., 150

252 | Index

Patton, M.Q., 145
Patton, W., 156
Payne, R., 146–47, 150, 157
Pedlar, A., 184
Pernice, R., 136, 144
Perrucci, C.C., 154, 156
Perrucci, R., 154
Pesavento Raymond, L.C., 1, 3, 179
Price, R.H., 156–57

Rantakeisu, U., 154, 157
Raymond, M., 146
Reid, D.G., 1, 179
Reynolds, S., 154, 156
Roberts, K., 2, 145
Rodriguez, Y., 145
Rosenberg, M., 133

Samdahl, D.M., 105, 133, 136, 138, 140, 144, 214, 222
Schwarzer, R., 154
Shams, M., 153–55
Shelton, B., 157
Sheeran, P., 152–53
Smit, P., 1
Smith, P., 149
Spigner, C., 1, 3, 179, 183
Sport Canada, 193
Starrin, B., 154, 157

Statistics Canada, 186
Strauss, A.L., 223
Stewart, C., 146

Targ, D.B., 156
Tiggemann, M., 159
Trew, K., 146, 148, 154

Ullah, P., 154, 157–58
Underlid, K., 150, 154, 159

Vinokur, A.D., 156–57

Wall, T., 133, 136, 138, 140, 214
Wanberg, C.R., 146, 148–49, 158
Warr, P.B., 133, 136, 138, 140, 145, 150, 152, 154, 214
Waterloo Recreation and Leisure Services, 242
Waters, L.E., 151, 157-58
Watkins, G., 155, 159
Weissinger, E., 136–38, 140, 144, 214
Whyte, L.B., 222
Winefield, A.H., 154, 159
Winefield, H.R., 159
Witt, P.A., 136–38, 140, 144
Wolcott, H.F.

YMCA of Kitchener-Waterloo, 243

Zeisel, H., 146

Subject Index

activity (leisure and recreation): *also see* sports, and passive and sedentary lifestyles 2, 5, 10, 40–43, 45, 50, 51, 54, 62, 64–65, 68, 70, 75, 78-80, 87, 89, 94, 117, 120–28, 130–31, 137, 141–44, 146, 149, 158–60, 168–75, 177–95, 198–99, 205, 213, 215–16, 219–21, 223, 232, 238, 242–43
  exercise, fitness, physical, 28–29, 68, 79–80, 82, 84, 88, 94, 120–21, 124–25, 128, 141–42, 168, 177, 182, 188–90, 194, 224
  recreation contexts, 28, 38, 58, 61, 78, 118, 121, 125
  purposeful, self-development focused, 29, 37, 43, 44, 61, 78–79, 109, 137, 158–60, 188–90
  sites, facilities, parks, 36, 64, 78, 84, 94, 123, 131, 169, 183, 192, 207, 237
affect (positive and negative), 34, 107–108, 145, 154, 157, 231
age, 11–12, 17, 18, 26–27, 33, 41, 47, 54, 59, 64, 67, 69, 72, 81, 86, 144, 151, 153, 156, 183, 198, 200, 206, 222–25, 232–33
agency approach, 147, 157
agency model, 147
anger (*also see* frustration), 145
Anti-Homebodies (*see* participant classification)
Asia (place locations), 55
  India, 55–56
at-risk behaviour, 82
Australia, New Zealand (place locations), 1, 136
automobiles, cars, transit, travel patterns, 60–61, 67–70, 80, 117, 121
autonomy, 107, 154–55

boredom, 42, 44, 53, 62–63, 82, 121, 128–29, 131, 223, 230

Breaking Ins (*see* participant classification)
brother (*see* family, siblings)
burn-out, 75

Canada Employment Centre, 7, 10, 16, 161
career socialization, 98, 136–40, 213–14
caregiver role, 114, 123, 223
Caregivers (*see* participant classification)
children:
  childcare, baby-sitting 59, 86, 109–14, 130, 132, 164, 170
  dependants, 13–15, 34, 48, 59–61, 64–65, 69–72, 78, 90, 93, 113–14, 119, 121, 123–24, 144, 168, 174, 180, 182–83, 188–89, 193, 200, 207, 218, 222–23, 240
  other children, 124, 127, 207
  single parent, 59, 72, 91, 173
chronic unemployment, 72
church (*see* religion)
cognitive functioning, 149
collaboration between agencies, co-operative endeavours, 183–84, 190–94
communication (*also see* information and marketing mix program information), 156, 164–65, 168, 172–75, 186–87, 190–92, 198
community development, 184
competence, 145
concentration, 145
confidence, mastery, 120
Connectors (*see* participant classification)
constraint (*see* leisure constraint)
coping behaviours and strategies, 3, 50, 53, 94, 149, 151–52, 159, 181
co-workers (*also see* social aspects of work), 52, 66, 76, 86, 95, 130, 154, 204, 219, 224

court, court dates, legal issues, 61–62, 81
creativity, 132

daily life patterns (*also see* time of day), 3, 97, 151, 160
  daily routine, 24, 27, 29, 31, 33–34, 36, 38–39, 42, 48, 51, 63, 65, 67, 84, 100, 106, 114–16, 119, 121, 148, 150, 160, 180, 187, 199, 204, 219, 223–24, 233
  daily structure, scheduling, 27, 30, 36, 39, 41–42, 48, 83, 106, 116, 119–20, 148–49, 152, 177, 197, 199, 204, 220, 233
  daily planning (*also see* sense of structure), 27, 30, 84, 122, 204–205, 209, 219
data
  completion rates, 7
  cross-sectional, 3
  Experience Sampling Method (ESM), 3–5, 7, 9–11, 21, 23, 67, 78, 96–39, 144, 149, 158, 184, 188, 194, 197–99, 207–209
  interviews, 4, 7, 10, 16, 23, 26–95, 100, 139, 144, 161, 188, 199, 203–206, 210–11, 218–21, 229
  longitudinal (*also see* Phase 2), 3
  mail-back survey, 7, 10, 139–44, 197, 199, 212–17
  qualitative, 4–5, 26–95, 98, 145, 147, 149, 161, 197, 222, 229
  quantitative, 4–5, 23, 98, 197, 199
  reliability, trustworthiness, triangulation 3, 10, 23, 117
  standardized scales, 4, 95, 106
  validity, 3, 225
depression, depressed mood state (*also see* moods), 39, 41, 42, 63, 82, 84, 86, 91, 128, 145, 149, 152, 155–56, 223–24

education, 11–12, 16, 19, 26, 34, 41, 47–48, 53–54, 59, 64, 72, 81, 85–86, 92, 189, 198, 206, 233
Efficacy-Seekers (*see* participant classification)
employment and career counselling, 165–66, 184
Employment Insurance (*see* Unemployment Insurance)
employment-related activities (*see* job search)

ethnicity, 11–12, 16, 19, 34, 41, 48, 54, 59, 64, 72, 81, 86, 144, 198, 206, 223, 225
Europe (place locations), 55
  Belgium, 73
  England, United Kingdom, 1, 56
  Germany, 55–56, 127
  Yugoslavia, 60
Experience Sampling Method (*see* data, ESM)
external validation, 38
extrinsic motivation, 42

family (*also see* children, parents), 28, 36, 48–50, 54, 58–59, 64, 69, 73–74, 78, 94, 115, 117–18, 120, 124, 126, 151, 198–99, 203–204, 207–208, 213, 218–19, 222–24, 238, 240
  activities, 39, 70, 122, 139, 198, 207
  conflict, 49, 74, 82, 84, 86, 91, 131, 181, 223
  contexts, 39–40, 58, 61, 121, 129
  functioning, cohesion, 32, 81–82, 86, 114, 155–56, 158, 199
  life, 64, 70, 86, 90, 94, 155, 207, 217
  siblings, 48–50, 62, 69, 90–91
  spouse (*see* marital status)
  stress, tension, 36, 70, 74–75, 82, 84, 86, 91, 97, 124, 155–56, 158
fear, 142, 145
financial
  constraint, deprivation, distress, hardship, insecurity, 33–34, 40, 45, 52, 54, 59–61, 64, 66, 68, 71, 75, 82, 86–87, 89, 139, 141–43, 157–59, 163, 173, 180–81, 197, 217, 223, 230, 232
  resources, support, 13–15, 49, 53–54, 66, 68, 74, 85, 158–59, 162, 164–65, 175
fitness (*see* activity)
flow, 5
free time, freedom, 52
friends, 36, 45, 46, 50, 51, 59, 73, 76–78, 100–101, 103–105, 113–14, 116, 118–20, 124–26, 130–31, 151, 204, 207–208, 219–20, 224, 233, 237, 240, 237
  companionship, 45, 51, 59, 68–69, 84, 86, 92, 114, 122, 124, 130, 131, 190, 220
  friendships, friendship networks, 30, 32, 34, 39–40, 41, 46–47, 49, 53, 55, 58–60, 63–65, 68–69, 73, 82–88, 92, 123, 130, 203–204, 219, 223

fun, enjoyment, pleasure 42, 52, 68, 79, 84, 109, 119–21, 125–27, 131–32, 174–75, 208, 216, 219
functional model, functionalist "deprivation" theory, functionalist theory, deprivation model, 146–47
frustration (see sense of)

gambling
    bingo, 83–84, 128–29
    blackjack, 27–28, 84, 120
    personality, 124
gender, sex of respondents, 11, 12, 16, 18, 28, 34, 59, 64, 67, 72, 81–82, 86, 139, 144, 151–53, 182, 195, 197, 222–24, 232–33
geographic
    dislocation, relocation, 54–55, 57, 72–73, 126–27, 223
    distance, 141–44, 185, 235
    groundedness, 49, 54, 56, 58, 72–73, 90, 224, 235
    neighbourhoods, 185, 217
global economy, 55
goals, 35, 53, 58, 79, 147, 150–51, 167, 171, 177
guilt, 41, 43, 57, 120, 122, 127, 182, 188, 223

hardship, 34, 123
health (also see well-being), 3, 217
    physical, 2, 84, 159, 177, 181, 233
    mental health, 2, 81, 84, 145–47, 151, 159, 177, 233
highlight of the day, 116–33, 209
home, 34–36, 38, 50, 55, 58, 61, 67, 72, 80, 85–86, 122, 158, 198, 207, 217, 218, 237–38
    home-related tasks, housework, cooking 35–36, 58, 61, 64, 82, 93, 117, 238
    homebound, 34–35, 41, 68, 82, 84, 86, 88, 97, 129, 158, 160, 171, 188, 198, 232, 237
Human Resources Development Canada (HRDC), 5, 161–72, 177, 179, 182–85

implications for local service providers (see marketing mix, and municipal and local level government agencies)
income
    constraints, 34, 59, 87, 157–59
    loss of, 71, 146, 157–58, 204
    of participants, 16, 19, 26

pre-unemployment, 13–15, 34, 47, 54, 59, 64, 72, 81, 86, 158, 198, 206, 233
In Controls (see participant classification)
industrial society, 1–2
information (also see communication, and marketing mix program information)
    dissemination, 164–65, 172, 183, 186, 190–92, 198
institutional supports, 168

job importance, 98, 136–40, 213–14
Job Importance Scale, 136, 138, 140, 213–14
job loss circumstances, 13–15
job search
    activities, work-search activities, 36, 38–39, 51, 53, 58, 61–64, 74–75, 78, 117, 122, 129, 132, 151, 163–67, 169, 170–71, 183–84, 207, 223–24, 237–38
    database expenses, transportation expense (also see subsidies), 168
job skills, skill upgrading, 27, 53, 85, 120, 159, 189, 232
job training, employment training, 27–28, 35, 76, 117–18, 120, 124, 126, 159, 166–68, 189, 232

lack of
    awareness of what's available (see program information, communication)
    entitlement, 139, 178, 180, 182, 187–88, 191, 198, 231
language-based constraints, 186
lazy, not contributing to society (also see sense of purpose), 33, 43–44
leisure
    and recreation spending (also see pricing, subsidies), 2
    benefits (also see activity, well-being), 2, 181
    boredom, 5, 10, 98, 136–38, 140, 144, 199, 213–14
    constraints, perceived constraints, 3, 5, 10, 40, 88, 98, 139–44, 189, 199, 213
    education, 183, 188–89, 191
    facilitation, facilitating leisure engagement, facilitating leisure participation in comparison with non-leisure, 105–14, 177, 198, 210

Leisure Boredom Scale (LBS), 136–38, 140, 144, 213–14
Leisure Diagnostic Battery (LDB), 136–38, 140, 215–16
leisure service agencies, leisure service delivery, 3, 177–95
life cycle, life stage, 5, 111, 125, 127, 139, 223, 231
life satisfaction, 3, 10, 72, 86, 96, 98, 133–38, 156, 177, 181, 187, 199, 217
Life Satisfaction Scale, 133, 136, 138, 140, 217
lifestyle, 5, 40, 51, 60–61, 170, 191–92
literacy, 186
local government (see municipal)
loneliness, 45–46, 68, 145
Lonely People (see participant classification)

Marginalized People (see participant classification)
marital status, 11–12, 28, 30, 34, 48, 59, 64, 80, 86, 88, 91, 180, 233
spouse, life partner, husband, wife, boyfriend, girlfriend, 30, 48, 51, 60, 65, 70, 77, 82, 93, 100, 102–105, 113–14, 116, 119, 122, 124, 129–31, 144, 155–56, 180, 203, 207, 218, 222, 240
marketing mix, 178–79, 182–90, 194
distribution issues (also see collaboration between agencies), 182–86
convenience, 184–85, 194
cost related issues, 194
program location, 185, 194
pricing issues (also see subsidies), 178, 180–82, 184, 188–90, 194, 242–43
pricing strategies, 180–82
programming issues (also see activity), 187–88
program development, 178
promotion, 178, 186–87
promoting recreation services, 186–87
program information, 183, 186, 190–92
market segmentation, 179–80, 188–90, 197, 199–201, 223
mental health (see health)
mood states, 5, 23, 26, 53, 63, 72, 83, 89, 97, 106–14, 129, 131, 141–42, 149, 151–52, 155–57, 171, 177, 181, 185, 187, 198–99, 208, 241

anxious/relaxed (also see anxiety, quiet time and relaxation), 106, 129, 208, 241
bored/involved (also see boredom), 106, 208, 241
happy/unhappy, 44, 53, 63, 76, 83, 121, 123, 129, 131, 208, 217, 241
irritable, grumpy/good humoured 44, 63, 82, 120, 208, 241
municipal and local level government agencies, 144, 177–92, 200

National Recreation Statement, 190–93
neighbours, 89, 120, 124, 130–31
Networkers (see participant classification)
New Democratic Party (NDP), 2
North America (place locations), 1, 3, 179, 181, 183
Canada (also see Ontario), 1, 4, 46, 179, 186, 190, 242
British Columbia, 73, 90–91
Calgary, 46
Maritime provinces, Nova Scotia, Newfoundland, New Brunswick, 55, 72–73, 91–92
Montreal, 91
Quebec, 91
Saskatchewan, 90
Vancouver, 46, 55, 91
Victoria, 73, 76
United States, 63
Ann Arbor, Michigan, 127

older workers (see age)
Ontario (place locations), 2, 7, 10, 47, 55
Barrie, 46
Brantford, 46, 70, 73
Cambridge, 73, 87, 127
Elmira, 69
Exeter, 90
Grimsby, 69
Georgian Bay, 74
Guelph, 55–56
Kitchener, 7, 10, 16, 46–47, 55–56, 61, 63–66, 72–73, 84, 86, 90–91, 126, 170–71, 174, 203, 224, 242–43
London, 56, 73, 90, 126
Oshawa, 56, 69
Ottawa, 56
St. Catharines, 56
St. Thomas, 90
Sarnia, 70

Sault Ste. Marie, 46
Toronto, 46–47, 56, 60, 63, 73, 86–87, 125
Waterloo, 7, 10, 46–47, 55–56, 63–65, 72–73, 90–91, 181, 186, 203, 224, 242–43
Whitby, 86

parent
  being one (*see* children)
  of participants, 47–49, 53, 60, 74–75, 81–82, 91, 94, 123, 158, 180, 222
participant classification, classification system
  Planners, 16, 18–22, 24–47, 98–99 106–108, 110–13, 115–16, 119–20, 134–35, 137–38, 141, 149, 151, 153, 158, 184–85, 188, 224, 226–28, 235, 237–41
    Routinizers, 16, 18–22, 26–34, 36, 41, 44, 47, 74, 98–100, 106–10, 112–15, 118–19, 121, 134, 139, 141, 148–49, 151–53, 159, 182, 188, 237–241
    Anti-Homebodies, 16, 18–22, 26, 28, 34–41, 44, 47, 97–100, 107–10, 112–15, 118–19, 121, 134, 139, 141, 152–53, 159, 180–81, 188, 226–27, 232, 237–41
    Efficacy-Seekers, 17–22, 26, 28, 36, 41–47, 78, 99–100, 106–10, 112–15, 118–19, 121–22, 134, 141, 143, 149, 158, 187–88, 237–41
  Vacationers, 16–22, 24–26, 47–58, 72, 98–99, 106–108, 110–13, 115–16, 118–19, 123–25, 134–35, 137, 139, 141, 151–52, 189, 227–28, 232–33, 237–41
    Breaking Ins, 17–22, 47–54, 58, 74, 82, 98–100, 107–108, 110–13, 115, 118–19, 126, 134, 139, 141, 148, 153, 156, 159, 180–81, 184, 189, 237–41
    In Controls, 17–22, 47, 50, 52–58, 72, 99–100, 106–13, 115, 118–19, 126, 127, 134, 139, 141, 143, 153, 180–81, 185, 189, 237–41
  Connectors, 16–22, 24–26, 58–72, 78, 98–99, 106–108, 110–13, 115–16, 118–20, 125–27, 133–35, 137, 139, 142, 185, 189, 237–41

Caregivers, 17–22, 58–64, 99–100, 106–10, 112–15, 118–19, 123–24, 134, 142–43, 153, 159, 182, 189, 223–24, 226–28, 237–41
Networkers, 17–22, 64–72, 99–100, 109–10, 112–13, 115, 118–19, 123–25, 134, 139–40, 142, 151–52, 154–55, 159, 182, 186, 189, 226–27, 232–33, 234, 237–41
Marginalized People, 16–22, 24–26, 72–95, 98–99, 106–13, 115–16, 118–19, 128–33, 137, 139, 142–43, 158, 185, 189, 237–41
    Rovers, 17–22, 72–81, 85, 90, 98–100, 107–15, 118, 127–28, 130–32, 134, 139–40, 142–43, 154–55, 157, 159, 180–81, 185–87, 189, 237–41
    Surplus People, 17–22, 72, 77, 81–86, 90, 97–100, 106–13, 115, 118–19, 128–32, 134, 142–43, 156–60, 185–87, 189, 223–24, 226–28, 237–41
    Lonely People, 17–22, 72, 77, 85–86, 95, 99–100, 106–13, 115, 118–19, 128–32, 134, 142–43, 154–55, 157, 182, 185, 189, 226–28, 232, 237–41
passive and sedentary lifestyles, passivity (*also see* activity), 68, 84, 122, 128, 150, 160, 173, 189
perceived freedom (in leisure), 5, 10, 98, 109, 136–38, 140, 199, 213–14
Perceived Freedom in Leisure Scale, 136, 138, 140, 213–14
personal care, 28, 38, 58, 61, 117, 127, 207, 238
personal time (*also see* quiet time), 68, 80, 125
personality, 76, 156, 224
pets, 30, 48, 59, 62, 77, 80, 88, 100–103, 105, 113, 117, 123, 125, 208, 223, 240
Phase 1 of the research, 7–11, 16, 21–96, 98, 133, 139, 162–63, 211, 222, 229
Phase 2 of the research, 7–11, 13, 16, 21, 28, 31, 33, 38, 39, 40, 45, 74, 82–84, 86–88, 92–93, 98, 126, 132–33, 137, 139, 157, 161–75, 211, 218–23, 229
physical activity, working out (*see* activity, fitness)
physical health (*see* health)
planning (long-range), planning orientation, 34–35, 38, 41–42, 44, 100

Planners (*see* participant classification)
post-hoc instrumentation, 3
proactive/pro-activity, 150–51, 185
procrastination, 45
Progressive Conservative (PC) Party, 2
provincial, regional, and federal level
  government response, 144, 178,
  190–94, 200
psychological
  benefits, 167, 181, 194
  distress, 159, 182

quality time, 61, 94, 130
quiet time, relaxation, 52, 68, 70, 79, 83,
  120–22, 125, 129, 131
quit (quitting jobs), 13–15, 59, 75–76

recreation (*see* activity)
recruitment (of research participants),
  7, 10
red tape, 116, 162, 175
religion
  church, 60, 65, 67–70, 92, 94, 117, 124,
    130, 183, 189
  religious affiliation, Christianity, 66,
    92–93, 125, 130, 144, 155, 189, 198
  spirituality, God, 65–66, 88, 117, 124,
    131
Routinizers (*see* participant
  classification)
Rovers (*see* participant classification)

sample characteristics (*also see*
  participant categorization), 11–20
self-concept
  self-affirmation, 159
  self-assessment, reflection, 57, 152–53,
    233
  self-esteem, 3, 5, 10, 62, 64, 72, 86, 96,
    98, 133–38, 144–45, 189, 197, 199,
    216–17, 223
    Self-Esteem Scale, 133, 136, 144,
      216–17
  self-defining activities
    self-development, 38, 98, 136–38,
      140, 213–14
    Self-Definition through Leisure
      Scale, 136, 138, 140, 213–14
  self-determination, 107
  self-doubt, 31, 33, 38, 152
  self-efficacy, 38, 47
  self-recrimination, 45

self-worth (*also see* sense of purpose),
  31, 67, 84, 126, 129, 139, 153, 230
  identity, 38, 145–46, 152–53, 208
  feeling sorry, 36
  feelings of confidence, 33–34, 54,
    145, 152–53
  rejection (*also see* stigma), 32, 152
sense of
  accomplishment, 31, 33, 122, 126
  control (*see* self-efficacy)
  discouragement, 41, 174
  disorganization, 45
  freedom, release, 125
  frustration, 32, 42, 75, 77, 87, 116, 123,
    162, 163, 183, 187, 224
  purpose, sense of non-productivity,
    feeling productive, loss of sense of
    purpose, wasted time, filling time,
    32, 34, 41–43, 45, 84–85, 122, 124,
    126, 149–51, 177, 188, 223–24, 230
  structure (*also see* daily structure),
    115, 177, 197
sex (*see* gender)
sleep, 52–53, 84–85, 89
sister (*see* family, siblings)
social aspects of work and volunteering
  (*also see*, co-workers), 66, 86
social
  contact, 29, 47, 63, 92, 124, 139, 146,
    159, 190, 199
  contexts and situations, 111, 114, 149,
    199
  distance, isolation, 36, 41, 45–46,
    72–74, 81, 86, 114, 145, 155, 158, 177,
    187, 197
  interaction, 5, 23, 41, 45, 60, 63, 77,
    151–56, 158–59, 175, 181, 189, 230,
    233
  networks, 3, 60, 71, 139, 154, 159, 224
  outlets, 45, 87, 188, 217
  support, 40, 49, 147, 154–55, 217
social service agencies, social service
  provision, social-based programs, 143,
  161, 163, 199–200, 221, 242–43
socializing (*see* family, friends)
sociodemographic characteristics (*also
  see*, age, education, ethnicity, marital
  status, sex), 4, 11, 180, 190, 197, 225,
  231, 235
sociotropic, 155
solitude, alone, solitary contexts,
  isolation, 37, 73, 77–79, 94, 100–105,

113–14, 117, 121, 124, 130, 155, 158–59, 171, 189, 198, 207, 230, 240

spending patterns (*also see* pricing, subsidies), 3

spontaneity (*also see* daily planning), 59

sports (*also see* activity)
   youth sports (*also see* volunteering), 29, 42, 62, 65–66, 117, 120, 126–27, 174

stigma, social embarrassment, prejudice, 27, 32, 33, 46, 87, 114, 153–54, 159, 173–75, 179, 182, 188, 197, 199, 204, 219, 232

stress relief, 42, 94, 121, 129, 230

structure in daily routine, sense of structure, structured activity (*see* daily life patterns)

subjective well-being (*see* well being)

subsidies (*also see* pricing)
   subsidized leisure programs, 168, 171–75, 178, 181–82, 188–90, 198, 242–43
   subsidized transportation, transit pass, bus pass, 168, 183, 185

substance abuse, alcoholic, alcoholism, drugs, 74, 80–81, 83, 131, 142, 223

suicide, 81, 131

Surplus People (*see* participant classification)

task involvement, task orientation, 23, 25, 37, 52, 60, 71, 90, 125, 198, 208, 239–40

television, television viewing, televised movies 34, 38–39, 41–44, 51, 68, 78–79, 85, 88–89, 93, 98–105, 117, 121–22, 124, 128–29, 141–42, 189, 226–28, 233

time of day, 109–12, 116, 149, 184–85

time diaries, 199

time pressure, time constraint, 23, 25, 37, 52, 71, 90, 141–43, 207, 220, 239

time structure, filling time (*also see* sense of), 37, 51, 85, 109, 146–47, 149, 150, 197, 199, 205, 209, 220

uncertainty, 33, 57

Unemployment Insurance, Employment Insurance, unemployment insurance system, 34, 157, 161, 163–64, 167, 169, 192, 221, 243

unemployment rate, 2, 200

Vacationers (*see* participant classification)

voluntary activities, volunteer activities, volunteer opportunities, volunteer organizations, volunteering, 61–62, 65, 69, 117, 124–25, 130, 174, 177, 189, 191, 199

welfare, 169, 173

well-being, 47, 82, 84, 86, 95, 122, 147, 156–57, 161, 178, 191, 193–94

withdrawal, 154, 188, 198